An Introduction to Corporate Governance

Mechanisms and Systems

Steen Thomsen

An Introduction to Corporate Governance

Mechanisms and Systems

DJØF Publishing Copenhagen
2008

*An Introduction to Corporate Governance
Mechanisms and Systems*
First Edition

© 2008 by DJØF Publishing Copenhagen

DJØF Publishing is a company of the
Association of Danish Lawyers and Economists

All rights reserved.
No parts of this publication may be reproduced,
stored in a retrieval system, or transmitted in
any form and by any means – electronic, mechanical,
photocopying, recording or otherwise – without the
prior written permission of the publisher.

Cover: Morten Højmark
Print: Narayana Press, Gylling
Binding: Damm's Forlagsbogbinderi, Randers

Printed in Denmark 2008
ISBN 978-87-574-1851-4

DJØF Publishing
17, Lyngbyvej
P.O.Box 2702
DK-2100 Copenhagen
Denmark

Phone: +45 39 13 55 00
Fax: +45 39 13 55 55
E-mail: forlag@djoef.dk
www.djoef-forlag.dk

Table of Contents

Introduction 9

I. An Introduction to Corporate Governance

Chapter 1. What is Corporate Governance? 15
What corporate governance is not 16
The basic governance problem 17
The extended agency problem 18
Why is corporate governance important? 21
Conclusion 22
References 23

Chapter 2. Agency Problems and Corporate Governance ... 25
The owner-manager problem 28
Agency theory 31
Types of agency problems 31
Information problems 32
Moral hazard 33
Adverse selection 34
Alternatives to the agency model 38
References 40

Chapter 3. The Mechanisms of Governance 41
Moral standards 42
Trust and reputation 44
Law 45
Large owners 49
Shareholder pressure 50
Boards 50

Table of Contents

Creditors 51
Incentive systems 52
Auditors 53
Analysts 54
Takeovers 54
Competition 55
The managerial labour market 55
Corporate governance codes 55
Media pressure 56
System effects 57
References 57

Chapter 4. International Corporate Governance 59
Theoretical considerations 60
International systems 64
Country models 71
Convergence 73
References 77

II. Understanding Mechanisms of Governance

Chapter 5. Understanding Corporate Ownership 85
Ownership of the firm 86
Ownership structure 87
Ownership and performance 89
Owner identity 90
Best owner 95
References 97

Chapter 6. What Boards do and Should do 101
Introduction 101
Board functions: facts and fiction 103
The theory of boards 109
The empirical evidence 115
Empowerment and overload 119
Discussion 122
References 126

Appendix 6.1. The tasks of the board according
to the combined code 129
Appendix 6.2 132

Chapter 7. Ethics as a Governance Mechanism 135
Business ethics as a governance mechanism 136
Optimal business ethics 141
Actual business ethics 143
Discussion 147
References 148

Chapter 8. Understanding Corporate Governance Codes 151
Code puzzles 152
Corporate governance codes in theory 154
Stylised facts and puzzles 156
Statistical evidence on codes 159
The contents 161
Discussion 165
References 167
Appendix 170

III. Understanding International Systems

Chapter 9. The Anglo-American Market Model and Shareholder Value 173
The ideal model: shareholder value 173
The market based system: ideal model 176
The US model 177
The UK corporate governance model 181
Evaluating the market model 183
References 186
Appendix 1. Sarbanes-Oxley 187

Chapter 10. Bank Governance in Germany 191
Bank governance in theory 191
Bank leadership in Germany 194
Two-tier boards with employee representation 195

Table of Contents

Other characteristics of German corporate governance 195
Why is Germany different? 196
Evaluation of the German model 197
References 198

Chapter 11. Relational Governance in Japan 199
Theoretical considerations 199
The Japanese model 200
The Keiretsu system 202
History of Japanese corporate governance 205
Changes in the Japanese model 206
Evaluation of the Japanese model 207
References 208

Chapter 12. Family Business with East Asia as an example 209
Family business defined 209
The costs and benefits of family ownership 211
Family ownership and economic performance 214
Family control mechanisms 216
Should dual class shares be prohibited? 219
Ownership and control in East Asia 219
References 223

Chapter 13. Corporate Governance in Scandinavia 225
Comparative governance 227
Evaluating the Scandinavian model 230
References 232

IV. Conclusion

Chapter 14. Corporate Governance beyond the Hype 237
Good corporate governance 239
Corporate governance reviews 242

Index 245

Introduction

This book is an introduction to corporate governance, a subject which is frequently misunderstood and occasionally – deliberately – distorted. In this book I hope to take you beyond the hype and to demonstrate that governance can be a useful subject.

The book can be used for a semester-long course in corporate governance. When you have read and understood it, you can congratulate yourself that you are now at the master's level. I have tried to write as informally as possible, so the determined reader should have no problem digesting it.

I owe a debt of gratitude to previous work done in this field. For example, 'Keeping Good Company' by Jonathan Charkham (1994, 2005) and the survey papers by Shleifer and Vishny (1997), Becht et al. (2002) and Tirole (2006) have all contributed to this field. More technical introductions to agency theory can be found in Mas-Colell et al. (1995). I try to combine a theoretical approach with an informal style and I pay constant attention to practice. Thus, the book is probably more theoretical than standard management textbooks, but much less so than textbooks in finance and economics.

Parts of this book are original work: some previously published and some not. Moreover, my ideas have matured over the years and now differ somewhat from other people's work. So I thought it was time to write them down.

The book is divided in 3 main parts:

I. Introduction to Corporate Governance and its Mechanisms. Here I present agency problems and the many mechanisms – laws, boards, owners, etc. – which address them.
II. Mechanisms of Governance. Here we study some of the mechanisms in more detail: ownership, boards, ethics, and codes.

III. International Systems: The US market model, the German bank model, Japanese relational capitalism, and family business in East Asia.

Finally, I briefly conclude in part IV how corporate governance can go beyond the hype and create value in business companies.

The focus throughout this book is on publicly listed companies. There are many interesting and important issues concerning governance of large and small unlisted firms, cooperatives, non-profits, foundations, and government-owned companies, but they will have to wait for another book.

There is no question that this book is a work-in-progress. Firstly, the whole corporate governance field is still changing, and we cannot yet predict where it will end. Will it, for example, converge with corporate social responsibility? Or will some clever economists come up with a general systems theory which can address the interrelationships between different mechanisms? Secondly, it would be good to have more and richer country studies; France, Italy, Russia, China and small countries like the Netherlands, Belgium, and Austria all have interesting corporate governance systems and governance problems of their own. Thirdly, corporate governance mechanisms like incentive pay, auditing, and corporate law could easily fill a book on their own – likewise topics including government ownership and privatization, institutional investors, and corruption. The topic of corporate governance deserves to be a brick of a book. In the meantime, however, you have this one.

I am grateful to Scancor – the Scandinavian Consortium for Organizational Research at Stanford University – for a summer stay which allowed me to finish this book in a wonderful atmosphere.

I am also grateful to Anne Sluhan Reich for language editing and to Filip Kolassa and Julie Blegvad for proof-reading.

17 August 2007

Steen Thomsen
Professor and Director of the Center for Corporate Governance
Department of International Economics and Management
Copenhagen Business School

References

Becht, Marco, Patrick Bolton and Ailsa Roëll. 2003. Corporate Governance and Control, *Handbook of the Economics of Finance*, edited by George Constantinides, Milton Harris and René Stulz, North-Holland, forthcoming.

Charkham, J., 1995, *Keeping Good Company: A Study of Corporate Governance in Five Countries*, Oxford: Oxford University Press.

Mas-Colell, Andreu, Michael D. Whinston, and Jerry R. Green. 1995. *Microeconomic Theory* New York: Oxford University Press.

Shleifer, A. and R. Vishny. 1997. 'A survey of corporate governance'. *Journal of Finance*, 52(2): 737-783.

Tirole, Jean. 2006. *Corporate Governance*. Chapter 1. The Theory of Corporate Finance. Princeton University Press. Princeton.

I An Introduction to Corporate Governance

CHAPTER 1

What is Corporate Governance?[1]

I define corporate governance as the control and direction of companies by ownership, boards, incentives, company law, and other mechanisms. This follows the widely-used definition by Cadbury (1992) as *'the system by which companies are directed and controlled'*.

There are many other definitions in the literature. To business people and in the management literature corporate governance is all about boards – what boards do, how they are composed, and so on. Among investors and in the finance literature there is a tendency to focus on the relations between the company and its shareholders--what rights shareholders have, whether the firm is protected against takeover by takeover defenses, etc. This varies from country to country and from company to company. Lawyers focus on company law and securities law. Accountants focus on how companies are held accountable to outside stakeholders through annual reports. Politicians and the media tend to focus on business ethics and corporate social responsibility – including financial scandals, fraud, and corruption. Sociologists focus on networks, socialization, and values. Psychologists focus on motivation – for example the intrinsic utility of 'good stewardship'.

It is natural that there should be different perspectives on this important subject. The views of various stakeholders may be expected to reflect their fields of experience and, to some extent, their vested interests. It is

1. Originally published in Festschrift for Morten Balling, professor of finance and former president at Aarhus School of Business. Morten has taken a keen interest in corporate governance for a number of years, has actively participated in the corporate governance group at the business school, and has contributed to the activities of the Danish Corporate Governance Network.

not surprising, for example, that financial investors try to make shareholder value the central objective in corporate governance.

Shleifer & Vishny (1997) define the subject of corporate governance as *'the ways in which suppliers of finance assure themselves of getting a return on their investment'*. This definition is focused on the financial aspects of governance and may be useful for many purposes, but it can be too narrow in other cases. For example, business efficiency might be more important than investor relations. Note, however, that suppliers of finance include both shareholders and creditors such as banks. These suppliers provide the firm with funding and are, of course, concerned with the payback. Cadbury's 1992 definition (above) is somewhat broader. For example, it does not exclude stakeholder concerns or corporate governance issues in privately-held companies that do not attract outside funding.

An even broader definition was given by Charkham (1994): *'The way companies are run'*. This is perhaps too broad because it includes everything that companies do. And a definition that includes everything is meaningless. But one thing is clear; corporate governance is influenced by national history, culture, and institutions. German or Japanese corporate governance is very different from what is found in the USA or the UK.

What corporate governance is not

A definition must also be clear about what it excludes.

For example, there must be a difference between governance and management. Although corporate governance is concerned with good management, it is not about management as such. Rather, corporate governance is about the control and direction of managers. Operationally, this means that important business functions like marketing, human resource management or financial management are not normally part of corporate governance. To be sure, managers can be controlled and directed by other more senior managers within the firm. Hiring managers to control managers just moves the control problem one level up; who will then control the managers who control the managers? It follows that top managers must necessarily be controlled by some other mechanism than management: in other words, by some governance mechanism. Juvenal's classic question 'Quis custodiet ipsos custodes?' – who is to guard the guardians? – captures the essence of the problem.

Moreover, corporate governance is not a religion. It is a field of practice and study. After all, if it was a religion, it could not be studied in business schools. We are concerned with corporate governance because we want companies to perform well and to create value for society. Good management is clearly an essential condition for good performance and corporate governance aims to ensure good management. There is no inherently 'right' kind of corporate governance since what works well in one firm does not necessarily work well in another. In practice, good corporate governance is about finding appropriate solutions – tailor-made, if you like – for the individual firm.

The basic governance problem

Another approach to defining corporate governance is to go back to theory. The basic problem of corporate governance is the so-called 'agency problem' which occurs because of the separation between ownership and management. This is also somewhat misleadingly termed 'the separation of ownership and control' by Berle and Means (1932).

The idea is that owners (shareholders) hire executives to manage companies on their behalf. In agency theory, we say that the agent (i.e. manager) acts on behalf of the principal (i.e. shareholder). The shareholders leave their money and other assets in the custody of the managers. The basic question to address is how to ensure that managers will manage the assets well? For example, what keeps them from taking the money and running away with it? Clearly, the law has some bearing on this and is, therefore, perhaps the most fundamental governance mechanism. It is worth noting here that stock markets have historically been able to flourish with little legal support. Thus informal mechanisms like reputation and trust may be even more basic control factors. Vigilant owners – for example owner-managers or large shareholders–represent another powerful control mechanism; self-interested owners will monitor what goes on in the firm and replace bad or opportunistic managers. Managers may be motivated to create more value for the shareholders through incentive systems (i.e. bonuses or stock options). The threat of being fired by an alert board could also be enough to make them work hard. Agency theory – by far the most important approach to corporate governance – is specifically concerned with devising efficient solutions to the agency problem when both owners and managers are rational and self interested.

There are more theories about corporate governance than agency theory, of course. As previously mentioned, corporate governance is a multidisciplinary subject which draws on economics, law, sociology, psychology, and political science. Within business studies it draws on management and organizational behaviour, finance, accounting, international business, and other topics. Economic theories of corporate governance include agency, transaction cost, and incomplete contract theory. The focus within these economic theories is, likewise, on relatively rational, selfish and sometimes opportunistic decision makers who interact with and create organizational mechanisms to further their own interests. This 'model of man' has been challenged by sociologists and psychologists who emphasize that human beings are not always rational and may not be motivated by self interest. But these challenges have thus far not been very successful. Therefore, almost all thinking on corporate governance is focused on agency problems.

The extended agency problem

In the real world, of course, there are more than two actors (i.e. principal and agent), so the picture becomes much more complicated.

Between owners and managers there is a board elected by the owners. Not all types of firms are required to have a board, but for most large firms this is a legal requirement. Boards are the straightforward solution to the corporate governance problem. A group of people are elected to the board to sanction major decisions and to monitor that managers are doing their jobs well. Boards usually meet regularly (e.g. 5 times a year, sometimes as often as 10 times a year).

The owners of a firm do not necessarily comprise a homogenous group. There may be many or few owners. Some owners may be private individuals (i.e. 'mom and pop' investors). Some may be founders or members of the founding family. Owners may be institutional investors, mutual funds, or hedge funds. There might be some owners who are actively concerned with corporate governance. Others may be passive investors who never vote and who mechanically match their portfolio to an index and choose to leave it to others to be active owners.

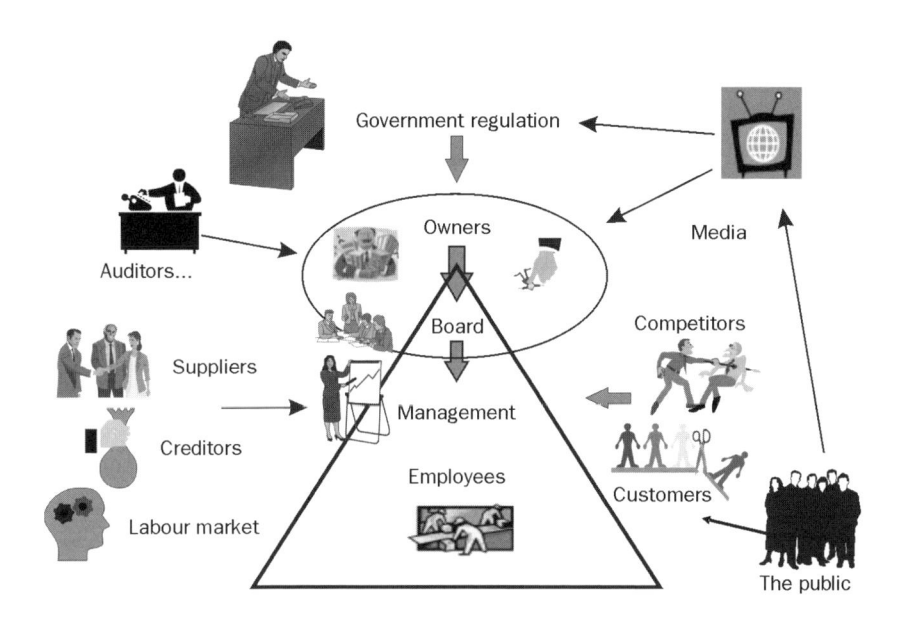

Moreover, most firms are associated with many stakeholders with whom they do business and who can directly and indirectly influence their corporate governance.

Banks and other creditors can play a powerful role in corporate governance for firms in need of external finance because they can sanction or veto investment projects, make demands on the composition of the board, and write debt contracts that include conditions (covenants) about what the firm should and should not do. In some countries, banks are so powerful that we talk about a bank-based corporate governance model. Banks may own large ownership stakes in other companies if the law permits.

Employees can also play a role in corporate governance. In some countries, employees are entitled to elect board members (e.g. Germany, Austria, and in Scandinavia). If labour unions are strong, they influence the strategic direction of the company since many decisions must be negotiated with them. The market for managers can play a particular role in corporate governance, since it can be easier for the board to control managers if they are easy to replace. Employees can also be owners: in owner-managed firms or in professional partnerships, for example, which are common structures for law firms, accounting firms, and management consulting firms. Employees may acquire shares as part of employee-ownership policies.

Suppliers can play a role in corporate governance as owners of firms: for example in cooperatives, where farmers jointly own the slaughterhouses or dairies to which they sell their product. A subsidiary relationship is another structure: for example, when IBM USA owns a sales subsidiary in France. In joint ventures, the participating companies will often share ownership and will appoint their own representatives to the board.

Customers can also own the companies from which they buy (e.g. retail cooperatives, investment funds) or they can influence them in other ways. The futurist Alvin Toffler once suggested that companies should appoint advisory boards composed partly by customers and through which the customers could get a formal channel of communication to the company. Many companies work hard to build customer relationships and to endorse the marketing concept according to which the customers should have priority over other stakeholder groups.

The most direct way in which customers exercise their influence, however, is through competition. In very competitive markets the job of controlling managers is effectively 'taken over' by the competition since the managers must continuously work hard to stay ahead of their competition. If there are many competitors in a market, shareholders can more easily evaluate the performance of their managers. They can compare their performance with other firms and owners can more easily replace their managers with those from competing firms.

Governments influence corporate governance by making the game rules (i.e. laws and regulations). For example – should banks be allowed to own firms? How much should family ownership be taxed by inheritance and wealth taxes? Should pension fund ownership be subsidized by tax benefits? Governments in different parts of the world address these questions in different ways.

Governments can also play a direct role as owners of business enterprises, although the popularity of this construction dwindles. Governments in former socialist countries and elsewhere have begun to implement large scale privatization programs.

In addition to the direct stakeholders, the media and various kinds of special interest organizations (NGOs, etc.) can influence corporate governance. Managers and shareholders fear public exposure and act to avoid scandal, sometimes by changing their policies to accommodate grassroots organizations like Greenpeace.

There are several other actors. Auditors, analysts, and stock exchanges play a special role by providing information to shareholders and to other stakeholders. Lawyers, stockbrokers, consultants, insurance companies, and others also have their roles to play.

In all this complexity, the primary focal point in corporate governance is the relationship between owners and companies – with particular focus on the board.

Why is corporate governance important?

A third approach to the definition of the subject is to examine why people are interested in corporate governance.

At the most general level, good management is obviously crucial to economic efficiency, productivity, firm performance, and social welfare. Corporate governance looks at how to ensure good management – meaning hiring the right managers, motivating them well through reward systems, giving them sufficient freedom to act and combining this freedom with a system of checks and balances to prevent the abuse of power. In this sense, good corporate governance has always been essential for good economic performance.

But there is another – more obvious – reason which can explain why corporate governance has become such a fashionable topic in the past few decades. An unprecedented amount of savings is currently flowing from pension schemes into the global economy. This money must be used as well as possible since its investment will directly influence the living standards of the future pensioners. In 1936, Keynes declared the coordination of savings and investment to be the Achilles heel of the capitalist economies. Keynes was concerned with the short-term macroeconomic impact of these imbalances. But there are also important microeconomic problems associated with them. How can we make sure that our pension money is put to good use? It is therefore no coincidence that pension funds have led the corporate governance debate around the world.

Recent scandals such as Enron, WorldCom, Tyco, Parmalat – as well as Maxwell and BCGI in a prior upsurge of scandal – are vivid examples that our pension money is not always being put to good use. Shareholders and debtholders suddenly realized they lost a significant amount of money – in some cases because they had been deliberately misled by fraudulent managers. Stunning examples of mismanagement often inspire action: for example, the implementation of new laws or codes of best practice to prevent a repeat of these errors.

But long before Keynes' declarations, another economist – Adam Smith (1776) – discovered that government intervention is not always the best way to create wealth. For example, corporate governance structures that invite scandals may, over time, be replaced by more efficient structures, if the rules and regulations allow it. Although most corporate governance regulation is based on the 'latest' scandal, it is doubtful whether the avoidance of scandals should be the overriding goal of corporate governance. Other famous economists – Frank Knight and Joseph Schumpeter, for example – have discovered that economic growth is to a large extent created by risk taking. Thus there are serious costs to regulation which makes firms more bureaucratic and more risk adverse. It may be better – in fact it probably is better – to tolerate a few scandals now and again than to slow down the capitalist engine of innovation and growth.

It is therefore important to find governance structures, which on the one hand allow managers and entrepreneurs to do what they do best and on the other hand to hold them accountable to investors if they also invest other people's money. Avoiding overregulation is another good reason to be interested in corporate governance.

Conclusion

At the most general level corporate governance is concerned with how to devise institutions (i.e. governance mechanisms) that lead to wealth-creating decisions in businesses. It should come as no surprise that there are different opinions about what mechanisms are most effective and about how to define wealth generation. This diversity of views may in itself be productive, since it allows for various solutions to compete in the marketplace. In many other business disciplines – including business strategy, innovation studies, and marketing – differentiation is considered to be an asset. Thus, it could also be argued that differentiation in corporate governance mechanisms at the firm level can be a source of advantage, since this enlarges the menu of choices available to investors and to other stakeholders.

However, it is important to remember that some of the most pertinent problems of corporate governance are associated with finance: in particular with how to best utilize the huge savings which are currently being accumulated in pension funds around the world.

References

Adolf A. Berle and Gardiner C. Means. 1932. *The Modern Corporation and Private Property*. New York: Harcourt, Brace & World, [1932] 1968.

Cadbury Commission. 1992. *Code of best practice: Report of the committee on the financial aspects of corporate governance*. London: Gee and Co.

Charkham, J.P. 1994. *Keeping good company – a study of corporate governance in five countries*. Clarendon Press. Oxford.

Keynes, John M. 1936. *The General Theory of Employment, Interest, and Money*. New York: Harcourt, Brace & World, Inc.

Knight, F. 1921. *Risk, Uncertainty and Profit*. Boston: Houghton Mifflin.

Shleifer, A & R.W.Vishny. 1997. A survey of corporate governance. *Journal of Finance*, 52(2): 737.

Schumpeter, Joseph A. *The Theory of Economic Development*, 2nd edition, Cambridge: Harvard University Press, 1934.

Smith, A. [1776] 1981. *An Inquiry into the Nature and Causes of the Wealth of Nations*. First edition. Indianapolis: Liberty Classics.

CHAPTER 2

Agency Problems and Corporate Governance

Agency problems arise whenever someone does something for somebody else. This somebody else we designate 'the principal' and the actor we denote the 'agent':

> '... an agency relationship has arisen between two (or more) parties when one, designated as the agent, acts for, or on behalf of, or as a representative for the other, designated the principal, in a particular domain of decision problems.' (Ross 1973)

Agency relationships lead to costly incentive problems. There are many examples of agency relationships – apart from the relationship between owners and managers – which comprise the core problem in corporate governance.

For example, there is an agency relationship between a boss and his employees. The boss would like the employees to work hard or to do certain tasks which he believes to be beneficial (although these tasks may not be beneficial to anyone else). In contrast, the employees will have their own ideas about what they would like to do. Only in rare cases (i.e. by luck) will these tasks coincide with what the manager would like them to do. For example, the employees may like to relax rather than to work hard, or they may prefer to hold meetings among themselves rather than to talk to the customers. The boss will therefore want to induce them to 'behave': for example the boss will tell them what to do and will threaten to fire them if they do not obey. Or he may be a more modern type of manager who prefers to motivate employees by more subtle means: for example through offering a bonus scheme or through psychological tricks. A hierarchical organization can be defined as a chain of such boss-employee relationships from top management to middle managers to workers on the shop floor.

Another example of an agency relationship is the affiliation between a house seller and a real estate agent (Posner, 2000). In this case, the house seller is the principal and the real estate agent acts on her behalf. The house seller would like the real estate agent to contact as many prospective buyers as possible, to bargain hard on her behalf to get a high price, and so on. But the real estate agent may prefer to take it easy and wait until the customers come along, or he may prefer to concentrate his energy on selling other people's houses. It may be difficult for the seller to verify whether the agent in fact devotes a reasonable amount of effort to the task, so this is a case of asymmetric information (the real estate agent is better informed than the house seller). In general, all relationships between firms and sales agents involve similar incentive problems.

More general problems with agency relationships include the relationships between citizens and their governments, where the citizens want the government to act on their behalf. In this light democracy can be seen as a (political) governance mechanism which allows the voters to replace inefficient politicians. In the absence of democracy, politicians become dictators that govern according to their own ideas (and very likely for their own benefit). Thus the citizens – much like shareholders in a firm – must organize a system to ensure that their interests are served.

Finally, the relationship between a patient and a doctor is a classical principal-agent problem (Arrow, 1963). The doctor is better informed than the patient about medicine and sickness; that is why the patient seeks his advice. So we again have a case of asymmetric information. And with that comes the incentive problem: the doctor could prescribe useless, expensive treatments and medicines (especially since many patients get better without treatment and since some patients get worse even with the best possible treatment). So how are the patients to know whether the doctor is fooling them? One solution to this asymmetry would be for the government to step in and require all practising doctors to have a university degree in medicine. Another solution would be the invention within the medical profession of a 'medical ethic' (Arrow, 1963) – e.g. the Hippocratic Oath – which is enforced through internalization (i.e. doctors identify with it) and through strong collegial pressure. The pressures may be so strong that doctors who are criticized by their peers have been known to commit suicide and they certainly can lose their license to practice.

Note that the doctors have an economic interest in this medical ethic; if they did not have it, they would get far fewer patients, since the patients would rationally fear being taken advantage of. The medical profession up to the 19th century is a vivid example.

We find similar social sanctions in corporate governance. For example, when an opportunistic manager gets a bad reputation this makes it more difficult for him to find a new job or to do business in the future. We note that law, reputation, and ethics can all function as governance mechanisms.

So how about the relationship between seller and buyers? This also involves a conflict of interest.

For example, when buying an apple from a grocer, I would like to get as good an apple as possible and to pay as little as possible for it. The grocer, however, would like to charge as much as possible. But we would not usually talk of an agency relationship in this case. As a customer I know what I will buy, and the grocer knows what he sells. So there is no asymmetric information here. To be sure there is always some asymmetric information in any transaction, but unless it is significant, we tend to disregard it. However, under certain circumstances, there are significant information asymmetries even in standard transactions. For example, if I buy an organic apple, I may not be able to tell whether it is really organic, whereas the grocer may know very well. Here a standard solution is to have a declaration of contents (a label) which is guaranteed by the government or some other body that can punish the grocer if he cheats people. Note that this kind of control may be in the grocer's own interest because it will encourage people to buy more. Similar guarantees –like the labels on foodstuffs – are found in corporate governance. We call them 'corporate governance codes'.

In summary, agency problems are universal. There are many different solutions to them: monitoring and sanctions, bonus systems, laws, and even ethical codes can be regarded as governance mechanisms. In chapter 3 we will see how these different mechanisms can be applied to corporate governance. For now we would like to take a closer look at the agency problems, which these governance mechanisms intend to solve.

The owner-manager problem

The owner-management agency problem begins with the separation of ownership and management or, as it is sometimes (confusingly) called, the separation of ownership and control (Berle and Means, 1932). Without this separation – in owned-managed firms – the basic agency problem disappears.

Owner-managers have a natural incentive to work hard and to employ somebody else if they are not the best managers. If they choose to use company funds for private expenditure (on the job consumption), they will only do so if consuming on the job is more beneficial to them than consuming at home (taxes and other complications aside). From the viewpoint of professional managers, the incentives look different since it is not their money which they manage. Their incentives may be to spend money on things which they like without thinking too much of the costs, and they may also have an interest in maintaining their jobs because they need the money.

A newly-appointed CEO of a Danish hearing aid company once described how his view of corporate expenditure changed after he bought 15 % of the company's stock. Every time he authorized the payment of a bill by using his signature, he questioned immediately whether this expense was really necessary.

By separation of ownership and management we get a specialization of resources where the principal/owner/investor is a supplier of finance, whereas the agent/manager supplies human capital. The idea is that managers act on behalf of the shareholders and the agency problem is to find ways in which shareholders can ensure that the manager will act in their interest, for example how they can make sure that she maximizes the stock price (value) of the firm.

From the viewpoint of the shareholders, a value maximizing manager is an entrepreneurial and creative leader, who is able to implement her ideas in the organization. She is hard working and economical with the shareholders' money and she delivers results. I am sure we could continue the list.

In reality, we expect the average manager to be more ordinary, but normally a very decent and conscientious person. But unfortunately, there are also many examples of managers who do not live up to this ideal.

The following are generic agency problems: some managers act criminally and embezzle (steal) shareholders funds. In a way, that is easy for the shareholder: it is a criminal act and the police will come after them. Some managers are known to undertake 'self dealing,' i.e. they use company money for transactions, which benefit themselves – for example with a company, which they own themselves. This was apparently the case in Parmalat, a publicly-listed Italian dairy controlled by a founding family. Parmalat transferred money to a company which was 100% owned by the family. This type of transaction is illegal in most countries but the police will typically be unable to uncover such problems on their own accord, so shareholders must be on their toes and monitor company activities.

Another classical agency problem is excess expenditure. The question here is when an expense is business-motivated and when it is really private consumption for the manager? Paper and pencils will typically not be much of a problem, but how about a company jet? The managers may argue that they need a company jet so as not to waste precious managerial resources in the airport and, if the board approves, they can buy one. So one jet might be OK, or perhaps it is not. But, how about two? Or three? At some point, this expense seems difficult to justify from a company viewpoint. Similar uncertainties apply to meals in expensive restaurants, luxurious headquarters, expensive thick carpets, and very good looking secretaries (i.e. do we really need a playboy secretary?). One American manager was known to let the company plane fly around with his dog. The problem with excess expenditure is that it is a grey area. It will usually be possible for the manager to make a case that this was necessary or beneficial from a business point of view – a nice looking secretary may charm business relations, it may be easier to close important deals over a meal, and the company jet saves time. Remember that a court must prove beyond a reasonable doubt that this was harmful to shareholders in order to send him to jail – and this is very difficult. Courts will be reluctant to do this because of the *business judgement rule:* a legal principle according to which managers are assumed to be in the right – unless proven otherwise. The underlying argument seems to be that if the shareholders do not like what the manager does, they can fire him. But we want managers to be dynamic and to do things: that is, to take risks, since that is part of their job. Sometimes this means that they make mistakes. If we sent them to jail every time they made a mistake, it would soon be difficult to fill CEO positions. Or – even worse – the CEOs would only think about how not to make mistakes and then would become risk averse.

Empire building – particularly through mergers and acquisitions – is another example of a conflict of interest between shareholders and managers. Usually managers like growth and size. It is more fun to lead a growth company, it is more prestigious to lead a large company, and managerial pay is positively correlated with company size. The risk of being taken over by another company also declines with firm size. So managers like to build their own little empires. But it is well known that many mergers and acquisitions fail to create value for the acquiring company, so shareholders often have a different view, particularly if the acquisitions are outside the company's core business. Usually, hidden private consumption is not what takes a company down – private consumption trifles compared to other business expenses. But, there are many examples of acquisitions which cost a company dearly. So in a way this is a more serious problem for shareholders, and they will typically be considered to be a normal part of doing business. Thus, courts would not accept a case against a manager because the company made an acquisition. Yes, there *are* examples of good acquisitions which create value.

Overinvestment falls into the same category as empire building. Oil companies are known to have overinvested in finding new sources of oil when it would have been much cheaper to buy it on the market (Shleifer and Vishny, 1997).

Entrenchment – when managers create barriers which make it difficult to fire them and they then stay on for too long – can also be regarded as an agency problem. The CEO likes his job, the prestige, and the money. But shareholders may prefer to have a new, more dynamic profile to head the company. This may be why some studies actually found that share prices actually rise when entrenched CEOs suddenly die. A 5 % increase in share prices would then indicate that the old manager cost the company 5 % of its value.

Finally, the inventor of 'shareholder value' Alfred Rappaport (and later, Jensen 1993) found that many – if not most – US companies did not cover their costs of capital during the 1970s and 1980s. In other words, they lost money for their shareholders. Jensen calculated that General Motors (GM) lost 100 billion dollars during the 1980s. Obviously, at the time, many managers could have done better in terms of maximizing shareholder value, and it is difficult to argue that they were unlucky over such a long period of time. So whatever else they did could, in principle, be attributed to agency problems.

Agency theory

Theoretically, the key elements of the agency problem are:

Separation between principal and agent
- Conflicting interests (selfishness), since principal and agent each have their own utility functions.
- Rationality: both principal and agent are rational and rationally further their own interests.
- Asymmetric information: the agent is better informed about his own abilities, his own activities, and what is going on in the firm than is the principal.
- Uncertainty (risk): the existence of 'other factors' – weather, bad luck, and unforeseen changes of any kind – means there is no one-to-one relationship between the activities of the agent and the outcome. If the information asymmetry problem disappeared, then the agency problem itself would disappear, since the principal would be able to deduce the behaviour of the agent by monitoring his performance.
- Risk aversion. Performance pay will usually involve some kind of risk for the agent (either over- or underpay), and the risk averse will demand compensation for this. If the agent is sufficiently risk averse, he will only want to work for a fixed pay to avoid economic uncertainty altogether. The risk will then be carried by the principal who, like entrepreneur capitalists, gets a variable profit while his employees are paid a fixed salary.

Types of agency problems

Type 1 agency problems (owner-manager problems) arise between shareholders (the principals) and managers (agents). They arise because the agents (managers) do not always act in the interests of the shareholders.

Type 2 agency problems between majority and minority investors occur if there are conflicts of interests between the two groups. A founding family in control of the firm may have different views than minority investors. The family in charge effectively acts on behalf of the other investors, so in this case the family is the agent, while the minority investors are the principals.

Type 3 agency problems between shareholders and stakeholders occur when shareholders make self-interested decisions which influence the welfare of stakeholders. For example, shareholders may decide to pay out high dividends or to pursue a risky strategy: both of which increase the risk of bankruptcy and reduce the welfare of creditors. In the same way shareholders may decide to close down a factory and this can harm the welfare of the employees, the suppliers, the local government, and perhaps the customers. Type 3 agency problems fall under the broad heading of corporate social responsibility. In the following section, we will pay more attention to type 1 and type 2 problems.

The three types of generic problems can be regarded as an expression of increasing responsibility. In the first instance, managers and the firm are responsible to the controlling owners, who decide whether they are hired or fired. In the second instance, the responsibility is extended to all shareholders – not just the controlling shareholders. In the third instance, the responsibility is extended further to cover all stakeholders – not just shareholders.

Information problems

There are two particularly important types of information asymmetry: moral hazard (i.e. hidden action) and adverse selection (i.e. hidden knowledge), which will be discussed in greater detail in the following sections.

To distinguish between moral hazard and adverse selection, it is useful to draw a timeline. Adverse selection problems tend to occur before the principal is to make a decision. Moral hazard problems tend to occur after the decision.

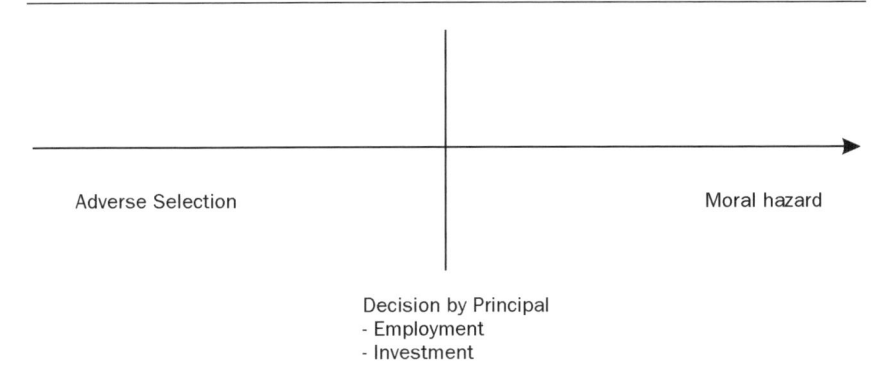

```
                              |
                              |
  ─────────────────────────────|──────────────────────────►
                              |
   Adverse Selection           |              Moral hazard
                              |
                   Decision by Principal
                   - Employment
                   - Investment
```

For example, to ensure good management of the company is perhaps the most important task in corporate governance. This task involves:

1) Selection: hire the right managers and replace bad ones, if necessary. The key problem here is 'adverse selection'.
2) Motivation: encourage management to do their best through incentives and monitoring. The key problem here is 'moral hazard'.

Since the moral hazard problem is easier to understand, we begin with that.

Moral hazard

Moral hazard (also known as hidden action) occurs when the activity of the agent cannot be observed by the principal. For example, as shareholders we do not know what managers are doing. We can observe some indicators, but most of their behaviour remains hidden. For all we know they could spend their time playing golf or checkers all day eating expensive lunches with their friends at the company's expense while demanding sky high salaries.

The term 'moral hazard' originates in the insurance literature. Insurers found that when people have fire insurance, the probability of fire increases. This can to some extent be attributed to direct fraud; some people may set their shop on fire in hopes of getting a new one financed with insurance money. But it is also possible that people become more careless when they know they are insured. For example, when you leave your

33

house you may ask yourself if you forgot a burning candle or if you forgot to turn off the stove. If you are not insured, agency theory would predict that you are more likely to go back and check an extra time. Thus, on top of the usual risk of fire, there is an additional element – a moral hazard – which insurance companies must take into account.

The moral hazard case illustrates a general principle: there is a trade off between risk and incentives. If you insure people against risk they also lose the incentive to do something about it. For example, insurers will routinely ask people to pay a minimum amount (deductable), when their car is insured and there is an accident. The argument for this is that the insured person will then share some of the risk and will therefore not lose all of the incentive.

In case of shareholders and managers, managers can be given incentives: for example, a bonus if profits are high or a stock option scheme so that the manager benefits if the stock price increases. In this case, the manager shares some of the shareholders' risk and receives an incentive to act in our interest as stockholders.

Monitoring is another strategy. Insurance companies may examine whether there is any indication of fraud or negligence before they pay out the insurance premium. When there is even a small chance of detection – or a small chance that one will not receive an insurance claim – people will be much more careful about negligence and fraud.

In the case of company managers, shareholders commission auditors to inform them annually (in the annual report) about the company's performance and management's performance. Although there are many examples of non-performance which auditors do not detect, at least some checks are probably better than no checks.

Adverse selection

Adverse selection – or hidden knowledge – occurs when there is some element in the situation which is known to the agent but not known to the principal. For example, when the shareholders (via the board) hire a new manager for the company, they may not know how capable she is. She may be more or less intelligent, more or less hard-working, but she may also be an alcoholic or a sex offender. Prior to appointment, shareholders can scan some signs of performance – her grades from business school or

Adverse selection

her references, for example – they cannot measure what they really want to know: How will she actually perform in the new job? The agent, of course, knows herself much better than principals do. Therefore, she has some hidden knowledge.

For the sake of the argument imagine that an agent – Susan – knows she is worth 40.000 DKK a month but she gets an offer of only 20.000. In this case, Susan may decide not to take the offer. Instead, she could choose to become self-employed and make 40.000 DKK per month plus incur a risk premium. In contrast, if she knows that she is worth only 10.000, she might want to take the job, because it is an attractive bargain from her viewpoint.

This means that the company will have selected the wrong employee – or rather – that the wrong employees were self-selected to work for the company. This is an adverse selection.

The term 'adverse selection' was suggested by George Akerlof who received the Nobel Prize in economics for highlighting this problem, amongst other ideas.

The now classic example is the market for bad cars – so-called 'lemons.' As the story goes, auto workers in the old days would not work on Sundays and they would take this opportunity to get drunk. When they returned to work on Mondays, the auto workers had hangovers. The result was that the cars produced that day would be full of errors. It would be referred to as a 'Monday car' or 'lemon' which was lower quality than cars produced on the other five weekdays. It would be impossible for a new buyer to tell the difference between Monday and Tuesday cars before they made their purchase. Post-purchase, however, there would be constant problems with Monday cars. They would need constant repairs. So let us say that a Monday car is worth nothing and that a normal weekday car is worth 100 000. People would then only be willing to pay 83 333 for the new cars because they knew there was a 16.666% chance of buying a lemon.[1]

A customer who bought a new car would quickly discover it was a Monday car and might want to sell it to buy another one. Used car buyers would consider that the fraction of Monday cars for sale in the used car

---

1. We assume that one out of six cars is a lemon because one out of six workdays is a Monday.

market would be substantially higher than 1:6, since many more owners of Monday cars would want to sell their cars than owners of Tuesday cars. Since some cars are worth 100 000 minus usage and some cars are worth 0, what could one expect the price of used cars would be? 0!

If the price was 50 000, the owners of good cars would not want to sell. Thus only Monday cars (lemons) would be on the market. The same is true for any price < 100 000 minus a little. Now suppose that the price was 100 000. All the Monday cars would then be put up for sale. For the sake of the argument, let us assume that the other cars would also be put up for sale because the price was slightly higher than what the cars were worth. The problem is, however, that nobody would want to buy at that price. Rational buyers would certainly not pay more than the 83 333 that they would pay for a new car – given that the probability of a lemon car was around the same for new and used cars. But at a price of 83 333, none of the good-car owners would want to sell. Thus there would be only lemons – worth 0 – on the market. Buyers would recognize this and not buy. Ultimately, the sellers would have to offer a lower price; in fact they would have to lower the price to zero before anyone would buy.

It is possible to make this example more realistic (and more complicated) by assuming that there would also be sellers of good cars at lower prices – for example because some of them had changed their mind and wanted to buy a new car or because they found that they could afford a better car because of increased income or wealth. Without going too much into detail, suppose that half of all car owners had good cars, but they would sell at a price of 60. But the lemon owners would of course also offer their cars for sale. This means that ½ + 1/6 = 4/6 of the cars would be up for sale, and 25 % of them would be lemons. Buyers would have to consider that the cars would not be worth 60 to them, but only 45, since ¼ of the used cars for sale would turn out to be lemons. So they would offer 45. But at that price, perhaps only 1/3 would be willing to sell. The lemon owners would still offer their cars, so now there would be 1/3 + 1/6 = ½ of the cars up for sale of which 1/3 would be lemons. So the cars on sale would on average only be worth 30 to the buyers, which would encourage even fewer good car owners to sell. The number of lemons on the market would increase and demand would fall. You can see where this leads. The market will collapse.

In the real world, of course, there is a market for used cars. In part this is because very few cars have no value at all, so prices will not fall to zero. Moreover, it is possible to examine cars to reduce the information asymmetry.

In corporate governance we would call this monitoring. Owners of good cars or the intermediaries (dealers) may signal to buyers that they are good –by offering a guarantee, for example. The law may also help the process by punishing cheaters. Nevertheless, used car dealers still have a bad name, and the prices for used cars are substantially lower than for new cars.

We can apply the same logic to the job market. Suppose that 1/6 of the applicants for a new job are no good (value 0), while the rest have a value of 100 to the firm. In order that the appointment creates value for the firm, the company cannot offer more than a salary of 83.3. But at that salary level, all the 'good applicants' might decide to start their own businesses or find another job offer. So the value of the new hires to the firm would be zero, and the firm would lose money if it offered them more. Alternatively, half of the good applicants might want to work for 60, since that was what they could make on their own. But there would still be 1/6 'good-for-nothings'. Thus the firm could only offer 45. You can work the rest out for yourself.

One solution to this problem is to screen – or monitor – incoming applicants. For example a human resource function can screen applicants prior to appointment. Another solution to this problem is incentive. If the firm offers performance-based pay, the good-for-nothings will not want to risk it, but the high-performers will.

Example 1. The IPO market. Adverse selection also occurs among firms that want to go public: an Initial Public Offering (IPO). Some firms go public because they need new capital. Others go public because the owners want to cash out. A third group wants to go public to sell out because the business is bad. It is difficult for investors to tell the difference. As a result, there is a discount on IPOs. In some cases, owners are better off to keep their ownership and live off the dividends which profitable businesses can generate. One of the solutions is that owners can signal to the market that they believe in the firm by retaining a high ownership share. During the dot.com boom, investors were apparently unable to tell the difference between good and bad. In hindsight, it might have been a good rule-of-thumb guide for investors to only buy stock in companies where the incumbent owners also had some money at stake rather than to buy stock in those companies where the owners ran away as fast as they could.

Example 2. Banking. The same problem occurs in banking. Some loans are bad and bankers try to sort the good from the bad, but they cannot perfectly do so ex ante (i.e. beforehand). Some of the bad borrowers have unrealistic expectations, some are gamblers, and some want to use the money for their own consumption. So banks have to charge a risk premium on their loans over the risk free rate of interest (e.g. treasury bills). This will make the 'good' borrowers less likely to borrow, but the bad borrowers will not be discouraged. So there can be adverse selection. In fact, one theory is that banks exist because they can specialize in handling adverse selection and moral hazard problems in the market for loans.

Alternatives to the agency model

While agency models appear to lead to many insights about real world models, and while agency is unquestionably the single most important theory in corporate governance, it cannot explain all human behaviour. For a better understanding of corporate governance we also need to draw on other theories within the fields of economics, psychology, law, political science, and sociology. An intelligent user will apply agency theory intelligently and will take into consideration, for example, that soft variables like ethics or prestige are sometimes more important to people than is monetary gain.

The fields of economics, microeconomics, and financial economics have much to say about markets. Contract theory (i.e. incomplete contracting) is important to understand ownership. Game theory (i.e. repeated games) is important to understand the importance of reputation.

Psychology is important to understand incentives, small group behaviour in boards, emotional ties (in the case of family business), and limitations on rationality. Emerging theories of behavioural finance and behavioural economics allow a more sophisticated understanding of both subjects.

Law regulates corporate governance to a surprising degree. Very often there is a specific legal reason for a certain governance practice. Law and economics are clearly central disciplines in the field of corporate governance.

Political science is important to understand law. Law is, after all, created by politicians. Moreover, the concept of governance is borrowed from politics. There is a parallel between political democracy and shareholder democracy, and there are commonalities in issues of voting procedures, representation, etc. Interestingly, political ideologies seem to be closely connected to preferences for corporate governance. For example, socialists prefer government ownership or employee ownership, while conservatives prefer private ownership.

Sociology (or social psychology) is important to understand social networks (interlocking boards), international cultural differences (e.g. Japanese corporate governance), and the social norms which shape ethics and morality.

Management researchers have developed their own toolbox. Concepts like corporate strategy, core competences, resource dependency, business ethics, and corporate social responsibility are useful to better understand corporate governance.

The urge to combine all of these approaches into one grand unified theory is a noble aim, but it will have to be left to basic research in order to move on with some more partial approaches to different aspects of corporate governance.

A thought experiment

Compare the two following statements:

'At The Coca-Cola Company, our publicly stated mission is to create value over time for the owners of our business. In fact, in our society, that is the mission of any business: to create value for its owners' (quote from the CEO 1981-1997, Robert C. Goizueta, 1996).

'Fundamentally, The Coca-Cola Company is built on a deep and abiding relationship of trust between it and all its constituents: bottlers ... customers ... consumers ... shareowners ... employees ... suppliers ... and the very communities of which successful companies are an integral part. That trust must be nurtured and maintained on a daily basis.' (Douglas N. Daft, Chair and CEO 2003).

Based on the above statements, how would you characterize the purpose of the Coca Cola Company in 1995?

How would you characterize it in 2003?

Has anything changed?

If so, how might this change matter to company behaviour?

What are the true goals of Coca Cola? Can you come up with some 'working hypotheses'?

References

Akerlof, George A. 1970. The Market for 'Lemons': Quality Uncertainty and the Market Mechanism. *Quarterly Journal of Economics* 84 (3): 488–500.

Arrow, K.J. 1963. Uncertainty and the welfare economics of medical care. *American Economic Review*, 53: 941-973.

Arrow, K.J. 1973. Social responsibility and economic efficiency. *Public Policy*, 21: 303-318.

Holmström, Bengt. 1979. Moral hazard and observability. *Bell Journal of Economics* 10.

Holmström, B. 1982. Moral hazard in teams. *Bell Journal of Economics,* 13(2).

Jensen, M. 1993. The modern industrial revolution, exit and the failure of internal control systems. *The Journal of Finance*, 48(3): 481- 531.

Jensen, M.C. & W.H. Meckling. 1976. Theory of the firm: managerial behaviour, agency costs, and ownership structure. *Journal of Financial Economics*, 3:305-360.

Eric A. Posner. 2000. *Agency Models in Law and Economics*. The Coase Lecture. Winter 2000

The Law School, The University of Chicago John M. Olin Law & Economics Working Paper No. 92 (2d Series). *The Chicago Working Paper Series* Index: http://www.law.uchicago.edu/Publications/Working /index.html

Rappaport, A. 1981. Selecting strategies that create shareholder value. *Harvard Business Review*.

Rappaport, A. 1986. *Creating shareholder value the new standard for business performance*. Free Press, New York.

CHAPTER 3

The Mechanisms of Governance

Given agency relationships, the central governance problem is how managers are controlled. How do we as shareholders ensure that they manage the company in our best interest? There are several mechanisms of governance, all of which serve to mitigate agency problems. I list some of them in figure 3.1

Figure 3.1: Governance mechanisms

Moral standards
Reputation and trust
Legal protection
Large owners
Shareholder pressure
Boards
Creditor monitoring
Incentive systems
Auditors
Analysts
Takeovers
Competition
Managerial labour market
Codes
Media Pressure

As you can see, there are many corporate governance mechanisms.

In this chapter I will argue that each of these mechanisms have their costs and their benefits. I argue that good corporate governance essentially consists of tailoring these mechanisms to the individual firm. The

Chapter 3. The Mechanisms of Governance

general logic is that of the Aristotelian golden mean (figure 3.2) or – from neoclassical economics – declining marginal productivity.

Figure 3.2

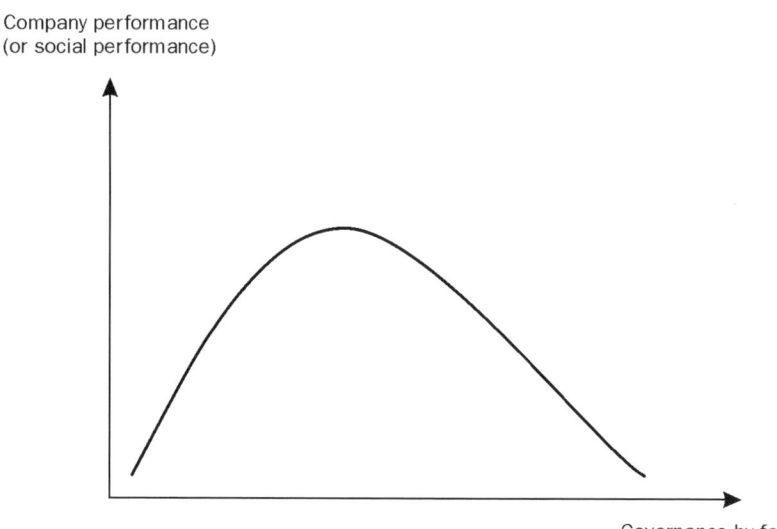

Company performance
(or social performance)

Governance by factor X

Up to a certain point, most corporate governance mechanisms will improve company economic performance, for example because the mechanisms pressure managers to work harder or to enable the shareholders to make better choices. Beyond this point – which is difficult to define and varies from mechanism to mechanism and from firm to firm – the costs start to kick in. Increasing use of this governance mechanism will destroy the value.

In other words, corporate governance is generally all about finding the golden mean – or – defining how a particular mechanism can create value in a particular situation. I will go through the different mechanisms of corporate governance and will point to some of their costs and their benefits.

Moral standards

At the most basic level corporate governance depends on morality. Suppose that a manager gets an opportunity to steal shareholder funds and knows it will never be detected. Will he do it? Economic man would. Would you? Suppose that it was a lot of money, so much that you could live on it comfortably for the rest of your life. Maybe the temptation is stronger in that case. There is a good chance that many people would, so morality is an imperfect solution to governance problems. On the other hand, there are many examples of people who would not steal and many cases in which most people would not steal. It would be difficult to run a modern society if people were completely amoral; the same applies to corporate governance.

Morality is related to what some management researchers call 'stewardship'. To the extent that managers act morally – as good stewards – there is a tendency for agency problems to disappear. However, they do not disappear entirely. As a manager, you may feel a moral duty to be an equal opportunity employer or help people in need, but your shareholders may not agree. Moreover, while some managers are highly moral, there are others who are not, and there are many who would be willing to compromise on their standards if the incentives were right. This can happen if the rewards are very high, but it may also happen if they are very low. For example, few managers hesitate to 'borrow' a pen at the office. Consider the classic story about Bernard Shaw:

> *George Bernard Shaw once found himself at a dinner party, seated beside an attractive woman. 'Madam', he asked, 'would you go to bed with me for a thousand pounds?' The woman blushed and rather indignantly shook her head. 'For ten thousand pounds?' he asked. 'No. I would not.' 'Then how about fifty thousand pounds?' he continued. The colossal sum gave the woman pause, and after further reflection, she coyly replied: 'Perhaps'. 'And if I were to offer you five pounds?' Shaw asked. 'Mr. Shaw!' the woman exclaimed. 'What do you take me for?' 'We have already established what you are,' Shaw calmly replied. 'Now we are merely haggling over the price.'*
> (Unconfirmed, but see the same story in Jensen (1998)).

Although shareholders cannot usually raise the moral standards of their employees, morality matters in corporate governance because moral standards differ between nations and may change over time. Some observers claim that corporate governance in the USA has become more of an issue because moral standards have fallen. Moreover, there may have to be more monitoring in countries where moral standards are low (or different). For example, corruption is more of a problem in some countries than it is in others. Finally, it is possible to influence morality among managers by carefully selecting who is hired (and fired) as well as it is possible to design corporate policies for what is and what is not acceptable behaviour.

It is clear, therefore, that good morals can increase company and social performance. But is it really true that moral standards can be too high? It is easy to think of examples of people who become so dogmatic that they are unable to act. From a strictly moral viewpoint we should perhaps give all our money to the poor, should only do business with the poorest countries, or should only employ people who have difficulties in finding a job. So it would seem that there is a limit to morality, after all. Many academics would then argue that true morals would take all the constraints into account, but this is no different from saying that there is a limit even to morality. More on ethics will be presented in chapter 7.

Trust and reputation

Informal governance mechanisms like trust and reputation are also important. Managers who cheat investors will not find it easy to obtain more money or to get a new job. This means they have an incentive to protect their reputations. Thus, reputation may be a powerful deterrent to both adverse selection and moral hazard problems.[1] Franks, Mayer, and Rossi document that the industrial revolution in the UK was financed to a large extent by informal governance, e.g. gentlemen agreements within the 'old boys' networks.' Specialized stock exchanges – for example the textile ex-

---

1. Following Kreps (1990) and the ensuing literature, it can be shown formally that under certain circumstances companies can overcome the prisoners' dilemma games with other market participants (buyers, sellers, employees, and investors). The common governance mechanisms are the emergence of reputation, culture, and social norms in repeated games that provide incentives for consistently honest and fair behaviour. But intuitively, such cooperative equilibriums are fragile and sensitive to informational problems and institutional constraints. For example, trust and reputation are difficult to sustain in large societies with impersonal exchange. Tadelis (1999) shows that a market for reputation, for example, when new owners unknown to the business partners acquire the reputations of other firms by acquisitions, gives rise to adverse selection problems and market failure.

change in Manchester – were places where everybody knew everybody else and it was more difficult to get away with bad behaviour.

Reputation is a powerful mechanism, but it is far from perfect. Reputation mechanisms can work in repeated games where bad behaviour is punished by other market participants in future transactions. For example, a fraudster may be excluded from the good society and others may refuse to do business with him. But if people have a finite time horizon, the reputation mechanism loses its force. This may be the case if a company has becomes self-financing and no longer needs external investors. In that situation, managers may cease to care about investors and they may focus more on their own self interests.

Moreover, the reputation mechanism works better in small societies where everybody knows everybody else and information flows easily. It cannot work if market participants are anonymous as they may be in large markets or large countries. Globalization will, therefore, tend to attenuate reputation mechanisms.

Finally, reputation is not a fine-tuned instrument. Suppose that a manger forgets to pay dividends to some Italian investors. He may not care very much about his reputation in Italy. And if there is disagreement among the parties, it may be unclear to what side public opinion will lean. One of the advantages of the law is that courts are able to take large amounts of information into consideration which could not realistically and accurately be handled by reputation.

Law

Legal protection of shareholder rights is clearly very important. For example, managers can be sent to jail if they steal from stockholders. Moreover, the law obligates companies to many practices which protect the interests of investors. For example, there must be a shareholder meeting at least once a year. All shareholders must be duly informed about the meeting. Boards are elected by shareholders. The decisions made at the shareholder meetings are binding for the company. In between meetings all major decisions including the choice of manager – must be ratified by the board. Managers must respect whatever shareholders decide to write into the bylaws and so on.

The law also stipulates duties for officers and directors in the corporation. Directors have a duty of loyalty (to shareholders) and a duty of care (to actively live up to their responsibility).

Shareholders may use the court system and sue the company if they feel that the company is being mismanaged. Knowing this also helps to keep managers on their toes.

The law also protects the interests of other stakeholders: for example creditors and employees. Banks can demand compensation from board members and managers who have acted recklessly with their money. In some countries, employees have the right to elect members of the company's board.

Law is essential. Corporate governance would not be possible without some enforcement of property rights, and it certainly helps shareholders control managers. But it is not a perfect mechanism. Sometimes managers break laws. And shareholders may not be satisfied with a manager just because he abides by the law. Too many rules and too large penalties would lead to a loss of flexibility and risk aversion, which would make it difficult to do business.

An example: Stock market regulation
Theoretically (see Thomsen and Vinten, 2007), a stock exchange is a firm that creates a market in shares (Mulherin et. al., 1991). The market is attractive to buyers and sellers of shares because it economizes on their transaction costs – that is their search, information, bargaining, decision, policing, and enforcement costs (Coase, 1992; Mulherin et al. 1991; Dahlman 1979). An important instrument in this is a certain standardization of the shares traded (Telser, 1981) which reduces the need for a continuous detailed assessment of individual firms and transforms their stock into 'homogenous, fungible securities' (Pirrong, 1995). Standardization and other rules are provided by the law, by the exchanges themselves (Coase 1992) through listing requirements and corporate governance codes (Cadbury Commission, 1992). This regulation applies to ownership and board structure, corporate governance practice, financial reporting, disclosure, capital structure, and firm size, but more subjective criteria like growth (NYSE listing requirements) may also be considered.

Governance rules and standards are valuable to investors and therefore also to issuers, because they reduce their cost of capital, but they come at a cost. There are direct costs, which include listing fees, fees for auditors and lawyers, liability and insurance costs, larger fees for non-executive and executive directors etc. In the USA the costs of compliance with the Sarbanes-Oxley act would fit into this category. Indirect costs would include costs of disclosure to competitors, loss of flexibility with regard to board structure, opportunity costs of top management time, box-checking, and bureaucratic procedures. Most of these costs will be fixed, while the variable cost of trading shares will be negligible (Foucault and Parleur, 2004).

It is difficult to determine the optimal level of regulation with any degree of precision because regulation is so multifaceted. It is not given, for example, that optimal regulation will maximize the number of listed companies or that it will minimize the number of delistings. However, it seems important to consider both costs and benefits. The widely used investor protection index originally proposed by La Porta et al. (1998) was justified to a large extent by a positive effect on the size of the stock market. This so-called 'anti-director rights' index summarized measures which were believed to strengthen the rights of minority investors vis-à-vis company boards.

The investor protection index constructed by La Porta et al. (1998) and updated by Pagano and Volpin (2005b) is a sum of six dummy variables:

1) whether proxy by mail is allowed,
2) whether shares are/are not blocked before a shareholder meeting,
3) whether cumulative voting for directors is allowed,
4) whether oppressed minorities are protected,
5) whether the percentage of share capital required to call an extraordinary shareholder meeting is less than 10 percent, and
6) whether existing shareholders have pre-emptive rights at new equity offerings.

There are clearly both costs and benefits associated with these provisions. For example, the right to file lawsuits against boards involves cost, as does the right to call an annual meeting or a prohibition against dual class shares.

Theoretically, it can be argued that the optimal level of investor protection for listed companies is greater than zero since stock exchanges use regulation to lower the costs of exchange. It is equally plausible that there are limits to the optimal complexity of regulation (Kaplow, 1995; Ehrlich and Posner, 1974) and that more regulation will at some point have a negative effect.

As an example, La Porta et al. assert that investors are better protected when an investor can call an extraordinary general meeting if s/he has more than 10 % of the stock. It is clear that an extraordinary meeting involves costs not just for the managers who have to defend their decisions, but also for the other shareholders who have to attend the meeting or live with the outcome if they stay away. But what would happen if this threshold was lowered to 5 %; would investor protection be higher? If so, what about 1 %? Or should any shareholder be able to call a shareholder meeting at any time? In most situations, the transaction costs for both the shareholder and for the company would probably become too high at some point; the other shareholders would consider delisting, or, at least, the company's market value would drop. In contrast, few would argue with the proposition that a qualified majority of the shareholders should be able to call an extraordinary meeting.

I therefore conjecture there is a cost to stock market regulation, that more regulation is not necessarily better, and that regulation beyond a certain point will lead to fewer listed firms and lower firm value. I summarize these propositions in figure 3.3 (Thomsen and Vinten, 2007).

Figure 3.3

Stock market performance
e.g. number of listed companies,
(Value of listed companies ...)

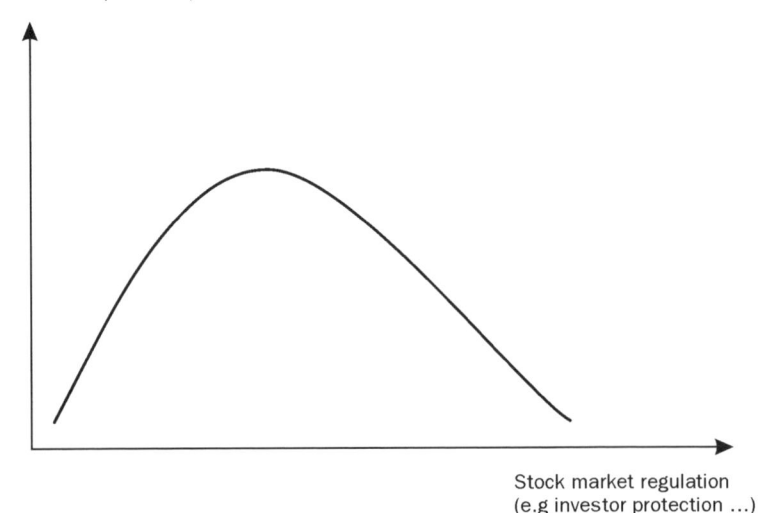

Stock market regulation
(e.g investor protection ...)

Large owners

The vast majority (most likely 99 %) of all companies are owned by one or two shareholders who also manage the company. It is not difficult to understand why. Owner-management aligns the interests of owners and managers. It is their own money so they have every incentive to manage it well. Owner-management also addresses the adverse selection problem. Suppose that you inherit a firm, but you know that you are not a good manager. Then you have every incentive to have someone else manage it; you might even see an incentive to sell it to somebody who can create more value than you can. It is your money and you have the incentives to manage it as well as you can. Both in theory and in practice it makes more sense to have a manager own the firm than somebody from the outside, because the manager has more information and is therefore in a better position to make decisions (Hart 1995).

Even for listed companies, a large owner can be a solution to a corporate governance problem because she has both the incentives and the power to influence what happens in the company. Large owners may therefore act as watchdogs on behalf of minority investors who can free ride on their efforts.

Nevertheless, large owners are not a perfect solution. First, as a rule they will be more risk averse than other investors because they have invested so much in this particular company (i.e. they have placed all their eggs in one basket), and this will influence corporate strategy. Secondly, there is a risk that they may exploit the minority investors, particularly in countries with low investor protection. Tunnelling occurs when controlling owners take money out of the company, for example by organizing transactions on unfavourable terms with companies which they themselves own (this seems to have happened in the Italian Parmalat case). Large owners may also have idiosyncratic preferences which do not maximize shareholder value. For example, they may prefer that the company is managed by a family member or they may want to retain ownership in the family despite an attractive offer from the outside which the minority shareholders would prefer. Failed succession – from a clever father to a stupid son – is the Achilles heel of family-owned companies. More on family-owned companies will be presented in chapter 13.

The effects of large owners on corporate governance and performance depends critically on owner identity. A financial investor with a clear preference for shareholder value might be expected to exercise ownership in a way that is aligned with the interests of minority investors. In contrast, a government owner will usually have objectives which differ very much from shareholder value maximization. Families are probably somewhere in between. More on ownership structure will follow in chapter 5.

Shareholder pressure

In the absence of a large owner, shareholders are much weaker, but it is not true that they have no power at all. They can turn up at annual meetings, they can criticize the management, and they can vote against it. Even if they lose a vote, the pressure can be unpleasant for the managers and it may damage their reputation. So managers have incentives to keep them happy.

Moreover, small shareholders may sell their shares – do the Wall Street walk. This will tend to lower share prices and increase the costs of capital for the corporation. Corporate bondholders may sell out, too. This could make it more difficult for managers to compete – e.g. to grow the company – which provides an additional incentive to try to please shareholders.

Shareholder pressure is obviously imperfect. Small shareholders cannot be expected to be well informed, and there are 'free rider' problems between them – if one shareholder makes an effort he bears all the costs while all the other shareholders benefit as well.

Boards

Boards are a generic corporate governance mechanism. They are elected by shareholders with the explicit aim to address corporate governance issues. Since it would be costly for shareholders to meet and to monitor the company, they hire a group of professionals to do it for them. Boards meet regularly to examine company performance, to ratify major investment decisions, and if necessary, to replace management.

Nevertheless, while there are no doubt many vigilant boards, and while corporate governance would no doubt be worse without them, boards are only a partial solution to the governance problem. For one thing, boards can be no better than the shareholders who elect them. If the shareholders are badly informed – or foolish – it is unlikely that they will elect the best board members, unlikely that they will monitor them well, and unlikely that they will replace bad board members. Secondly board members have little knowledge about what goes on in the company compared with the CEO. Board members should not know too much, since they should not interfere with the day-to-day management of the company. Moreover, board culture appears to make it psychologically difficult for an outside board member to voice a critical opinion, c.f. the following quote by the second richest man in the world, who has extensive board experience:

> 'It's almost impossible, for example, in a boardroom populated by well-mannered people, to raise the question of whether the CEO should be replaced. It's equally awkward to question a proposed acquisition that has been endorsed by the CEO, particularly when his inside staff and outside advisors are present and unanimously support his decision. (They wouldn't be in the room if they didn't.) Finally, when the compensation committee – armed, as always, with support from a high-paid consultant – reports on a mega grant of options to the CEO, it would be like belching at the dinner table for a director to suggest that the committee reconsider ...' Buffet (2003).

More about boards is found in chapter 6.

Creditors

If companies need to borrow, creditors exercise tremendous influence over what they do. Banks may make demands on board composition, management, and capital structure as a condition for lending. They may also insist on covenants which limit their strategic flexibility (for example, new investments may need to be approved by creditors). In some cases a meeting with a major creditor may be more important than a board meeting for deciding the future of the company.

Loan contracts are relatively simple to enforce, and this is probably why loans are much more important than equity as a source of company finance. Moreover, debt finance is attractive as a way to motivate managers to perform in order to be able to pay off debt since the alternative is bankruptcy.

Some countries – e.g. Germany – are known for a governance model which relies so much on bank finance that we talk about a bank-based model of corporate governance as an alternative to the market-based model. In recent years private equity funds appear to have reinvented this model and have much higher financial gearing (i.e. much more debt) than listed companies.

There are also limitations to creditor monitoring. First of all, it only works when companies have significant debt. Secondly, creditors are naturally risk averse – they do not gain when things go better than expected, but they lose when things go worse than expected. Since there is a trade off between risk and return, lower risk will lead to lower returns – and lower overall performance. Thirdly, there are many kinds of companies which banks are reluctant to finance: for example, those companies with highly specialized and immaterial assets which cannot be used as collateral. In contrast, businesses with collateral value – property, land, and inventory – are easier to debt finance.

As an alternative to both equity and bank loans, companies may also issue corporate bonds to the market. Since bondholders have no voting rights, they have less of an influence on corporate governance, although bond prices may influence the company's cost of capital.

Incentive systems

By incentive systems I mean the incentives given to managers. Managerial pay (compensation) consists of fixed salary, bonus, stock options, stock grants, and other benefits (i.e. health insurance, fringe benefits, and a pension scheme). Changes over the past decades mean that US managers in large listed companies are currently paid mostly according to performance (i.e. bonus or stock options schemes) while the greater part of management compensation in continental Europe is still fixed (i.e. a fixed amount per month).

Incentive systems can clearly give managers incentives to work in the interest of the shareholders; they can help address governance problems both of the moral hazard and the adverse selection variety. But incentive systems are not perfect solutions. Badly-designed incentives are more part of the disease rather than the cure since they involve large transfers of money from the shareholders to the managers; this is exactly what we want to avoid in corporate governance. Moreover, programs may lead to perverse incentives – for example earnings management, accounting fraud, or excessive risk taking. Finally, because of risk aversion, performance-based pay should theoretically be higher than fixed pay, which is consistent with what we observe in practice.

Auditors

Auditors are part of the corporate governance system. With a little exaggeration, they can be regarded as spies who are sent by the shareholders to the company to ensure that managers and the board are doing a good job. Auditors must audit the accounts and ensure that they present a 'true and fair view' of the company's performance and its financial situation.

There is no doubt that accurate information is crucial in addressing corporate governance problems if they reduce the information asymmetry which is at the core of the agency problem. Shareholders are in a much better situation to assess whether the management is doing a good job and whether the stock is attractive if they have access to trustworthy financial reports. Thus, auditors are clearly important contributors to corporate governance along with other mechanisms like disclosure requirements which provide information to investors.

Nevertheless, auditors cannot completely solve corporate governance problems. First of all, audit and accounting are not free, so there is a limit to the demand for auditing services. Secondly, more information does not always lead to greater transparency. The number of figures and words in annual reports have increased rapidly over the past decade, but it is not clear whether they have become more informative. In fact, for some users, they have become more confusing and less transparent. Thirdly, the move from historical cost accounting to market-based valuation has unfortunately made accounts more subjective and easier for managers to manipulate. Auditors who are paid by companies have a strong incentive to accommodate the wishes of company managers for 'creative accounting.'

To be sure, auditors are not normally regarded as spies. If they were, it would be more difficult for them to do their job, since managers would hesitate to volunteer information which would later be used against them. Thus, here we have another 'give-and-take' situation.

Analysts

Analysts employed by investors, stock brokers, and rating agencies issue reports which help shareholders and creditors understand companies and reports which evaluate company performance. This provides information which is useful for shareholders that have neither the capacity nor the time to do their own analysis and can help shareholders act more intelligently in corporate governance. A reasonably correct stock price is an important signal for shareholders.

But the value of analysis for corporate governance is limited by incentive problems. For example, analysts have been criticized for issuing too many 'buy' recommendations in order to stimulate trading and commissions, which is how their employers make their money.

Takeovers

Hostile takeovers are a famous and dramatic governance mechanism. If company performance is bad, the stock price drops, and a raider can make a tender offer for its shares, acquire control, fire the management, restructure, and sell his shares again at a significant gain.

However, empirically we observe few hostile takeovers. Thus, while they can make a contribution in some cases, they only rarely work in practice. One simple reason is that most companies around the world (including the USA) employ takeover defences specifically geared to prevent hostile takeovers. Another reason is that hostile takeovers may not create value for the acquirer, since significant costs are involved, whereas the gains to a very large extent go to the incumbent shareholders who almost always get a value premium. Finally, it is not clear whether hostile takeovers are directed at companies with both bad corporate governance and bad performance. This should be the case if they were to function as a corporate governance mechanism. Empirical studies indicate that many hostile takeovers are directed at companies with relatively good governance and good performance.

Competition

Competition in the market for products and services is a fundamental correction mechanism for any kind of inefficiency in a market-based system, and this also includes inefficiency in corporate governance. Bad management will ultimately lead to higher costs, loss of competitiveness, and bankruptcy. But competition will tend to lower profit rates and shareholder returns. Thus, from a shareholder viewpoint, competition is not a satisfactory solution even though it works well for society as a whole. However, shareholders can derive some benefit from the ability to benchmark their company against competitors. This can make it more transparent whether bad performance is attributable to bad management or to more general conditions.

The managerial labour market

Managers have an interest in a good track record if they want to advance in their careers. Even if the top managers do not care – because they plan to retire after their present job – their mid-level managers may. Moreover, a good track record will be helpful to managers who would like to have a few board positions after they retire. Therefore, the managerial labour market can also be regarded as a corporate governance mechanism. One of the correction mechanisms available to mid-level managers is 'whistle blowing'. They can leak information to the press so that shareholders or government organizations can take action before a scandal takes the whole company down (and the employee loses his job). Sarbanes-Oxley – an American corporate governance law enacted in 2002 – specifically recognizes the social value of whistleblowers and tries to protect them against reprisals.

Corporate governance codes

Corporate governance codes are recommendations about best practice in corporate governance issued by a government authority or a stock exchange, but which are typically prepared by respected top executives from the national business community. Usually these codes are not laws, but they are adopted on a 'comply-or-explain' basis so that companies must not comply, but they can instead choose to explain why they do not comply. Recommendations are very similar across countries and they typically include recommendations concerning the independence of board members, committees, board obligations, etc. Corporate governance codes seem to have had a significant effect on practice since the majority of companies have chosen to voluntarily comply with the provisions.

It is unclear why corporate governance codes have been so influential since there is little theoretical or empirical justification for most of the recommendations that they contain. One reason may be that they received the backing of institutional investors and that companies felt forced to comply. Another reason might be that best practice from leading companies became formalized and was eagerly imitated.

As with other governance mechanisms, it seems reasonable to assume that corporate governance codes have contributed to addressing agency problems; but they are not a perfect solution. In particular, the accompanying tendency to box checking may have imposed 'one-size-fits-all' solutions on a number of companies for which they were not suited. This, in turn, creates new governance problems. More on codes can be found in chapter 8.

Media pressure

As Dyck and Zingales (2003) emphazise, the media can be a corporate governance mechanism. Bad corporate governance and bad company performance can lead to media exposure, which is unpleasant for the managers and which may induce them to change their ways. Media exposure seems to work for both listed and unlisted companies regardless of ownership structure. Exposure may have a more pervasive effect than the other mechanisms mentioned. However, there is little doubt that media exposure is a very blunt instrument which often targets the wrong cases and which overlooks other cases which should have been addressed.

System effects

Altogether there is an impressive array of corporate governance mechanisms. In the real world these mechanisms are not independent; on the contrary, there are strong causal connections between them. For example, boards are elected by shareholders. Thus there must be a causal connection between ownership structure and board structure. In other words, governance mechanisms are parts of a system (Milgrom and Holmstrom, 1997). There may be both substitutability and complementarity between mechanisms so that some mechanisms tend to substitute for each other (i.e. if you have one, you do not need the other), while other mechanisms tend to coexist. In the next chapter we look at national systems of corporate governance as an application.

References

Fama, E.F. 1980. Agency Problems and the Theory of the Firm. *Journal of Political Economy* 88(2).

Franks, J., C. Mayer and S. Rossi. 2004. Ownership: Evolution and Regulation. European Corporate Governance Institute *Working Paper 09/2003* (revised 12/2004).

Hart, Oliver. 1995a. *Firms, contracts and financial structure.* Oxford University Press. New York.

Michael C. Jensen, *Foundations of Organizational Strategy.* Harvard University Press, Harvard Ma.1998.

Kreps, D.M. 1990. Corporate Culture and Economic Theory. Alt, James, E.; Shepsle, Kenneth, and A., eds. *Perspectives on Positive Political Economy.* Cambridge University Press, 90-143.

CHAPTER 4

International Corporate Governance

There are many different corporate governance mechanisms – pressure by large owners, company law, boards, pay and incentive systems, reputation and trust, etc. These mechanisms are used to varying degrees in different countries, and that is why we can discuss different corporate governance systems. For example, the USA and the UK have traditionally relied upon the stock market to finance and to regulate a substantial share of their businesses, while Germany has relied more upon banks, and the Keiretsu (i.e. cross-ownership) system is prevalent in Japan.

Before we start to analyse these differences, it is important to note they are to some degree fictional. Not all US firms are listed. In fact, the vast majority of firms are not listed. The banks are not active participants in the governance of all German companies, but they concentrate on the largest firms. Moreover, there are powerful banks in the Japanese and US systems as well. When we characterize 'systems' we tend to focus on the largest, most visible companies in a nation. But most companies in any nation are small and unlisted and in all nations they account for the bulk of business activity. As far as we know, these small- and medium-sized companies tend to be similar in their corporate governance – closely-held by founders or by families. Thus we may exaggerate the differences.

There is another substantial part of corporate governance which is not normally visible in international comparisons; this is the role of non-profits, government organizations, cooperatives, associations, and subsidiaries of foreign firms. We find these organisations in all countries – in the USA as well as in Europe. With the exception of government organizations, we know little about their importance and their relative efficiency.

Moreover, the characteristics of each system change over time. France used to be known for government ownership, but much has now been privatized. German banks try to reduce their shareholdings in German companies, so the German bank model might be obsolete in the near fu-

Chapter 4. International Corporate Governance

ture. Then again, it might not. Thus, it is important to adopt a dynamic perspective on international corporate governance.

Theoretical considerations

I define a governance system simply as a set of governance mechanisms in use in a given country or context. The fact that they are used in combination indicates some degree of consistency.

Corporate governance mechanisms are not independent. There are logical and causal ties between them. I propose a simple model in figure 4.1.

Figure 4.1: A schematic model of corporate governance

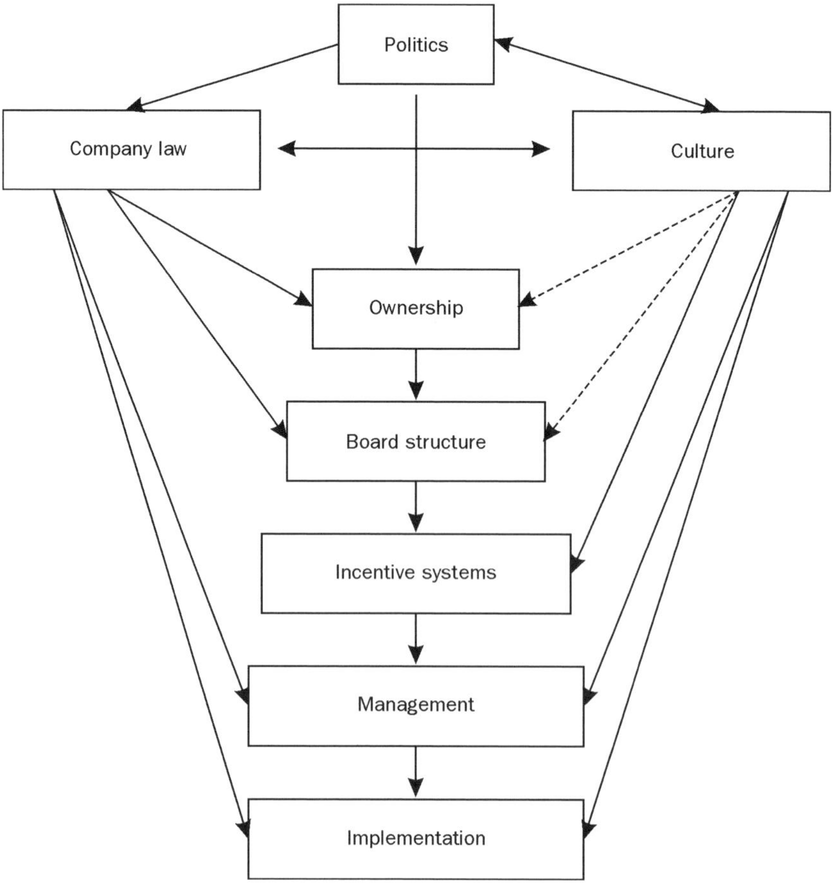

Theoretical considerations

In terms of causal structure, macro factors like culture and politics logically precede company law which logically precedes ownership structure. There are quite specific laws which regulate how much a bank or an institutional investor can own, and these laws differ between nations. This is an important cause of system differences (Roe, 1994). For example, a political change will often lead to the creation of new laws, which in turn can influence corporate ownership structure. However, a change in corporate ownership structure will not directly change the law. Board structure is decided by the owners under the limits laid down by law, which are often quite specific. The board decides on management incentives and on a number of other issues, but it delegates significant responsibility to managers, who again delegate to their employees the implementation of their decisions. We have here a series of agency relationships.

Another type of dependency is complementarity or substitution between mechanisms (Milgrom and Holmstrom, 1997). In figure 4.2, I sketch some hypothetical relationships.

Figure 4.2: A Hypothetical Sketch of Substitution (-) and Complementarity (+) between Governance Mechanisms

	Reputation	Law (investor protection)	Large owners	Boards	Incentives (performance pay)	Banks
Reputation						
Law (investor protection)	−					
Large owners	+	−				
Board control	−	−	−			
Management incentives	−	+	−	−		
Banks	+	+	+	+	−	

For example, there seems to be some degree of substitutability between law and informal governance by reputation. If laws are well defined there

61

is no need to rely on reputation to sanction corporate governance (see Poppo and Zenger 2002 for a counterargument).

Moreover, law – e.g. investor protection – enables atomistic share markets and dispersed ownership (i.e. the market model) to function, while strong owners are necessary to control firms in systems with weak investor protection, so there is substitutability between law and large owners (La Porta et al. 1998).

Large owners, in contrast, appear to rely heavily on reputation, but this is more difficult and less necessary for small investors who can (individually) buy and sell without much of an effect on the firm. Large owners will usually have a longer time horizon since they retain their shares for a longer period of time. This will make the mechanism of building reputation more attractive.

Boards have their key rationale when there is separation of ownership and control with dispersed ownership, whereas large owners do not have to rely on the board to represent them vis-à-vis managers. First, large owners often participate directly in the management of the firm, and in this case it is superfluous for the board to monitor the managers on behalf of the owners. The relationship between boards and law or reputation is more uncertain, but it seems possible to argue that boards need to do less when the governance problem is already addressed by either of the two other mechanisms.

Management incentives seem less necessary if there is already a strong ownership incentive. Board monitoring to reduce information asymmetries will also tend to reduce the need to incentivize. Moreover, by focusing on profit maximization in the short or medium term, management incentives may attenuate reputation building. Put differently, if managers are adequately motivated by reputation concerns, there is no reason to give them more incentives. The direct relationship between law and incentives is more uncertain, but I tentatively hypothesize a positive association because well-developed share markets with a strong legal infrastructure will need additional motivation of managers.

Because banks focus on risk, they will prefer flat rate pay over performance-based pay. There could be a trade off between shareholder and creditor protection but it is also possible to argue (with La Porta et. al. 1998, Djankov et al. 2005) for complementarity. A strong bank system will make it possible to debt finance more activities which should help large owners retain control compared to equity finance, which would require them to sell out. Moreover, banks will thrive with reputation whereas banking is more difficult without some prior knowledge of the debtor.

I do not claim that the hypotheses outlined in table 4.2 are rock solid. They should rather be regarded as work in progress, which serves to demonstrate the possibility of interaction effects between governance mechanisms more than a specific theory of such interactions.

The dependency between governance mechanisms serve to demonstrate their systemic character. But why are there systems? Where do they come from?

The dominant streams of research have emphasized the role of formal institutions, for example the legal system and investor protection rules, as determinants of these differences (Shleifer and Vishny, 1997; La Porta et al. 1998; 1999; 2002a). The legal systems perspective has led to a growing number of supportive empirical studies (Classens et al., 2000; Denis and McConnell, 2003; Durnev and Kim, 2002; La Porta et al., 1999). The implication here seems to be that countries develop constitutions and basic institutions which have a deep and lasting impact on their corporate governance systems.

This emphasis on formal institutions is also characteristic of the so-called political theory of corporate governance (Roe 1991; 1994), which emphasizes the regulation of financial institutions as a source of corporate governance differences. The pervasiveness of these differences within systems and the persistence of differences between systems is explained in terms of complementary institutions and rent seeking, which may effectively block changes in corporate governance (Coffee, 1999; North 1991; Roe, 1994). The argument is that the organizations created in a specific system – e.g. banks or institutional investors – will tend to lobby politicians to protect their own interests including the system which supports them. However, the political theory indicates that corporate governance systems can change when the policies change.

Licht (2001) has proposed a cultural theory of corporate governance. If countries differ systematically in terms of risk aversion, time horizons, obedience to authority, and other cultural factors, this could influence their choice of corporate governance system. It is also possible that the legal origins are related to differences in ideology (e.g. liberalism vs. socialism).

Chapter 4. International Corporate Governance

International systems

Figure 4.3 summarizes a large amount of information on corporate governance in six countries. For simplicity we count the 3 small Scandinavian countries (Norway, Sweden and Denmark) as one. The columns list countries. The rows list corporate governance mechanisms.

Starting with the first two countries – the USA and the UK – we observe from the two bottom rows that they have bigger stock markets both in terms of the **number of listed firms** and in terms of **stock market capitalization relative to GDP**. Stock market capitalization is the total value of all listed firms (stock price * number of shares) divided by the gross domestic product in the country. There are 7000 listed firms in the USA – which is probably more than in all of Europe. However, as a share of GDP, the stock market matters even more in the UK; it is almost 3 times as large as in Germany.

The German economy is much larger than the UK economy, but the number of listed British firms is more than double that of Germany's. In this way, we can distinguish between market-based governance systems – in the USA and the UK – and the control or bank-based systems found in continental Europe and Japan (Bebchuck and Roe, 1999).

Market-based systems are characterized by diffuse stock ownership (low ownership concentration). On average the largest owner in a large US corporation will hold only a few percent of the stock, in the UK less than 5% (Barca and Becht, 2001). The dispersion of ownership is obviously related to the size of the market. When more small shareholders invest, the size of the market increases and the average ownership share declines. Moreover, the increasing liquidity is attractive both for buyers and sellers of shares, and this leads to even more market participants (investors, companies).

The typical shareholders both in the USA and the UK are institutions (i.e. pension funds, insurance companies, mutual funds, etc.). In the USA, there are many individual 'mom and pop' investors. While many institutions are also large enough to take a high share of ownership in individual firms without undue risk to their portfolio, they are prevented from this by legal placement limits (which limit the share ownership of many investors to less than 5% of an individual company) as well as by an obligation to diversify risk (Roe, 1991). In comparison, the control-based systems are characterized by higher levels of ownership concentration by

International systems

Figure 4.3 International Governance Systems

	USA	UK	Japan	France	Germany	Scandinavia
Legal System	Common	Common	Civil	Civil	Civil	Civil
Investor protection	High	High	Low	Medium	Medium	Medium
Ownership concentration	Low	Low	Medium	Medium	Medium	High
Identity of owners	Institutions Individuals	Institutions	Cross Ownership Keiretsu	Cross Ownership Government	Banks Families	Families
Board System	One Tier	One Tier	One Tier	Optional	Two Tiers	Two Tiers
Insider share	+	+	++	+	-	(-)
Employees on board	0	0	0	0	50 %	33 %
Bank Influence	-	-	+	+	++	(+)
Performance pay	++	+	(+)	(+)	(+)	(+)
Listed firms 2004	7069	2073	3755	830	872	650
Market Cap % GDP	142	158	69	89	55	80

65

founding families, corporate investors (cross holdings), banks, and governments (Barca and Becht, 2001).

As a result, it is impossible for US and UK managers to have an ongoing dialogue with their shareholders. If the shareholders are not satisfied, they will sell and the stock price will fall. In contrast, in the European system a founder or a founding family will probably be able to express his/its opinion verbally (and probably in no uncertain terms). Management responsibility in the USA and the UK is diffuse (to the public), whereas it is direct and personal in Europe. In the USA and the UK, we find strong managers and weak owners, while the situation in Europe is the opposite (Roe, 1994).

The **dominant owners** in Japan and France are other corporations. Japan has the so-called keiretsu system in which members of a company group (a keiretsu) hold shares in each other. In the Mitsubishi group Mitsubishi heavy industry will own shares in Mitsubishi motors. They will both own shares in the Mitsubishi bank, which in turn holds shares in the other two. See chapter 11 for more on the Japanese model. Although each shareholding is small, when they are summed up, they constitute an effective defence against takeovers.

With regard to **board systems,** the USA, the UK, and Japan have one tier systems, while Germany and Scandinavia have two tier systems.[1] The difference between one and two tier systems is illustrated in figure 4.4.

In two tier systems (Germany, Scandinavia, Finland, Austria), shareholders elect supervisory board members – which are part time non-executive directors – and occasionally also a minority of executive directors to a supervisory board which evaluates company performance, hires and fires the management (the executives), and must approve all major decisions. This is similar to one tier systems, but unlike one tier boards,

1. I define a two tier system simply as a system in which the law requires companies to have two levels of management. This is the case both in Sweden and Norway, and so I define these countries as two tier systems. Some people would disagree and claim that for example all decision power in Swedish companies is vested in the board which only delegates some of these functions to the management as a practical issue. I would maintain that Sweden is a two tier system, although it is different from the German two tier system. The difference of opinion is attributable to the definition of a two tier system which I maintain because I believe that the two tier model is reflected in practice as well as in form in all the Scandinavian systems.

Figure 4.4: Board Systems

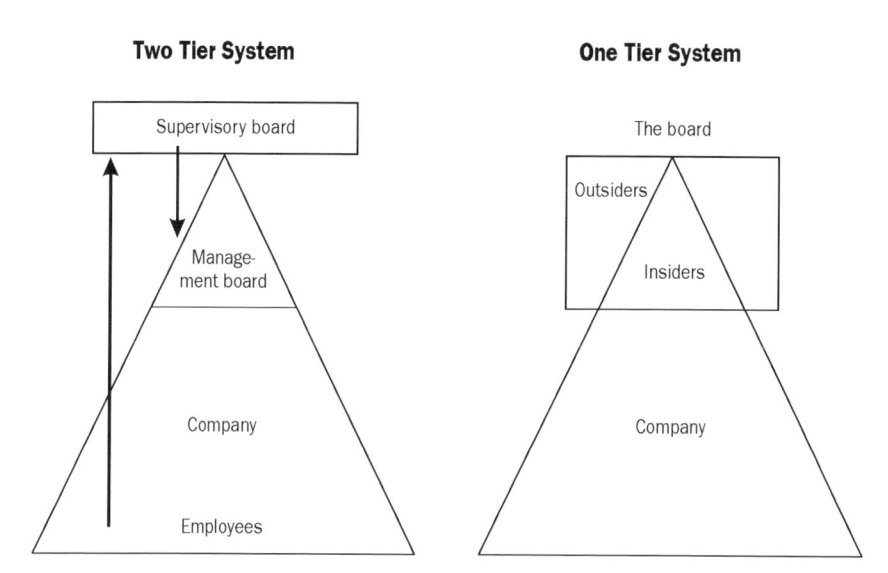

Two Tier System

- Supervisory board
- Management board
- Company
- Employees

One Tier System

- The board (Outsiders / Insiders)
- Company

supervisory boards cannot run the company on their own. They must appoint a management board.

In one tier systems, shareholders elect the board, which then appoints the executives. Executives may or may not be board members, but typically some of them are. In Europe and the USA most of the board members are now non-executive directors (this holds in the USA and Europe, but not in Japan). Non-executive directors are typically part-time, and generally – in accordance with best practice codes – a majority are independent also in the sense that they have no other material ties with the firm (e.g. the company lawyer, for example, is not an independent board member). Many non-executive directors have demanding jobs as executives, managers in other firms, lawyers, or even professors.

French companies have a choice between one- and two-tier boards, and the vast majority of them have chosen to stay with the traditional one-tier system. This is interesting, since it indicates that the one tier board structure would win if the choice between one-tier and two-tiers was left to the market participants. It may be that the one-tier model is more effective or it may be that managers dislike the added control. However, it is also possible that many French companies hold on to the old board structure because of conservatism.

Turning to board composition, **insiders** (i.e. executives) are prohibited from taking a seat on German supervisory boards, but the US, the UK, and the French companies have a fairly large percentage of managers on their board – although not a majority. In Scandinavia, the majority of the supervisory board members by law must be non-managers. In Denmark it is now regarded as best practice that managers do not sit on the supervisory board at all. Japan is famous for a very large percentage of insiders on boards. Boards in Japan are often quite large – with 30 or 40 members – which is perhaps too many for the board to make effective decisions. In the USA and France, the chief executive can also be chairman of the board (i.e. duality), but this is prohibited in two-tier systems. The French title is PDG – President + Director General. In the UK, the two positions – chairman and managing director – are now typically separated following corporate governance recommendations (Cadbury, 1992).

Employee Representation. In Germany and Scandinavia employees of a company have a right to elect members of the supervisory board: typically 1/3 of the board members (Denmark, Norway, Sweden, Austria). But in some large German companies, up to 50% of the board will be employee representatives. Despite employee representation, the shareholder-elected board members have a majority of the votes (e.g. in Germany the vote of the chairman is decisive in case of a split). Employee representation is not found on the shareholder-friendly US and UK boards, nor is it found in France. Interestingly, French unions have historically been unwilling to assume responsibility by employee representation. The differences are directly attributable to company law. In some countries, employee representation is mandatory by law and this is where you will find it. In other countries, employee representation is not mandatory, and the result is that most companies choose not to have it.

Banks have little influence in the (stock) market-based systems in the USA and the UK, but they continue to play a pivotal role in German corporate governance. Figure 4.5 illustrates the key difference between market-based and bank-based governance systems. In a market-based system, savers invest directly in shares and bonds of listed companies. In a bank-based system, they put their money in the bank which then lends it to the corporations or invests some of it directly in their shares. In the bank-based system, the bank acts as an intermediary and we therefore talk about intermediation. In the market-based system – or in a transition to a market-based system – we refer to 'disintermediation'.

Figure 4.5: Bank vs. Market Governance

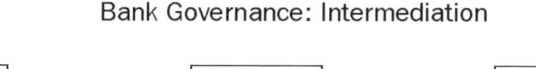

Bank Governance: Intermediation

Savers → BANK → Companies

Market Governance: Disintermediation

Savers (Investors) → Companies

To be sure, even in market-based systems many people prefer to invest in a mutual fund rather than investing directly in stocks, but in this case, the role of the intermediary is much more limited. Banks used to be central actors in most corporate governance systems but the worldwide growth of stock and bond markets have shifted the balance towards disintermediation in recent years.

In Germany the importance of banks for corporate governance is magnified by a number of special characteristics. First, banks are allowed to make large investments in stock even to the point of controlling some of the largest German corporations. Secondly, bankers often act as custodians for German shareholders and they may be entitled to vote on their behalf at shareholder meetings. Thirdly, bankers are allowed to sit on the boards of non-financial companies. So, despite a recent trend towards the reduction of their shareholdings in Germany, banks remain powerful actors in the German system. More can be found on the German system in chapter 10.

Japanese banks are also considered to be powerful actors in the Japanese corporate governance system since they play a role as 'main banks' at the centre of many keiretsus.

Again, there are very concrete legal reasons for why banks are less powerful in the USA and the UK. Commercial banks are prohibited to take large positions in non-financial companies in the USA and also (albeit less formally) in the UK. Moreover, traditionally US banks have been kept small by a forced specialization among investment and commercial banks (due to the Glass Steagal Act). For a long time in the USA banks were prevented from merging across state boundaries (due to the bank holding company act). Only recently in 1999 were some of these restrictions lifted.

The extent of **performance pay** for senior managers differs widely across systems although recently there appears to have been some convergence. Total pay levels for CEOs are much higher in the USA and, to a lesser extent, in the UK than in continental Europe and Japan. Moreover, a much larger percent (e.g. 80%) of US executive pay depends on performance (in the largest companies). Overall, this means that US managers have much stronger performance incentives than do European managers.

Legal systems also differ from one another around the world. Some researchers claim that these differences have important implications for corporate governance (La Porta et al. 1998). In the common law system which is used in the English-speaking world, law is in principle made by the courts based on specific decisions which thus create precedence, and thereby influence future decisions. In short, law is made from the bottom up, and the courts are regarded as private institutions which side with other private institutions against government in the protection of property rights. In contrast, in civil law systems the law is in principle regarded as an instrument which the government uses to achieve its goals, and it is by nature much less protective of property rights. Law is made top down by politicians, civil servants, and law professors. So the theory goes that common law systems are more likely to protect property rights, including the rights of minority investors, and that this is why the stock market is so well developed in common law countries.

In practice, the distinction between common and civil law countries is less clear. Why should lawmakers in continental Europe not be able to adopt the rule which they consider most conducive for stock market development (even to imitate common law countries if necessary)? Moreover, there are many examples of top-down legislation in the US: Sarbanes-Oxley is a recent example.

However, there is considerable empirical support for the hypothesis that company law in the USA and the UK tends to be more protective of shareholder rights than law in other countries. One important and widely-used measure is the investor protection index constructed by La Porta et al. (1998) and updated by Pagano and Volpin (2005b) – known as the LSSVPV index. The LSSVPV index is correlated with other kinds of minority investor protection: for example the Djankov et al. (2007) anti self-dealing index.[2] The anti-self dealing index measures legal limitations to self-dealing by controlling owners. For example, self-dealing can include transactions with other entities (i.e. those owned by the controlling owner) at inflated or reduced prices which will benefit their own interests and which harm minority investors. These limitations can include mandatory disclosure, a mandatory approval by the minority investor, the ability to challenge such transactions in court, etc.

European – particularly North European – countries score higher on an alternative, broader governance measure: the World Bank governance index, which combines measures of political freedom (e.g. freedom of speech, association, voting), regulatory quality (e.g. costs of regulation, efficient enforcement, presence of generally accepted codes, company law) and quality of the legal system (e.g. quality of contract enforcement and court system). Every second year since 1996 the World Bank has published a set of six different country level governance indicators for 209 countries (see Kaufman et al. 2005, 2006). The six governance indicators are: i) Voice and accountability, ii) Political instability and violence, iii) Government effectiveness, iv) Regulatory quality, v) Rule of law, and vi) Control of corruption.

Country models

Instead of comparing corporate governance mechanisms, it is interesting to examine the individual countries to explain their historical and cultural characteristics (Pedersen and Thomsen, 1997). Charkham (1994) makes an interesting – if somewhat speculative – attempt.

Great Britain was the first nation to industrialize, and funds for large enterprises had to be attracted from a number of individual investors. The fortunes of the landed gentry and the merchant class were to a large extent channelled into manufacturing at arms' length via the city of London.

---

2. The USA and the UK score high on the anti-self dealing index.

Social prestige dictated that finance and economics enjoyed a higher status than engineering.

France has a historical tradition for government intervention and centralization which, according to some, can be traced back to Louis XIV (Charkham, 1994). Features of the French system like the almighty chairman-CEO (the PDG combined President and Director General) also fit a hypothesis of centralization. More recently, the large share of government ownership in France which is partly a consequence of nationalization after the Second World War and partly a result of the Mitterand government in the early 1980s now undergoes large-scale privatization. The French tradition for government intervention is no doubt strengthened by strong personal ties in the elite that graduate from 'grand ecoles' and who occupy top jobs in business and government (Charkham 1994).

Another interesting feature of French ownership structure is the role played by holding companies which were originally established by industrial companies to overcome financing constraints (Levy-Leboyer 1980). This helps to explain the frequency of cross holdings. After privatization there seems to have been a tendency for this system to reappear, as companies join in a hard core of cross ownership to avoid being taken over by 'Anglo-Saxons'.

In Germany, banks played an active role in the industrialization process and financial institutions continue to exercise dominant minority control over many large companies (Feldenkirchen 1988), although founding families have often continued to exercise some control (by large minority shareholdings) even in listed companies (Pohl 1982). Furthermore, individual company profiles reveal that bank participation has often come about unintentionally and at a later stage – e.g., as the result of a financial crisis (Charkham 1994). In addition, Socialdemocratic politics have clearly played a role in the emergence of employee representation both in Germany and in Scandinavia. Both countries are characterized by more friendly relations between capital and labour than in the market-based governance systems.

A high frequency of family, foundation, and cooperative ownership in Scandinavia is partly attributable to scarcity of large companies in Norway and Denmark which have a relative factor advantage in agricultural products and shipping which are still dominated by coops and family-owned companies.

Convergence[3]

Corporate Governance systems are quite stable in the short run (e.g. from year to year), but they do sometimes change over longer periods of time (e.g. decades).

Recently, a consensus seemed to emerge amongst academics and executives alike that the Anglo-American corporate governance model had won and that European systems were converging to US/UK standards (e.g. Hansmann and Kraakman, 2000, 2002; Coffee 1999, 2002, Denis & McConnell, 2002). During the 1990s, examples were easy to find. Examples included the growing importance of stock markets in most economies, the increasing importance of institutional investors (Coffee, 1999; van den Berghe, 2002), the increasing number of hostile takeovers (The Economist, 2000) and suggestions to open the European markets further by a break-through rule (Bolkestein report, 2001), the spread of stock option-based managerial compensation (Murphy, 2000), or increases in leverage through share buy backs and higher dividends (Warner 1998).

However, contrary to general beliefs, it is possible to argue for a mutual convergence hypothesis (Thomsen, 2003). Not only has European corporate governance converged to US standards, US corporate governance has also effectively converged to European standards in several important respects since the 1980s. Comparative research in corporate governance has emphazised that Anglo-American corporate governance is characterised by low ownership concentration, one-tier boards and shareholder value norms, whereas high levels of insider ownership, two-tier boards and stakeholder concerns are more characteristic features of continental Europe (Baums, 1994; Roe, 1994; Prowse, 1995, Gugler, 2001; Vives, 2000; Barca and Becht, 2001). But during the 1990s ownership concentration in the USA/UK increased due to growing managerial ownership and institutional investment (Holderness et al., 1998, Meyer, 1998, Investor Relations Business, 2000). Moreover, management and control in the USA/UK have increasingly been separated by the appointment of non-executive directors (Monks and Minnow 2001), subcommittees com-

---

3. This section draws heavily on my paper "The Convergence of Corporate Governance Systems to European and Anglo-American Standards', European Business Organization Law Review, 4 (1), 2003.

posed of non-executives (Cadbury Code, NYSE code), and separation of the roles of CEO and board chair (e.g. the Cadbury and Higgs codes in the UK). Furthermore, the stakeholder approach has attracted increasing attention in US management research and practice during the 1990s (Clarkson, 1995. Donaldson and Preston, 1995; Jones, 1995; Mitchell et al., 1997; Agle et al., 1999; Jones and Wicks, 1999; Jawahar & Mclauglin, 2001). Finally, financial deregulation has relaxed the separation of investment and commercial banking and has allowed banks to assume a more prominent role in the America economy (Financial Services Modernization Act, 1999; The Economist, 1999). That too is a step in a European direction.

The leading convergence theorists, Hansmann and Kraakman (2000), point to three mechanisms of governance convergence: logic (persuasive arguments for the superiority of one model), example (of competitive success of one model), and demonstrated competitive advantages. These forces work in the same direction when influential shareholders or company managers adopt international governance structures that are perceived to work better, for example, when European managers adopt US/UK governance principles because comparable companies in the US/UK have higher market value, lower capital costs, or other advantages. In global capital markets this may be the direct result of an attempt to attract capital from the same investors, or it may be a more indirect imitation of new management practices. Studies by van der Elst reported in van den Berghe (2002) document the significant internationalisation of European equity markets which implies global competition to attract shareholder funds. Among listed companies international share ownership has increased considerably as a percent of total ownership in most European countries over the period 1990 to 1998. In rough figures international ownership increased from 12 to 15% in Germany, from 14 to 35% in France, from 8 to 12% in Italy, from 16 to 36% in Spain, and from 12 to 24% in the UK. It also increased significantly by more than 30% in the Nordic countries (Thomsen, 2001), but only marginally in the US from 7 to 7%+. Likewise, Coffee (2002) documents an increasing tendency for foreign firms to list on the New York Stock Exchange up to 2001 which was significant given the size and importance of the large companies in question (e.g. Daimler Benz) although the numbers (20-50 new firms a year during the 1990s) are probably too small to affect global changes in corporate governance in their own right.

Hansmann and Kraakman (2000) also mention harmonisation and changes in corporate law as a weak force towards convergence. Convergence in regulation may come about if politicians imitate the laws and policies of other countries because they are persuaded by logical arguments and/or the desire to improve international competitiveness, economic growth, or employment. For example, a case in point is the proposed EU takeover directive (Bolkestein, 2001, EU Commission, 2002) which aims to stimulate the market for hostile takeovers in Europe. Alternatively, governance structures may converge if corporate decision makers respond in the same way to similar challenges (e.g. the growing importance of institutional investors).

Clearly, these forces must be weighed against other powerful forces which block convergence or even promote divergence – for example the same factors that created corporate governance differences in the first place. Bebchuck (1999) and Bebchuck and Roe (1999) explain why ownership concentration will not automatically adjust to efficient levels, particularly why a controlling shareholder structure with high ownership concentration (which I will call a control structure) does not automatically develop into a non-control structure (which I will call a market-based structure), even when the market-based structure maximizes the financial value of the firm.

One important reason is the existence of private benefits to controlling shareholders, which are not shared with minority investors (Bebchuck 1999; Bebchuck and Roe, 1999). When firms have already adopted a mixed ownership structure with some minority investors, prospective gains by selling more shares to the public must be shared by these investors, and this reduces the incentive to give up private control benefits (Bebchuck and Roe, 1999). Bebchuck (1999) therefore predicts that control-based governance systems will emerge when the private benefits of control are large. In market-based systems, managerial control benefits may give rise to persistence of market-based governance structures (dispersed ownership). Because of vested interests in maintaining the status quo incumbent managers may resist the formation of controlling blocks (Bebchuck and Roe 1999) and fight hostile takeovers. Gains from the formation of large blocks of control will again be shared with the market reducing the incentive to form such blocks in market-based systems (Shleifer and Vishny, 1986).

Other factors at the system level also create barriers to change of ownership structure (Bechuck and Roe, 1999). Ceilings and other limitations on ownership by financial institutions, as in the USA, limit their ownership shares of individual firms (Roe, 1991). The existence of complementary institutions in a given system, e.g. a large and well-functioning stock market as in the USA/UK or an active bank sector as in Germany, may influence the ownership and capital structures of firms based in that system (Roe, 1994). Legal systems may provide varying degrees of protection of minority investors (La Porta et al., 1998). Finally, the incumbent organizations/institutions will lobby for continuation of their own existence (North 1991).

However, even though the formal governance structure is unchanged, there may be convergence in behaviour. Gilson (1999) – and later La Porta et al. (2000) – makes the important distinction between formal and functional convergence: companies within a particular institutional framework may change their behaviour in order to succeed or survive in international competition even though the formal structure is unchanged. Coffee (1999) argues that a number of forces pull and push towards convergence: the growth of European stock markets, disclosure harmonisation, the growth of institutional investors, harmonisation of international accounting standards, and the need for global economies of scale. But these forces clash with path dependency, complementarity, and other strong forces that block formal changes in the legal system. The outcome of this dilemma, Coffee argues, is that formal governance structures change very little, but that functional convergence in corporate governance takes place as European companies change behaviour to align with American standards.

Theoretically, functional convergence can be seen as a special case of Coasian contracting (Coase, 1960). If there are gains to trade or coordination, market participants have an incentive to contract around the prevailing formal structures of law and ownership to approach a first best allocation of resources. An obvious channel for this type of convergence is the internationalisation of equity markets in which profit-seeking investors can strike mutually-advantageous deals with companies in other governance systems and thus they may conduct transactions around formal barriers. This may, for example, have resulted in a functional reorientation of corporate governance in continental Europe.

References

Agle, B.R.; R.K. Mitchell; J. A. Sonnenfeld. 1999. Who matters to CEOs? An investigation of stakeholder attributes and salience, corporate performance, and CEO values, *Academy of Management Journal* 42(5): 507-525.

Aguilera, R. and Jackson, G. 2003. The Cross-National Diversity of Corporate Governance: Dimensions and Determinants. *Academy of Management Review*. Forthcoming.

Allan, F. and D. Gale. Corporate Governance and Competition. Vives, Xavier (ed.), 2000. *Corporate governance. Theoretical and empirical perspectives*. Cambridge University Press. Cambridge, UK.

Barca, F. and M. Becht. 2001. *The Control of Corporate Europe*. Oxford University Press, Oxford, UK.

Bebchuk, L.A. and M. Roe. 1999. A Theory of Path Dependence in Corporate Ownership and Governance. *Stanford Law Review*. 52 ( ), 127-170.

Baums, T. 1994. The German Banking System and its Impact on Corporate Finance and Governance. Aoki, M. and Patrick, H., eds. *The Japanese Main Bank System*. Oxford University Press, Oxford, UK.

Baums, T., Buxbaum T. & Hopt . K. J. (Eds). 1994. *Institutional investors and corporate governance*. Berlin: De Gruyter.

Barclay, M.J., & Holderness, C.G. 1989. Private benefits from control of public corporations. *Journal of Financial Economics*, 25 (2): 371-396.

Barza, F. and M. Becht. (Eds.). 2001. *The Control of Corporate Europe*. Oxford University Press. Oxford.

Becht, M. and Mayer, C. Introduction. Barza, F. and M. Becht. (Eds.). 2001. *The Control of Corporate Europe*. Oxford University Press. Oxford.

Bechuk, L. 1999. A rent protection theory of corporate ownership and control. Cambridge, Mass. *NBER Working Paper 7203*.

Bebchuck, L. and Roe, M. 1999. A theory of path dependence in corporate ownership and governance. *Stanford Law Review*, 52(1): 127-170.

Becht, M. and C. Mayer. Introduction. Barza, F. and M. Becht (Eds.). 2001. *The Control of Corporate Europe*. Oxford University Press. Oxford.

Berghe, Lutgart van den. 2002. *Corporate Governance in a Globalising World: Convergence or Divergence?* A European Perspective. Kluwer Academic Publishers. Dordrecht.

Berle, A., &. Means, C. 1932. *The modern corporation and private property*. New York: Macmillan.

Blair, M.M. & Roe, M.J. 1999. *Employees and corporate governance*. Brookings Institution, Washington D.C.

Blair, M. 2002. Post-Enron Reflections on Comparative Corporate Governance. Georgetown University Law Center. 2002 Working Paper series in Business, economics and Regulatory Law. *Working Paper no. 316663* (SSRN id=316663).

Bolkestein report. 2001.http://europa.eu.int/comm/internal_market/en/company/companynews/hlg01-2002.pdf).

Bolton, P.; von Thadden E. 1998. Blocks, liquidity, and corporate control. *The Journal of Finance*, 53(1):1- 25.

Burkart, M. 1997. Large shareholders, monitoring, and the value of the firm. *The Quarterly Journal of Economics*, 112(3):693-729.

Burkhart, M.; Gromb, D.; Panunzi, F. 1998. Why takeover premia protect minority shareholders. *Journal of Political Economy*, 196:172-204.

Calian, S.S. and Booth, T. 2000. Ethical Investing Grows in the United Kingdom. *Wall Street Journal*. New York, N.Y.; Jun 19.

Carlin, W. and Mayer C. How do financial systems affect economic performance. In Vives, Xavier (ed.), 2000. *Corporate governance. Theoretical and empirical perspectives*. Cambridge University Press. Cambridge, UK.

Chung, K.H., & Pruitt, S.W. 1994. A simple approximation of Tobin's q. *Financial Management*, 23: 70-74.

Claessens, S., S. Djankov, and L.H.P. Lang. 2000. The Separation of Ownership and Control in East Asian Corporations. *Journal of Financial Economic*. 58(1-2), 81-112.

Clarkson, M.B.E. 1995. A stakeholder framework for analysing and evaluating corporate social performance. *Academy of Management Review*, 20, 92-117.

Coase, R.H. 1960. The problem of social cost. *The Journal of Law and Economics*, 3:1-44.

Coffee. J.C. 1999. The Future as History: The Prospects for Global Convergence in Corporate Governance and its implications. Center for Law and Economic Studies. Columbia University School of Law. *Working paper No. 144*. Northwestern University law review 93: 641-.

Coffee, J.C. 1999. The Future as History: The Prospects for Global Convergence in Corporate Governance and its Implications. *Northwestern University Law Review*. 93, 641-708.

Coffee, J.C. 2002. Convergence and Its Critics: What are the Preconditions to the Separation of Ownership and Control. McCahery, J.A.; Moerland, P.; Raaijmakers, T.; Renneborg, L. Eds. 2002. *Corporate Governance regimes. Convergence and Diversity*. Oxford University Press. Oxford.

Coffee, J.C. 2002b. Racing Towards the Top? The Impact of Cross-Listings and Stock Market Competition on International Corporate Governance. Columbia Law School. The Center for Law and Economic Studies. *Working Paper no. 205*.

Coffee, J.C. 2002c. Understanding Enron: It's about the Gatekeepers, Stupid! Columbia Law School. The Center for Law and Economic Studies. *Working Paper no. 207*.

Cohen, S. and Boyd, G. 2000. *Corporate Governance and Globalization*. Edward Elgar. Cheltenham.

Demirguc-Kunt, A., and R. Levine. 1999. Bank-based and market-based financial systems: Cross-country comparisons. *World Bank Policy Working Paper No. 2143*.

Demsetz, H. 1983. The structure of ownership and the theory of the firm. *Journal of Law and Economics*, 26(2): 375-394.

Demsetz, H., & Lehn, K. 1985. The structure of corporate ownership: Causes and consequences. *Journal of Political Economy*, 93 (6): 1155-1177.

Denis, D.J., & Sarin, A. 1999. Ownership and board structures in publicly traded corporations. *Journal of Financial Economics*, 52(2):187-223.

References

Denis, Diane K. McConnell, J. K. 2002. International Corporate Governance: A Survey. *Working Paper*.

Denis, D.K., and J.J. McConnell. 2003. International ational Corporate Governance. *Journal of Financial and Quantitative Analysis*. 38 (1), 1-36.

Donaldson, T. & Preston. 1995. The stakeholder theory of the corporation: concepts, evidence, and implications. *Academy of Management Review*, 20 (1).

Durnev, A. and E. Han Kim. 2002. To Steal or Not to Steal: Firm Attributes, Legal Environment, and Valuation. *Working Paper*, University of Michigan Business School.

Dyck, A. and Zingales. L. The Corporate Governance Role of the Media. *Working Paper*. University of Chicago. August 2002

Dyck, A. and Zingales. L. 2002. 'The Corporate Governance Role of the Media,' R. Islam, The Right To Tell: *The Role Of Mass Media In Economic Development*. Washington, D.C.: World Bank, 2002, pp. 107-40.

Dyck, A., and Zingales, L. 2004. Private benefits of control: An international comparison. *The Journal of Finance*, LIX: 537-600.

Easterbrook, F.H. 1997. International Corporate Differences: Market or Law. *Journal of Applied Corporate Finance*, 9/4:23-29.

The Economist 2000. Europe's new capitalism: Bidding for the future; Feb 12, 2000; Vol. 354, Iss. 8157; pg. 71-74.

The Economist 1999. Finance and economics: The wall falls. 353 (8143):79-81.

EU Commission (Commission Of The European Communities): Brussels, 2.10.2002. Proposal For A Directive Of The European Parliament And Of The Council On Takeover Bids. Com (2002) 534 Final 2002/ 0240(Cod).

Fama, E.F., & Jensen, M. C. 1983. Agency problems and residual claims. *Journal of Law and Economics*, 26(2): 327-49.

Ferran, E. (1999). *Company Law and Corporate Finance*. Oxford University Press. Oxford.

Flynn, J. 1999. Use of Performance-Based Pay Spreads Across Continental Europe, Survey Says. *Wall Street Journal*. Nov. 17. New York, N.Y.

Freeman, R.E. 1984. *Strategic management: A stakeholder approach*. Pittman Books.

Friedman, Benjamin M. 1996. Economic implications of changing share ownership. *Journal of Portfolio Management*, 22(3): 59-71.

Gilson, Ronald J. Globalising Corporate Governance: Convergence of Form or Function. Columbia Law School. The Centre for Law and Economic Studies. Working Paper No. 174. 2000. *American Journal of Comparative Law*, Spring, 329.

Granovetter, M. 2005. The Impact of Social Structure on Economic Outcomes. *Journal of Economic Perspectives*. 19(1), 33-50.

Gugler, K., 2001. *Corporate governance and economic performance*. Oxford University Press. Oxford.

Guilen, Mauro F. 2000. Corporate Governance and Globalization: Is There Convergence Across Countries. Published in *Advances in International Comparative Management*.

Hamilton, J.D. 1994. *Time series analysis*. Oxford University Press. Oxford.

Hansmann, H. and R. Kraakman. 2000. The End Of History For Corporate Law. *Working Paper*.

Hansmann, H. and Kraakman, R. 2002. Towards A Single Model for Corporate Law. McCahery, J.A.; Moerland, P.; RaaijMakers, T.; Renneborg, L. Eds. 2002. *Corporate Governance regimes. Convergence and Diversity*. Oxford University Press. Oxford.

Healy, P.M.; Palepu, K. 2002. Governance and Intermediation Problems in capital markets: Evidence from the Fall of Enron. *Harvard NOM Research Paper O*. 02-27. August.

Hellwig, M. On the Economics and Politics of Corporate Finance and Control in Vives, Xavier (ed.), 2000. *Corporate governance. Theoretical and empirical perspectives*. Cambridge University Press. Cambridge, UK.

Himmelberg, C.P., Hubbard, R.G., & Palia, D. 1999. Understanding the determinants of managerial ownership and the link between ownership structure and performance. *Journal of Financial Economics*, 53: 353-384.

Holderness, C.G. 2001. A Survey of Blockholders and Corporate Control. *Economic Policy Review* (forthcoming).

Holderness, C., & Sheehan, D. 1988. The role of majority shareholders in publicly held corporations. *Journal of Financial Economics*, 20 (1): 317-346.

Holderness, Clifford G., Kroszner, Randall S., Sheehan, Dennis P. 1998. Were the Good old days that good? Changes in Managerial Ownership since the great depression. *The Journal of Finance* 54(2).

Investor Relations Business. 2000. Reversal of Fortune: Institutional Ownership Is Declining May 1: 8-9.

Jawahar, I.M. & G.L McLaughlin. 2001. Toward a descriptive stakeholder theory: An organizational life cycle approach. *The Academy of Management Review*, 26(3): 397-414.

Jensen, M.C., & Meckling, W.H. 1976. Theory of the firm: Managerial behaviour, agency costs, and ownership structure. *Journal of Financial Economics*, 3: 305-360.

Johnson, S. and Shleifer, A. 2001. Coase and Competence in Development. Harvard University. *Working Paper*.

Jones, T.M. 1995. Instrumental Stakeholder Theory: A Synthesis of Ethics and Economics, *The Academy of Management Review* 20(2):404-437.

Jones, T.; Wicks, A. 1999. Convergent stakeholder theory. *The Academy of Management Review* 24(2): 206-222.

Khanna, T., J. Kogan, and K. Palepu. 2002. Globalization and Corporate Governance Convergence? A Cross-Country Analysis. *Working Paper*, Harvard Business School.

La Porta, R., F. Lopez-de-Silanes, A. Shleifer and R. Vishny. 1997. Legal Determinants of External Finance. *Journal of Finance*. 52 (3), 1131-50.

La Porta, R. Lopez-de-Silanes, F., Shleifer, A. & Vishny, R.W. 1998. Law and finance. *Journal of Political Economy*, 106: 1113-1155.

La Porta, R., Lopez de Silanes, F., Shleifer, A., & Vishny, R.W. 1999. Corporate ownership around the world. *The Journal of Finance*, 54(2): 471-519.

La Porta, R., Lopez de Silanes, F., Shleifer, A., & Vishny, R.W. 2000. Investor protection and corporate valuation. *Journal of Financial Economics*, 58: 3-27.

References

La-Porta, R., F. Lopez-de-Silanes, and A. Shleifer. 2002b. Government ownership of banks. *The Journal of Finance*, 57(1): 265-301.

Licht, Amir N. 2001. The mother of all path dependencies. towards a cross cultural theory of corporate governance systems. *Delaware Journal of Corporate Law*, 147-205.

McCahery, J.A.; Moerland, P.; RaaijMakers, T.; Renneborg, L. Eds. 2002. *Corporate Governance regimes. Convergence and Diversity*. Oxford University Press. Oxford.

Meyer, Paul. 1998. Board stock ownership: More, and more again. *Directors and Boards*. 22(2): 55-61.

Mitchel, R.K., B.R. Agle & D.J. Wood. 1997 .Toward a theory of stakeholder identification and salience. *Academy of Management Review*, 22(4): 853-886.

Morck, R., Shleifer, A., & Vishny, R. 1988. Management ownership and firm value: An empirical analysis. *Journal of Financial Economics*, 20(1): 293-315.

Most, B. 2002. Socially responsible investing: An imperfect world for planners and clients. *Journal of Financial Planning*, 15(2):48-55.

Myers, S.C., & Majluf, N.S. 1984. Corporate financing and investment decisions when firms have information investors do not have. *Journal of Financial Economics*, 13: 187-222.

Monks, R.A. and Minnow, N. 2001. *Corporate Governance*. Blackwell. Oxford.

Murphy, Kevin J. 2000. Executive compensation. Working paper. April 1998. Published in *Handbook of Labour Economics*.

New York Stock Exchange Corporate Accountability and Listing Standards Committee. 2002. Report submitted to the NYSE's Board of Directors Thursday, June 6, 2002.

North, D.C., 1991. Institutions. *Journal of Economic Perspectives*. 5(1), 97-112.

Oxelheim, L. 1998. 'Regulations, institutions and corporate efforts – The Nordic Environment' in Pagano, M., and Volpin, P. F. 2005. The political economy of corporate governance. *The American Economic Review*, 95(4): 1005-1030.

Pedersen, T., & Thomsen, S. 1997. European Patterns of Corporate Ownership. *Journal of International Business Studies*, 28(4): 759-778.

Pedersen, T., & Thomsen, S. 1999. Economic and systemic explanations of ownership concentration among Europe's largest companies. *International Journal of the Economics of Business*, 6(3): 367-381.

Poppo, L., and T. Zenger (2002). Do Formal Contracts and Relational Governance Function as Substitutes or Complements? *Strategic Management Journal*, 23(8): 707-726.

Prowse, S. 1995. Corporate Governance in an International Perspective: A Survey of Corporate Control Mechanism among Large Firms in the U.S., U.K., Japan and Germany. *Financial Markets, Institutions & Instruments*. 4(1), 1-63.

Roe, M.J. 1991. A Political Theory of Corporate Finance. *Columbia Law Review*, 1: 10-67.

Roe, M.J. 1994. *Strong Managers, Weak Owners: The Political Roots of American Corporate Finance*. Princeton University Press, Princeton, New York.

Roe, M.J. 1994b. Some Differences in Corporate Governance in Germany, Japan and America. In: T. Baums, T. Boxhaul & K.J. Hop (Eds.), *Institutional Investors and Corporate Governance*. Berlin: de Gruyter.

Roe, M.J. 2000. The Shareholder Wealth Maximization Norm and Industrial Organization. *University of Pennsylvania Law Review*, 149.

Shleifer, A., & Vishny, R.W. 1997. A survey of corporate governance. *Journal of Finance*, 52(2): 737-83.

Short, H. 1994. Ownership, control, financial structure and the performance of firms. *Journal of Economic Surveys*, 8(3): 203-249.

Tadelis, S. 1999. What's in a Name? Reputation as a Tradable Asset. *American Economic Review*. 89(3), 548–563.

Thomsen, S.; Pedersen, T. 1998. Industry and Ownership Structure. *International Review of Law and Economics*, 18: 385-402.

Thomsen, S., & Pedersen, T. 2000. Ownership structure and economic performance in the largest European companies. *Strategic Management Journal*, 21: 689-705.

Thomsen, S. Convergence goes both ways: An alternative perspective on the convergence of corporate governance systems. In Neville, M. and K. E. Sørensen. *The internationalisation of companies and company laws*. DJØF, Copenhagen, 2001.

Vives, X. 2000. Corporate governance: Does it matter? X. Vives, eds. *Corporate Governance*. Cambridge University Press, Cambridge, UK, 1-15.

Vives, Xavier (ed.), 2000. *Corporate governance. Theoretical and empirical perspectives*. Cambridge University Press. Cambridge, UK.

Warner, J. 1998. Buyback Fever Hits Europe; Continental companies are snapping up their shares. *Business Week*. Iss. 3577; pg. 46

Zeckhouser, R., & Pound, J. 1990. Are large shareholders effective monitors? An investigation of share ownership and corporate performance. In G. R. Hubbard, (Ed.), *Asymmetric information, corporate finance and investment*. Chicago: University of Chicago Press.

II. Understanding Mechanisms of Governance

CHAPTER 5

Understanding Corporate Ownership

In this and the following chapters we examine corporate governance mechanisms in greater detail. We begin with ownership structure.

Ownership is a set of rights concerning assets:

- user rights (usus): right to use an asset
- profit rights (usus fructus): if you own a piece of land you also own the fruits of the land
- control rights: right to determine who is going to use the asset, or even destroy it if you wish
- transfer rights: rights to sell the asset

In addition, ownership confers responsibility. For example, if you are a farmer you are responsible to not let your livestock trample over another person's land. If you own a handgun, you are responsible to store it in a way so that your neighbour's children cannot easily find it.

These rights may be endlessly combined and recombined. Doing so can be an important source of value creation.

Consider some of the combinations. If you rent an apartment you may have the right to use a washing machine (user rights), but you would not have the right to sell laundry services (profit rights); to determine whether, when, and how the other tenants can use the washer (control rights); nor to sell the machine; nor, for that matter, would you have the right to sell your user rights. But suppose you go on a vacation and the machine stands idle during the summer. Would it not be economically beneficial to be able to lease your rights to somebody else during that period of time? In a larger setting, reconfigurations like this can create a lot of value for everyone.

Or consider your body. You can use it, you can profit by using your muscles and brain, you can control it, but you cannot sell it, since slavery is forbidden. Yet some people die of hunger. Would everyone be better off if they were allowed to sell themselves as slaves? What about body parts? Should you be allowed to sell your liver?

For a less controversial application, much new deregulation is based on the premise that you can distinguish between the infrastructure (the railway, the telephone lines, the airport, etc.) and the services they provide. Property rights to the infrastructure do not necessarily mean that infrastructure service cannot be provided by many different firms.

Ownership of the firm

In a typical limited liability joint stock company owners (shareholders) do not have the rights to use corporate assets. They can dissolve the company if they wish, but they cannot just grab corporate assets for their private use. However they do have the right to profit, a right to control (vote), and a right to sell their shares. Moreover, in a limited liability company, owners are usually free of responsibility for how the company is managed and they do not pledge for the debt which the managers incur beyond the share capital which they have invested. This means that they must not constantly keep track of what happens in the firm. This is a major convenience making it much more attractive to buy shares – which is perhaps the foundation for modern capitalism.

However, not all companies share these characteristics.

Companies may for example issue different types – or classes – of shares: some with and some without voting rights (to the extent this is allowed by law). In this case, owners of the non-voting shares will have no voting rights, but they will have the same rights as other shareholders to buy and sell shares and to receive dividends. In the literature on dual class shares, profits rights are sometime called cash flow rights.

Owners may also have profit and control rights without transfer rights. This is true in cooperatives in which you are a member; you can vote, you can receive dividends, but you cannot sell your membership to another person. Moreover, in cooperatives, farmers often have the right and the obligation to do certain kinds of business with the coop. For example, members may be obligated to sell all their milk to the cooperative dairy; the dairy, in turn, is obliged to accept it. This certainty of supply is a key competitive advantage for agricultural cooperatives.

Shareholder agreements may limit the rights of family members and others to sell their shares and they may oblige them to vote together on certain issues. In general, corporate ownership is simply one large shareholder contract so that shareholder agreements can restructure ownership completely – within the confines of the law.

Hedge funds may buy shares in a company and hedge their risk (e.g. by an options deal). They can then vote their shares without any economic responsibility (i.e. they are insured against losses or gains). They can even go short in a stock, buy voting rights, and influence the firm to activities which will reduce the stock price. This is a decoupling of voting rights from profit and transfer rights.

Ownership structure[1]

In publicly-listed companies, there are two key elements of ownership structure: ownership concentration and owner identities. Or in other words: who are the owners and how much of the firm does each of them own? Whereas ownership concentration measures the power of shareholders to influence managers, the identity of the owners has implications for their objectives and the way they exercise their power. This is reflected in company strategy with regard to profit goals, dividends, capital structure, and growth rates (c.f. the work of Henry Hansmann (1988, 1996)).

Ownership concentration can be measured as a first cut approximation by the share of the largest owner of total stock. According to agency theory, the choice of a privately optimal ownership structure involves a trade off between risk and incentive efficiency (Jensen and Meckling, 1976; Fama and Jensen, 1983; Demsetz, 1983; Shleifer and Vishny, 1997). Ceteris paribus, larger owners will have a stronger incentive to monitor managers and they will have more power to enforce their interests. This should increase the inclination of managers to maximize shareholder

---

1. This and the next sections borrow heavily from my paper with Torben Pedersen: Ownership Structure and Economic Performance in the Largest European Companies. The Strategic Management Journal. 21(6). 2000. 689-705.

Chapter 5. Understanding Corporate Ownership

value. But generally the owner's portfolio risk will also increase the larger the ownership share becomes. To the extent that companies differ in terms of firm-specific risk, the privately optimal ownership share of the largest owner will therefore vary. Furthermore, the nature and complexity of activities carried out by individual firms may also vary, which will influence the marginal effect of monitoring individual firms (e.g. Demsetz and Lehn, 1985, Zeckhauser and Pound 1990). Finally, the relationship between ownership concentration and economic performance need not be uniform (Fama and Jensen, 1983; Morck et al., 1988; Shleifer and Vishny, 1997). Fama and Jensen (1983) suggest that managerial ownership above a certain level will allow managers to become entrenched and expropriate the wealth of minority shareholders.

This leads to the idea of a bell-shaped relationship between ownership concentration (share of the largest owner) and economic performance, which we can measure by firm value, accounting rates of profitability, shareholder value creation, or other variables (figure 5.1).

Figure 5.1

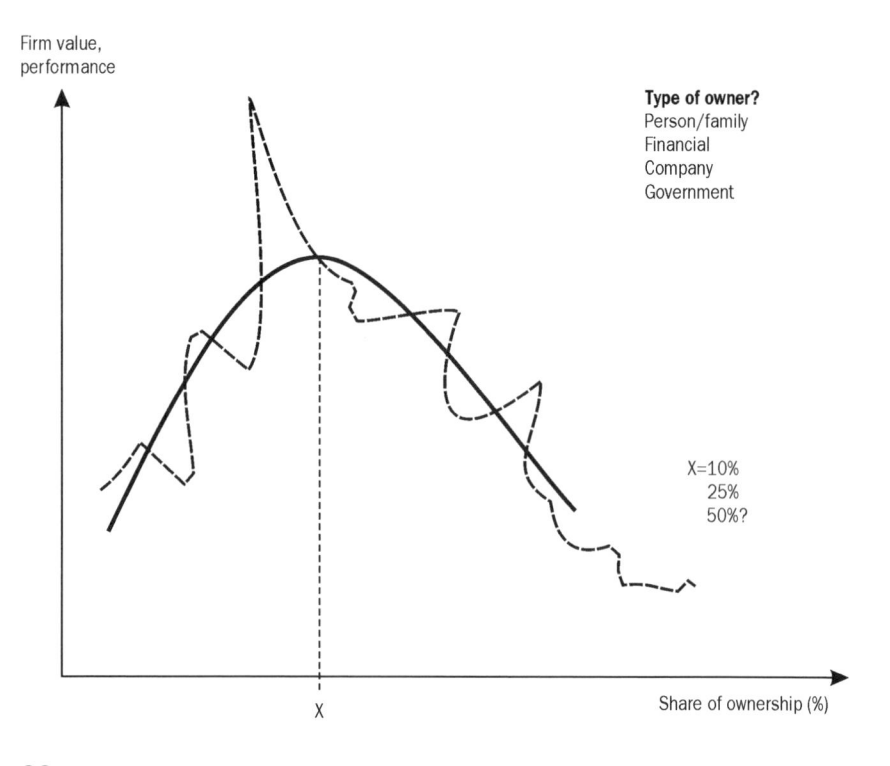

Up to a certain point, all shareholders benefit from greater ownership concentration because a large owner has the power and incentives to maximize firm performance or – what results in the same thing – to see to it that the management maximizes performance. The larger the share of the largest owner, the greater her incentive will be and the more certain she can be of her ability to influence the managers.

Beyond a certain point, however, the entrenchment effect kicks in. The largest owner nears complete control and, in effect, manages the company. But she is very difficult to get rid off and she may start to enjoy private benefits of control – e.g. fringe benefits and all sorts of other things which reduce the value of the firm. Moreover, her risk aversion becomes more and more serious because of an increasingly unbalanced portfolio.

Once the point of full control (entrenchment) is reached, the curve may turn upwards again. From this point on a higher ownership share means that the majority owner now has less and less of an incentive to deviate from value maximization (i.e. she will be paying for it out of her own pocket).

Ownership and performance

The implication of figure 5.1 would be that owners of firms with low ownership concentration could benefit from buying more shares, while the owners of firms with high ownership would benefit from selling out (this would increase the value of their shares). So why do they not do so? Demsetz (1983) argued theoretically that the ownership structure of the firm is *'an endogenous outcome of competitive selection in which various cost advantages and disadvantages are balanced to arrive at an equilibrium organization of the firm'* (Demsetz 1983 p. 1164). So again, if owners could increase their profits by rearranging their portfolios, why do they not do so?

One answer to this question could be that the estimated performance effects of ownership concentration are statistical artifacts. In support of this view, Loderer and Martin (1997) and Cho (1998) recently found the performance effect to be insignificant in a simultaneous estimation of causes and effects of ownership concentration.

Another answer may be free rider problems among small investors (Shleifer and Vishny, 1986): if one shareholder attempts to acquire a large ownership stake the gains will (largely) be captured by the other shareholders who sell their shares at a premium price reflecting the anticipated increase in the value of the firm. But while free riding among small shareholders provides an argument for a positive effect on company economy performance, the strength and significance of this effect is an empirical question.

A third answer may be that the tacit agency-theoretical assumption of value maximizing shareholders is incorrect. In other words, owners may have their own reasons for not reshuffling their portfolios to capture the gains from arbitrage. The *identity* of owners may be important with implications for corporate strategy and performance. I develop this idea in the following section.

Owner identity

The standard assumption in agency theory is that owners want the company to maximize economic profits or – in modern terms – shareholder value. Although this assumption may be sufficient for many purposes, it is strictly speaking only an approximation of the more general idea that owners (like managers) may be expected to maximize their utility which may depend on other factors. One simple reason is that many owners (institutional investors, banks, other companies, and governments) act as intermediate agents for final owners. Furthermore, even theoretically, profit maximization is only well-defined when markets are complete (e.g. when all risk is diversifiable). When markets are incomplete, even profit maximizing owners may disagree about corporate strategy because of different preferences regarding risk and the time profile of expected cash flows.

Following Hansmann (1988, 1996) and Pedersen and Thomsen (1999), we can use the relative costs and benefits of ownership for each owner category as a benchmark for assessing its dominant objectives. To model the firm as a nexus of contracts with a number of different stakeholders such as (in this case): institutional investors, banks, business partners, managers, or the government there are transaction costs associated with each of these contracts. Ownership can in principle be assigned to any one of these stakeholders who will then incur the costs of ownership, but is relieved of the costs of market contracting. The (opportunity) costs of assigning the ownership rights to another stakeholder therefore consist of the sum of added ownership costs plus added costs of market contracting. All else equal, the optimal ownership type – j – minimizes transaction costs which consist of ownership costs (CO) and costs of market contracting (CC) (i.e. it solves the optimization problem):

$$\text{Min } (CO_j + \Sigma_{i \neq j} CC_i) \text{ by } j,$$

where i is an index of the firm's stakeholders. Furthermore, regardless of the optimality of the present owners, the economic behaviour of individual ownership types is likely to be influenced by their ownership costs and benefits.

An example

Table 5.1 gives a numerical application of Hansmann's formula. Imagine that there are 4 'patrons' (you can also call them stakeholders or just 'possible owners'): investors, suppliers, managers, and government. And imagine that the cost of contracting and ownership are given by the numbers in the table.

Table 5.1: Applying Hansmann's Formula. A Numerical Example.

Patron	Costs of Ownership	Costs of Contracting	Total Cost
Investors	1	8	19
Suppliers	2	7	21
Managers	3	6	23
Government	4	5	25

From the investor viewpoint, the cost of acquiring ownership would be the sum of the direct ownership costs + the costs of market contracting with other participants, that is total transaction costs of

$$1 + 7 + 6 + 5 = 19$$

For suppliers, the total transaction costs would be:

$$2 + 8 + 6 + 5 = 21$$

Chapter 5. Understanding Corporate Ownership

If you go through the last two you will see that estimated transaction costs are still higher. It follows that investors – whose transaction costs of ownership are the lowest in this case – should take ownership (provided that the benefits of ownership exceed the cost).

In Hansmann's framework, the costs of market contracting include the conventional losses attributed to market power distortions (double marginalization, Tirole, 1992 p. 170-171), ex post transaction costs associated with asset specificity (of the type emphasized by Williamson, 1985), and information costs (Arrow, 1975). Transaction costs of this kind incurred by one particular stakeholder or group of stakeholders can be avoided to some extent if these stakeholders become owners and thereby internalize their transactions with the firm. The costs of ownership include monitoring and risk-bearing costs (as emphasized by Jensen and Meckling, 1976), but also costs of collective decision making (Hansmann, 1988), which may be large if the owners are a large and heterogeneous group.

For example, companies run by an owner-manager avoid the transaction costs by hiring the services of professional managers (i.e. the incentive and information problems studied in standard agency theory), but have to incur market transaction costs in financing (i.e. to use debt rather than equity capital) since the firm cannot at the same time internalize its transactions with managers and outside investors. In contrast, investor-owned companies can obtain equity finance from the stock markets, but have to contract out for the services of professional managers. Hybrid solutions (e.g. when shareholders share ownership with managers) are clearly possible, but they may give rise to conflicts of interest between the two owner categories, in which case the objectives of the dominant category seem more likely to prevail (although the exact relationship between ownership concentration and owner 'power' is complex, Cubbin and Leech, 1983).

Furthermore, the objectives imposed on the company by any given dominant ownership category are likely to reflect the ownership costs and benefits of that category. In the case of owner-managed companies ('proprietorships'), financial problems due to capital rationing, short time horizons, and risk aversion are particularly likely to influence the company (Fama and Jensen, 1985). For example, compared to investor-owned companies, owner-managed companies seem less likely to undertake ambitious investment programs to exploit economies of scale and are more likely to pursue niche strategies related to flexibility or differentiation. For the same reason Chandler (1977, 1990) regarded separation of ownership and control as an essential part of the enduring logic of industrial success in exploiting scale economies.

Investor ownership is therefore likely to imply advantages in terms of finance, low risk aversion and a relatively long time horizon. Furthermore, institutional investors are characterized by portfolio investments and arm's length relationships with the firms. In comparison with other owner categories, they are relatively specialized as owners, their performance is often measured in terms of financial success, and their objectives can therefore be described as shareholder value and liquidity. Although their usually low ownership shares impair their ability to influence management, this leads to the hypothesis of a positive expected impact of institutional investor ownership on shareholder value for a given ownership share. Previous findings (McConnell and Servaes, 1990; Levin and Levin, 1982; Nickel et. al., 1997) have supported this hypothesis.

Family ownership is often associated with a double role for the family as owners and managers of the firm. In economic terms, families make firm-specific investments in human capital which makes them reluctant to give up control (Maug, 1996). This – and the fact that founding family owners of larger corporations are likely to be relatively wealthy – may create a long-term commitment to the survival of the company. However, since a disproportionate share of their wealth is invested in the company, and since families often do not want to risk losing control by attracting equity from the stock markets, family-owned companies may be relatively risk averse, and they are more likely to be capital-rationed than other companies. Furthermore, families may derive private benefits from running the company at the expense of minority shareholders (expropriation) (Fama and Jensen, 1983; La Porta et al., 1998). In support of the expropriation hypothesis, Johnson et al. (1985) find that the stock market reacts favourably to the unexpected death of CEOs with large ownership stakes.

Bank ownership is illegal in the USA and generally avoided in the UK, but it plays an important role in the so-called German model (Charkham, 1994) in which banks function as universal providers of financial services (Hausbanks) to industrial companies. Since bank-owned companies have (at least partly) internalized their banking relationships, they may have privileged access to capital, information, and other services which the banks have to offer. In support, Cable (1985) finds a positive performance effect of bank ownership among West German firms, and Hoshi et al. (1990a, 1990b, and 1991) and Ramirez (1995) indicate that members of bank-based business groups are less likely to be credit-rationed.

Corporate ownership ties are an integral feature of the Japanese Keiretsu, the French cross-holding structures, and Swedish business groups (Kester, 1992; Charkham, 1994). Vertical ties between companies at different stages of the value chain appear to play an important role in those groups which are not bank-based. In this case, the company has internalized its transactions with the providers of a critical input which makes sense under conditions of high asset specificity and transaction frequency (Williamson, 1985). As demonstrated by Caves (1996), the multinational company's choice of foreign direct investment over exports reflects similar reasoning. In particular corporate ownership ties may facilitate knowledge transfers. Nevertheless, as recognized by Kester (1992) the advantages of business group membership come at a cost: for example loss of flexibility and risk of deficient mutual monitoring. Hundley and Jacobson's finding (1998) that Keiretsu members do worse in terms of export performance than non-members indicates that the costs may sometimes exceed the benefits.

Government ownership internalizes the relationship between government and company which may or may not make overall sense, but which functions as an institutional alternative to regulation. With regard to economic performance, the literature (e.g. Shepherd, 1989; Laffont and Tirole, 1993; Hart et al., 1996) suggests that governments are likely to pay special attention to political goals such as low output prices, employment, or external effects relative to profitability. In fact, non-profit maximizing behaviour is a key rationale for government ownership in welfare economics (e.g. Arrow, 1969), since it is expected to correct market failures by acting differently than private firms (e.g. Shepherd, 1989). Ceteris paribus, government-owned enterprises are therefore expected to be low performers in terms of conventional performance measures. On the other hand, governments are usually relatively wealthy, which implies a relative advantage for government-owned companies in terms of credit, liquidity, or costs of capital.

In conclusion, we conjecture that each of the ownership categories have different objectives with implications for corporate strategy and performance. The analysis indicates that institutional investors are more focused on conventional performance measures like shareholder value while the other ownership types typically have other business relationships with the firm (e.g. the bank that is both owner and creditor). Accordingly, these owners try to optimize across the entire range of relationships with the firm, so that their objective vis-à-vis the company becomes a composite of ownership and the other stakeholder interests.

Best owner

While corporate ownership used to be taken for granted, it is increasingly becoming part of business strategy and value creation. Private equity funds believe that they can create value by new ownership and so do the many other acquirers. New financial instruments like hedging or advanced combinations of debt and equity can decouple ownership rights from cash flow rights and make it easier to finance new ownership structures.

A third increasingly important part of the ownership calculus is outsourcing, which is addressed by the make or buy decision: should we have an IT department or outsource it to IBM (or CSC)? Should we run our own call centre or outsource it to India?

The 'best owner' of a company – or an asset – is the owner which can create most value with it, which involve weighing costs and benefits of ownership. In an open auction, this 'best owner' will win because he will be paying the highest price for the company. It is interesting therefore to inquire what makes one owner better than another. While a complete theory remains to be developed, it is possible to identify some important determinants.

At the core this is a matching problem where a range of potential owners with given characteristics are matched with firms which also have different characteristics.

Capital is the traditional reason for going public. If some owners have capital and others do not, the firm may be more valuable for the capital risk owners who can invest more in it.

Risk aversion. The more risk averse the potential owner is, the less likely it is that she will take ownership.

Information. All else equal, the individuals who run a company are the best owners since they have more and better information than anybody else.

Competence. Some potential owners have acquired an expertise in running businesses which others do not have. Owner competence may be industry and country specific. The 'stupid son' does not automatically inherit the competence of the 'clever father.'

Strategic fit. Sometimes a business unit does not fit into the overall strategy of a corporation which would like to concentrate its effort elsewhere. It may, therefore, be put up for sale.

Business relations. Other companies are more likely to acquire a company with which they have ongoing business relations – particularly if they involve mutual dependency (asset specificity).

Preferences. Individuals have different preferences, and preference may change over time. Some may be interested in acquiring ownership and some in divesting it.

Government regulation. Some companies or individuals are occasionally not allowed to acquire certain companies – for example because of anti-trust legislation or national security. There may also be legal ceilings on the amount of stock that investors can own in an individual firm.

References

Alchian, A.A. and H. Demsetz (1972). 'Production, Information Costs, and Economic Organization', *American Economic Review*, 62(5), pp. 777-795.

Amihud, Y. and B. Lev (1981). 'Risk reduction as a managerial motive for conglomerate mergers', *Bell Journal of Economics*, 12, pp. 605-617.

Arrow, K.J. (1969). 'The organization of economic activity: issues pertinent to the choice of market versus nonmarket allocation'. *In The Analysis and Evaluation of Public Expenditure: The PPB System.* Vol.1, U.S. Joint Economic Committee, 91st Congress, 1st Session, US. Print Office, Washington DC.

Arrow, K.J. (1975). 'Vertical Integration and Communication.' Bell Journal of Economics, 6, pp. 173-183.

Bergström, C. and K. Rydqvist (1990). 'The Determinants of Corporate Ownership. An Empirical Study on Swedish Data', *Journal of Banking and Finance*, 14 (2), pp. 237-253.

Bergh, D.D.: (1995-). 'Size and relatedness of units sold', Strategic Management Journal 16(3), pp. 221-240.

Berle, A and C. Means (1932). *The Modern Corporation and Private Property.* Macmillan, New York.

Bethel, J.E. and J. Liebeskind (1993). 'The effects of ownership structure on corporate restructuring', *Strategic Management Journal*, 14 (Summer Special Issue), pp. 15-31.

Blaine, M. (1994). 'Comparing the Profitability of Firms in Germany, Japan and the United States', *Management International Review*, 34(2), pp. 125-148.

Cable, J. (1985). 'Capital Market Information and Industrial Performance: The Role of West German Banks', *The Economic Journal*, 95(377), pp. 118-132.

Charkham, J.P. (1994). *Keeping Good Company – A Study of Corporate Governance in Five Countries.* Clarendon Press, Oxford.

Caves, R. (1996). *Multinational Enterprise and Economic Analysis.* Cambridge University Press, Cambridge, UK.

Chandler, A.D. (1977). *The visible hand: The managerial revolution in American Business.* Bellknap Press, Cambridge, MA.

Chandler, A.D. (1990). *Scale and Scope.* Harvard University Press, Cambridge MA.

Cho, M. (1998). 'Ownership Structure, Investment, and The Corporate Value: An Empirical Analysis', *Journal of Financial Economics*, 47(1), pp. 103-121.

Cubbin, J. and D. Leech (1983). 'The Effect of Shareholding Dispersion on the Degree of Control in British Companies: Theory and Measurement', *The Economic Journal*, 93(370), pp. 351-369.

Demsetz. H. (1983), 'The Structure of Ownership and The Theory of the Firm', *Journal of Law and Economics*, 26(2), pp. 375-394.

Demsetz, H. and K. Lehn (1985). 'The structure of corporate ownership: Causes and consequences', *Journal of Political Economy*, 93(6), pp. 1155-1177.

Dennis, D.D., D.K. Denis and Sarin, Atulya. 'Agency Problems, equity ownership and corporate diversification', *The Journal of Finance* 52(1), pp. 135-160.

Fama, E. (1980). 'Agency Problems and the Theory of the Firm', *Journal of Political Economy*, 88(2).

Fama, E.F. and M.C. Jensen (1983). 'Agency Problems and Residual Claims', *Journal of Law and Economics*, 26(2), pp. 327-49.

Fama, E.F. and M.C. Jensen (1985). 'Organizational Forms and Investment Decisions', *Journal of Financial Economics*, 14(1), pp. 101-119.

Gedajlovich, E. and D. Shapiro (1998). 'Management and Ownership Effects: Evidence from 5 Countries', *Strategic Management Journal*, 19(6), pp. 533-555.

Gerson, J. and G. Barr (1996). 'The Structure of Corporate Control and Ownership in a Regulatory Environment Unbiased toward One-Share-One-Vote', *Corporate Governance*, 4(2), pp.78-93.

Gibbs, P.A. (1993). 'Determinants of corporate restructuring: The relative importance of corporate governance, takeover threat, and free cash flow', *Strategic Management Journal*, 14, pp. 51-68.

Hansmann, H. (1988). 'Ownership of the Firm', *Journal of Law, Economics and Organization*, 4(2), pp. 267-305.

Hansmann, H. (1996). *The Ownership of Enterprise*. The Belknap Press of Harvard University Press, Cambridge: MA.

Hart, O. (1983). 'The Market Mechanism as an Incentive Scheme', *Bell Journal of Economics*, 74.

Hart, O., A. Shleifer and R.W. Vishny (1996). 'The Proper Scope of Government. Theory and an Application to Prisons', *National Bureau of Economic Research*, Working Paper 5744, September.

Hill, C.W.L. and S.A. Snell (1989). 'Effects of ownership and control on corporate productivity', *Academy of Management Journal*, 32(1), pp. 25-46.

Holderness, C. and D. Sheehan (1988). 'The Role of Majority Shareholders in Publicly Held Corporations', *Journal of Financial Economics*, 20(1), pp. 317-346.

Hoshi, T., A. Kashyap and D. Sharfstein (1990a). 'Banking, Monitoring and Investment. Evidence from the Changing Structure of Japanese Corporate Banking Relationships'. In G.R. Hubbard (ed.), *Asymmetric Information, Corporate Finance and Investment*. University of Chicago Press, Chicago.

Hoshi, T., A. Kashyap, and D. Sharfstein (1990b). 'The Role of Banks in Reducing the Costs of Financial Distress in Japan', *Journal of Financial Economics*, 27(1), pp. 67-88.

Hoshi, T., A. Kashyap and D. Sharfstein (1991). 'Corporate Structure, Liquidity and Investment. Evidence from Japanese Industrial Groups', *Quarterly Journal of Economics*, 106(1), pp. 35-60.

Hoskisson, R.E., JR.A. Johnson, and D.D. Moesel (1994). 'Corporate divestiture intensity in restructuring firms. Effects of governance, strategy and performance', *Academy of Management* Journal 37(5), pp 1207-1238.

Hundley, G. and C.K. Jacobson (1998). 'The effects of the Keiretsu on the export performance of Japanese companies: Help or hindrance?', *Strategic Management Journal* ,19(10) , pp. 927-937.

Kester, C.W. (1992). 'Industrial Groups as Systems of Contractual Governance', *Oxford Review of Economic Po*licy, 8(3), pp. 24-44.

Jensen, M. (1986). 'Agency Costs of Free Cash Flow, Corporate Finance and Takeovers', *American Economic Review*, 76, pp. 323-329.

References

Jensen, M. (1989). 'Eclipse of the Public Corporation', *Harvard Business Review,* 67(5), pp. 61-75.

Jensen, M. (1993). 'The Modern Industrial Revolution, Exit and the Failure of Internal Control Systems', *The Journal of Finance*, 48(3), pp. 481-531.

Jensen, M.C. and W.H. Meckling (1976). 'Theory of the Firm: Managerial Behaviour, Agency Costs, and Ownership Structure', *Journal of Financial Economics.* 3, pp. 305-360.

de Jong, H. (1995). 'European Capitalism: Between Freedom and Social Justice', *Review of Industrial Organization,* 10, pp. 399-419.

Johnson, W.B., R.P. Macgee, N.J. Nagarajan and H.A. Newman (1985). 'An Analysis of the Stock Price Reaction to Sudden Executive Deaths. Implications for the Managerial Labour Market', *Journal of Accounting and Economics,* 7(1), pp. 151-74.

Lane, Peter J., A.A. Cannella Jr. and M.H. Lubatkin (1998). 'Agency Problems as antecedents to unrelated mergers and diversification: Amihud and Lev reconsidered'. *Strategic Management Journal* 19(6), pp. 555-578.

Laffont, J.J. and J. Tirole (1993). *A Theory of Procurement and Regulation.* MIT Press, Cambridge: MA.

La Porta, R., F. Lopez-de-Silanes, A. Shleifer and R.W. Vishny (1998). 'Law and Finance', *Journal of Political Economy*, 106, pp 1113-1155.

Leech, D. and J. Leahy (1991). 'Ownership Structure, Control Type Classifications and the Performance of Large British Companies', *Economic Journal,* 101(409).

Levin, S.M. and S.L. Levin. (1982). 'Ownership and Control of Large Industrial Firms: Some New Evidence', *Review of Business and Economic Research*, pp. 37-49.

Li, M. and R. Simerly (1998). 'The moderating effect of environmental dynamism on the ownership and performance relationship', *Strategic Management Journal*, 19(2), pp. 169-179.

Lloyd, W.P., J.H. Hand and N.K. Modani (1987). 'The Effect of the Degree of Ownership Control on Firm Diversification, Market Value, and Merger Activity', *Journal of Business Research,* 15(4), 303-312.

Loderer, C. and K. Martin (1997). 'Executive stock ownership and performance', *Journal of Financial Economics*, 45, pp. 223-255.

Maug, E. 1996. 'Corporate control and the market for managerial labour: On the decision to go public', *European Economic Review*, 40(3), pp. 1049-57.

Mazzolini, R. (1990). 'The International Strategy of State-owned Firms: An Organizational Process and Politics Perspective', *Strategic Management Journal* 1(2), 101.

McConnell J.J. and H. Servaes (1990). 'Additional evidence on equity ownership and corporate value', *Journal of Financial Economics,* 27(2), pp. 595-612.

Morck, R, A. Shleifer and R. Vishny (1988). 'Management Ownership and Market Valuation: An Empirical Analysis', *Journal of Financial Economics,* 20(1), pp. 293-315.

Nickel, S., D. Nicolitsas and N. Dryden (1997). 'What makes firms perform well?', *European Economic Review,* 41(3), pp 783-796.

Nobes, C. and R. Parker (1998). *Comparative International Accounting*. Prentice Hall, London.

Oswald, S.L. and J.S. Jahera Jr. (1991). 'The influence of ownership on performance: An empirical study', *Strategic Management Journal*, 12(4), pp. 321-326.

Pedersen, T. and S. Thomsen (1997). 'European Patterns of Corporate Ownership', *Journal of International Business Studies*, 28(4), pp 759-778.

Pedersen, T. and S. Thomsen (1999a). 'Industry and Ownership Structure', *International Review of Law and Economics*, forthcoming.

Pedersen, T. and S. Thomsen (1999b). 'Economic and Systemic Explanations of Ownership Concentration among Europe's Largest Companies', *International Journal of the Economics of Business*, forthcoming.

Ramirez, C.D. (1995). 'Did J.P. Morgan's Men Add Liquidity? – Corporate Investment, Cash Flow, and Financial Structure at the Turn of the Twentieth Century', *Journal of Finance*, 50(2), pp. 661-678.

Sexty, R.W. Autonomy Strategies of Government Owned Business Corporations in Canada. *Strategic Management Journal*, 1(4), pp. 371.

Shepherd, W.G. (1989). 'Public Enterprise: Criteria and Cases'. In H.W. de Jong (ed.). *The Structure of European Industry*. Kluwer Academic Publishers, Dordrecht.

Shleifer, A. and R.W. Vishny (1986). 'Large Shareholders and Corporate Control', *Journal of Political Economy*, 95(3), pp 461-488.

Shleifer, A. and R.W. Vishny (1997). 'A Survey of Corporate Governance', *Journal of Finance*, 52(2), pp. 737-83.

Short, H. (1994). 'Ownership, Control, Financial Structure and the Performance of Firms', *Journal of Economic Surveys*, 8(3), pp. 203-249.

Tirole, J. (1992). *The Theory of Industrial Organization*. MIT Press, Cambridge MA.

Zeckhouser, R. and J. Pound. (1990). 'Are Large Shareholders Effective Monitors? – An Investigation of Share Ownership and Corporate Performance'. In G.R. Hubbard (ed.), *Asymmetric Information, Corporate Finance and Investment*. University of Chicago Press, Chicago.

Williamson, O. (1985). *The Economic Institutions of Capitalism*. Free Press, New York.

Worldscope-Disclosure (annually). *Compact D – CD-ROM*. Disclosure Inc., Bethesda, MD.

CHAPTER 6

What Boards do and Should do[1]

Compared to other actors like managers, large owners, and auditors, boards have a comparative advantage in classical board functions such as monitoring, management replacement, control, and the ratification of major decisions. While the expertise accumulated by doing these jobs may also be useful in business strategy, risk management, shareholder and stakeholder relations, I argue that the marginal value of additional board work declines steeply and becomes negative if boards are overloaded with responsibility. Because of the empowerment of boards, the risk of overload appears to have increased in recent years with potentially dysfunctional effects like passivity, delay, box checking, risk aversion, strategic mistakes, and insufficient control. Boards may respond to these challenges by organizational innovations like the formation of committees, and other actors like shareholders, auditors, and managers may substitute for weak boards by assuming more important governance roles.

Introduction

There is no doubt that boards are central to the corporate governance discussion. In fact, to many observers and researchers, the concepts of 'boards' and 'corporate governance' are almost synonymous. In this chapter I will argue theoretically and empirically that boards have an important but limited role to play in corporate governance, and that on average boards do not – and should not – matter much. I go on to assess the recent

1. This chapter draws heavily on my working paper 'A minimum theory of boards' prepared for presentation at the Scancor Seminar 13. August 2007, Stanford University. The chapter has benefited greatly from discussions with Lars Nørby Johansen.

empowerment of boards in the light of this and argue that boards are likely to become overloaded and either fail to live up to expectations or are likely to have dysfunctional effects on company behaviour and performance.

To clarify the proposition I do not claim that management does not matter. There is a great deal of empirical evidence which indicates that top managers make a difference for company performance, although perhaps not quite as much of a difference as popular opinion would have it (Dennis and Dennis, 1995, Hayes and Schaefer 1999, Huson, Malatesta, and Parrino 2004, Bennedsen, Perez-Gonzalez, and Wolfenzon 2006). The proposition is concerned with the board, particularly the non-executive directors or (in two-tier board systems) with the function of supervisory boards.

Nor do I claim that no board will ever under any circumstances make a difference. The proposition is that the average board does not have much of an influence on company behaviour or performance. The strong form proposition is that the average board might as well be replaced by a new team. It might be cut in half, double in size, introduce or abolish board committees, have meetings with or without the executives. It would make no difference. Again, the proposition is concerned with 'normal' boards within the range of behaviour which we observe in normal companies; what would happen in extreme cases is another matter. For example it might – or might not – make a difference if the non-executive board members were replaced by chimpanzees. But this question will not be analysed in the present chapter.

Finally, I do not claim that boards have no role to play in corporate governance, although this might be a more entertaining case to make. Summarizing recent board research I propose that boards are just one of many corporate governance mechanisms that they play a valuable, but limited role in certain key decisions and that overextending their responsibilities beyond these functions will most likely have detrimental effects on company performance.

In the theory of boards, it is customary to refer to board behaviour as a 'black box '. This is a metaphor which is borrowed from the theory of the firm and which resonates well with the mystique surrounding board work. My proposition is that most of what we call corporate governance takes place 'outside the box'. However, because of the procedural formality of board meetings and best practice codes, I argue that the black box metaphor is ill-founded; we actually know more about what goes on in boardrooms than about many other kinds of company behaviour.

The chapter is structured as follows. In section two, I present some stylized facts which demonstrate a gross imbalance between the limited resources available to boards and the daunting list of responsibilities with which they are burdened. I recall the important distinction between formal and real authority. Boards have a great deal of formal authority, but since they have very limited information, their real authority is much more limited. In section three I argue theoretically that boards are designed to address a limited set of decision problems in which managers have conflicts of interest. Drawing on the distinction between formal and real authority (Aghion and Tirole, 1997), I propose that extending board work to other functions is subject to declining marginal returns and beyond some point is likely to lead to overload and value destruction. In section four, I review the empirical evidence on board performance and find it to be consistent with the minimum theory. In section five, I analyze what happens when boards are overloaded and argue that overload can lead to organizational innovation as well as substitution by other governance mechanisms. In section six, I conclude by discussing hypotheses for empirical testing and management implications.

Board functions: facts and fiction

Following the warning against 'blackboard economics' (Coase 1991) or 'armchair economics' (Simon, 1988) I begin by describing some stylized facts about boards in large listed companies.[2] The idea is to define a nor-

2. Most of the paper is concerned with topics which cut across international differences in board structure. For example the key issues are the same in one- and two-tier boards. In two-tier boards (Germany, Scandinavia, Finland, Austria) shareholders elect non-executive directors – and occasionally also a minority of executive directors – to a supervisory board which evaluates company performance, hires and fires the management (the executives), and must approve all major decisions. In one-tier systems, shareholders elect the board, which then appoints the executives. Executives may or may not be board members, but typically some of them are. In both systems, most of the board members are now non-executive directors (this holds in the USA and in Europe, but not in Japan). Non-executive directors are typically part-time, and

mal board and to get some intuitive appreciation of what boards can and cannot do. I show that boards face severe limitations in terms of manpower, time, information, and decision processes, which appear to be inconsistent with the wide range of tasks which they are expected to undertake.

It is true that boards have enormous formal power. Company law across the world stipulates that all important decisions must be made (i.e. at least approved) by the board. However, we know that formal authority does not always imply real authority (Aghion and Tirole, 1997). In particular boards – much like shareholder meetings – may have much less real than formal authority because they do not have sufficient information to exercise their authority. Unlike shareholder meetings which occur in the public domain, board meetings are confidential, and this lack of transparency is usually fertile ground for myths. We know – or rather we think – there is not much going on at shareholder meetings. It is tempting, therefore, to assume that the important decisions are made in the board room. But this is evidently a *non sequitur*.

The available facts indicate that boards are relatively small entities who only account for minute fraction of overall business activities. In terms of size, boards consist of a limited number of members, e.g. twelve,

> generally – in accordance with best practice codes – a majority are supposed to be independent also in the sense that they have no other material ties with the firm (the company lawyer for example is not an independent board member). Many non-executive directors have demanding jobs as executives, managers in other firms, lawyers, or even professors. Despite these differences, boards in the two systems have similar responsibilities and in both systems the corporate governance discussion has been directed primarily at what non-executive directors do and what they should be doing. The same applies to other system differences. In some countries (e.g. the USA, France) the chief executive can also be chairman of the board (duality), but this is prohibited in two-tier systems. In the UK the two positions are now typically separated following corporate governance recommendations (Cadbury, 1992). But in all three countries there are similar discussions about the responsibilities of non-executive directors. Likewise the corporate governance debate cuts across differences in employee representation. In some two-tier countries employees have a right to elect members of the supervisory boards, typically 1/3 of the board members, but in some large German companies, up to 50 %. But despite employee representation, the shareholder-elected board members have a majority of the votes (in Germany the vote of the chairman is decisive in case of a split).

which can be greater in large organizations, but rarely larger than 20 members (e.g. de Andres, Azofra and Lopez. 2005, Conyon and Peck 1998). Boards tend to meet between six and eight times per year, and occasionally will meet more often: but rarely more than twelve times a year (Vafeas, 1999). There is little scientific evidence on the duration of board meetings, but a normal meeting is believed to take from 3-4 hours up to a whole day in large corporations. Company directors interviewed by consulting companies indicate that they spend some 180-200 hours a year (i.e. 4-5 work weeks) on board-related tasks (Price Waterhouse Coopers, 2005; USC and Mercer/Delta, 2005), but this includes both executive directors and chairs (who probably spend more time preparing the meeting), the time spent by directors with several board positions (some only do board work), and preparation time. Nevertheless, the survey studies agree that the time spent on board work has increased significantly over the past few years.

If we count seven meetings a year multiplied by twelve board members multiplied by two days of work (to account for preparation) we total 168 work days – or in total half a year's work – invested by the average board. If we compare this to the number of employees measured in tens of thousands (e.g. 16 558 in the study by Brick et al.), the work of non-executive directors accounts for 0.004% of the work put in by the corporation as a whole. This does not necessarily mean that boards are useless, but rather that their contribution is limited. In fact – much like penicillin – they may be essential for a limited range of very important tasks, and companies might find it difficult to function without them. But on the margin their contribution is probably negligible. If boards were very useful – for example if more board effort or better qualified board members could add 5% to company value it would be relatively simple, inexpensive, and profitable to double the number of board meetings or to double the fees to attract better board members.

Non-executive directors get paid in tens of thousands of dollars – for example USD 67 225 in a study of US directors (Brick, Palmon and Wald, 2006), whereas CEOs get paid in hundreds of thousands or millions (e.g. an average of 4.054 million dollars in the same study). Sales, however, are counted in billions of dollars ($2.8 billion in the study by Brick et al.), so that director compensation accounts for a minute fraction of sales, value-added, and total salaries paid by the corporation. A rough estimate is that total director compensation accounts for 0.03% of company sales or perhaps 0.06% of value-added (total income generation) in the average company. Basic microeconomics would indicate that the marginal product of non-executive directors should equal their marginal compensation[3]. Assuming that average director compensation equals marginal compensation this would indicate that the average non-executive director accounts for a minute fraction – something like a percent of a percent – of total value creation in the average company. If we assume that marginal director pay should be equal to director effort and marginal director productivity (Vafeas 1999), boards apparently do not make much of a difference.

Moreover, boards are relatively inefficiently organized by collective (i.e. non-hierarchical) decision making. Voting is democratic. Decisions are officially made in plenum. In almost all cases decisions are unanimous. Informal contacts between board members are often discouraged on suspicion of coalition building. In agency terms, group work like this is likely to create free rider problems since individual non-executive directors can free ride on the activities of others. In a 4-hour board meeting between eight board members, each member gets in principle only 30 minutes to express her opinions. However, the executives and the chairman use much more time because they need to convey messages, to make proposals, and to make presentations. In addition most of the dialogue will be questions to and answers by the executives. A total of 1-2 hours of interactive dialogue is therefore more realistic, and for non-executives, 5-10 minutes voice per meeting. This is unlikely to be sufficient for questions and answers or for any in-depth analysis.

The black box metaphor notwithstanding, we actually know much about what happens in boardrooms. Very often this is even written down in the rules of procedure. Most board meetings tend to follow a standard agenda with minor modifications (Colleney et al. 2003):

1. Quorum/approval of agenda
2. Approval/signature of minutes
3. Messages (non-decision/consent items)
4. Committee reports (if any)

---

3. On the margin, director pay should also be equal to director effort (disutility). Adams (2005) applies this principle when using pay as a proxy for board effort.

5. Current financial status
6. Proposals
7. Briefings
8. Any other business

In the vast majority of cases, the board ratifies decision proposals by the managers (McNulty and Pettigrew 1999). The chair controls what items are put on the agenda and will often not include proposals which are not likely to be approved.

It is instructive to compare the above-mentioned stylized facts to the relatively detailed recommendations in corporate governance codes concerning what boards should do. As an example of this I focus on the tasks and duties of the board as outlined in the UK combined code: the 'mother of all codes'. Similar codes are found around the world (e.g. the NYSE and NASDAQ codes). For a full view of director responsibilities these codes must be supplemented with national law, listing requirements, etc.[4]

In the appendix (table 1) I summarize the key tasks and responsibilities of the board according to the British combined code of best practice in corporate governance. The 'to do list' is daunting. The board should be

---

4. For example contrary to views commonly expressed in textbooks on corporate finance, directors now face a complex set of responsibilities to ALL stakeholders. Consider the UK 2006 companies act: § 172. Duty to promote the success of the company, part (1):
   'A director of a company must act in the way he considers, in good faith, would be most likely to promote the success of the company for the benefit of its members as a whole, and in doing so have regard (amongst other matters) to
   (a) the likely consequences of any decision in the long term,
   (b) the interests of the company's employees,
   (c) the need to foster the company's business relationships with suppliers, customers and others,
   (d) the impact of the company's operations on the community and the environment,
   (e) the desirability of the company maintaining a reputation for high standards of business conduct, and
   (f) the need to act fairly as between members of the company.'
   Whatever benefits there may be in adopting a stakeholder view, a multi-valued – and possibly partly conflicting – objective function beyond profit or value maximization does not make it easier for company directors to make decisions or for shareholders to hold them accountable (Jensen, 2001).

entrepreneurial, contribute to strategy, monitor performance, assess risks, and set the company's values and standards.

There are even more elaborate best practice recommendations for chairs, lead directors, and committees. According to the UK best practice code, the chair and a 'senior non-executive director' have special tasks with regard to self evaluation and shareholder relations (appendix table 1). In addition to meeting without the executives present, non-executive directors (including the chair who is a non-executive in the UK system) should hold meetings on their own. A third control – a control of the control – is undertaken by mandatory meetings between non-executive directors excluding the chair. In these meetings the senior non-executive director (lead director) acts as a second chair. Moreover, both the chair and the lead directors should spend time meeting with major shareholders: particularly institutional investors.

In large listed US firms board committees meet separately in 3-4 meetings per year (Adams, 2005). The committees are primarily composed of independent non-executive directors since they deal with issues in which the executives may have a private interest. Auditing committees, for example, deal with financial reports, control systems, and choice of auditor. Intuitively, the rationale seems to be to ensure that information provided to the board is reliable and not biased by the executives in their own favour. Remuneration (compensation) committees set the pay of the executives, in which they also have a vested interest. Finally, the nomination committee is concerned with selecting board members and managers, so independence is intended to ensure that managers do not bias board composition in their own favour.

Given the complexity and importance of the companies involved – the world's largest multinational companies are formally governed by boards as described above – it is not easy to see how these tasked can be adequately solved with two to three weeks effort per board member. While boards play a prominent formal role in the company, the few available stylized facts tend to indicate a discrepancy between the very important formal role of boards and the limited resources which they have at their disposal.

The theory of boards

Drawing on institutional economics (Coase, 1937; Williamson 1984, 1985, 2005), boards can be characterized as one of many other governance mechanisms (institutions). The current consensus view among researchers is that corporate governance – defined as 'the control and direction of companies' – consists of a set of mechanisms which include company law, monitoring by large owners, the threat of hostile takeover, managerial incentives, creditor monitoring, product market competition, as well as boards (Shleifer and Vishny 1996, Becht et al. 2002, Tirole 2006). Given this broader theoretical understanding, it is surprising that so much attention has been directed exclusively at boards in the contemporary discussion. For example, the vast majority of the recommendations in corporate governance codes across the world are concerned with board structure and board behaviour.

I examine the comparative advantage of boards relative to those institutions. I characterize the board as a partially internalized, non-hierarchical corporate institution based on collective decision making. While non-executive directors are paid by the firm, they are elected by shareholders and work only on a part-time basis, which distinguishes them from executives (McNulty and Pettigrew, 1999). Given the existence of boards the central problem (as for any other institution) is to determine the range of their activities. I use the board activities suggested in the US literature (Monks & Minnow, 2001, Colleney et al. 2003) as a starting point:

- Evaluate the financial situation and strategy of the company
- Select, evaluate, and if necessary replace the CEO and other chief executives
- Negotiate CEO pay
- Nominate of new board members
- Control major strategic decisions (M&A, capital investments)
- Establish stakeholder policies (philanthropy, environmental protection, business ethics)
- Advise the executives on strategy and other policies
- Ensure lawfulness of company activities
- Ensure appropriate risk management
- Facilitate good shareholder relations
- Form and maintain business relationships

Then, I consider whether boards can be expected to do better or worse than other governance institutions when undertaking these activities. Some of the key concerns are avoiding conflicts of interest (opportunism) and aligning responsibility and information access.

The division of labour between boards and management can be analysed as a delegation decision: How much should the board do, and how much should be left to the management? Impartiality concerns imply that management cannot control itself – e.g. evaluate its own performance, approve its own strategy, hire or fire itself, set its own pay or the non-executive director pay. However, it is at least possible – to some extent – for boards to share these tasks with shareholders and with external consultants.

Shareholders will often be asked to approve major decisions (like mergers) and, when voting on the annual report, they also get a say on company strategy. But it is impractical (i.e. costly) to have a large group of shareholders meet regularly, so the board steps in as an intermediary. Fama and Jensen (1983) therefore suggest that boards will arise as a control mechanism when there is separation of ownership and control. Information asymmetries, costs of collective decision making, and free riding problems all imply excessively high transaction costs for direct shareholder democracy. Compared to shareholder meetings, boards can give more continuous and flexible feedback to the management which will often be in the company's best interest. To some extent, collective action problems and information costs can be reduced by large shareholders who have both the incentive and the power to act (Shleifer and Vishny, 1996, Anderson and Reeb, 2004). However, ownership concentration is costly, and a large owner may not be available. Moreover, ownership concentration gives rise to a new set of impartiality problems related to possible conflicts of interest between large and small shareholders.

The board can also outsource some jobs to external consultants. For example, it can solicit proposals for compensation packages from pay consultants or monthly performance reviews from the auditors. Professional service firms do not face the same time and information constraints as non-executive board members. Impartiality concerns would dictate that auditors and other consultants should be selected by an entity which is independent of the management (i.e. by the shareholders or if this is impractical by the board). So here is a role for the board.

Altogether, boards seem to have a comparative advantage in a small set of classical board functions which they are designed for – overseeing performance evaluations, CEO replacement and executive pay, and approval of major decisions. It is not clear, however, that board control is particularly effective. A large literature in management and economics argues otherwise. Adam Smith (1776) held that 'negligence and profusion' must generally prevail in boards because directors are watching over other people's money. Berle and Means (1932) argued that executives were effectively in control of the board because of their control of proxy committees. Mace (1971) and Lorsch and MacIver (1989) emphasise the power of the CEO over the board and downplay the importance of board control. Warther, (1998) summarizing the earlier literature, argues that critical board members who voted against the management tend to leave or be ejected. Hermalin and Weisbach (1998) show how successful CEOs can accumulate power over time by influencing the composition of the board. From a social psychology viewpoint, Westphal argues that non-executive directors display 'pluralistic ignorance' (i.e. underestimate that other board members may also be critical of the CEO) (Westphal and Bednar, 2005), that the CEO appeases them through ingratiation (Westphal, 1998), and that troublesome directors are subjected to 'social distancing' through personal networks (Westphal and Khanna, 2003).

To the classic board functions ('the control role') some management scholars would add 'service' and networking (Johnson et al. 1996). Service involves giving advice and input to strategy discussions. For example, a lawyer on the board may advise on legal issues (Daily et al. 20003). Networking consists of establishing and maintaining contacts to important constituencies, including investors (e.g. Pfeffer & Salancik, 1978 Stearns & Mizruchi, 1993). A transaction costs argument for these other roles would be that boards acquire firm-specific knowledge through the control function, and that this knowledge can be efficiently applied here as well.

Nevertheless, there are strong reasons to assume a relatively steep decline in the marginal productivity of board effort beyond the classical 'minimum functions':

– Non-executive board members have an information disadvantage compared to managers and will therefore make worse decisions if they delegate less

Chapter 6. What Boards do and Should do

- Despite the recent emergence of organizational structure at the board level, boards have very limited resources in terms of time and organizational support compared to company managers
- Group decision making – which is believed necessary for mutual monitoring – reduces the decision making efficiency of boards (Hermalin & Weisbach, 2003)
- There is a trade off between management and control. The more effort boards put in, the more they will become involved in management and the less objective can they be in controlling the self same management (Adams and Ferreira, 2007)
- There appear to be relatively strong social and psychological mechanisms which reduce the influence of non-executive board members (cf. Westphal's work and Buffet 2003).

The implication is first that the marginal productivity of additional board work will decline rapidly and become negative as boards put in more effort (figure 1), and second that value creation will become value destruction if boards overextend their reach (figure 2).

A formal argument for board inactivity or 'rubber stamping' of CEO proposals can be found in the distinction between formal and real authority (Aghion and Tirole, 1997, Weber, 1968). Although boards have formal

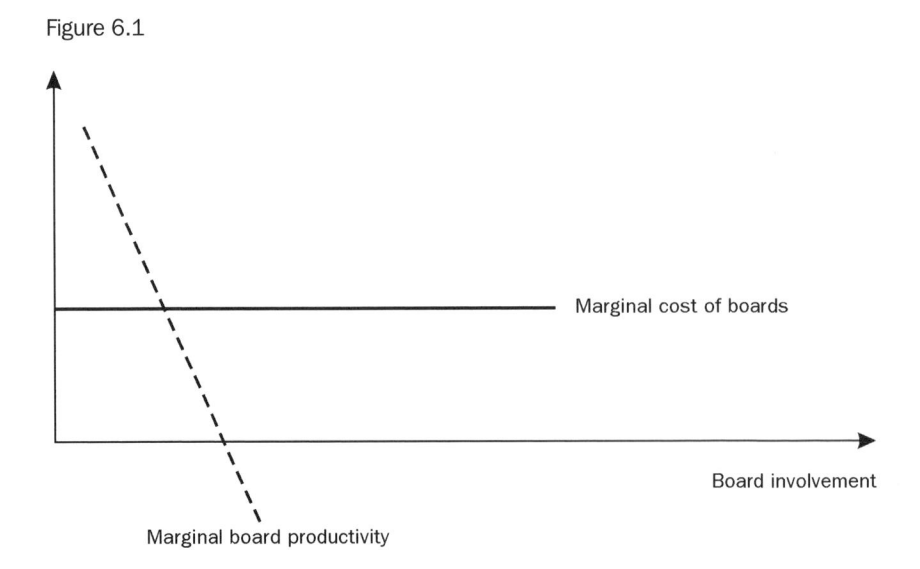

Figure 6.1

Figure 6.2

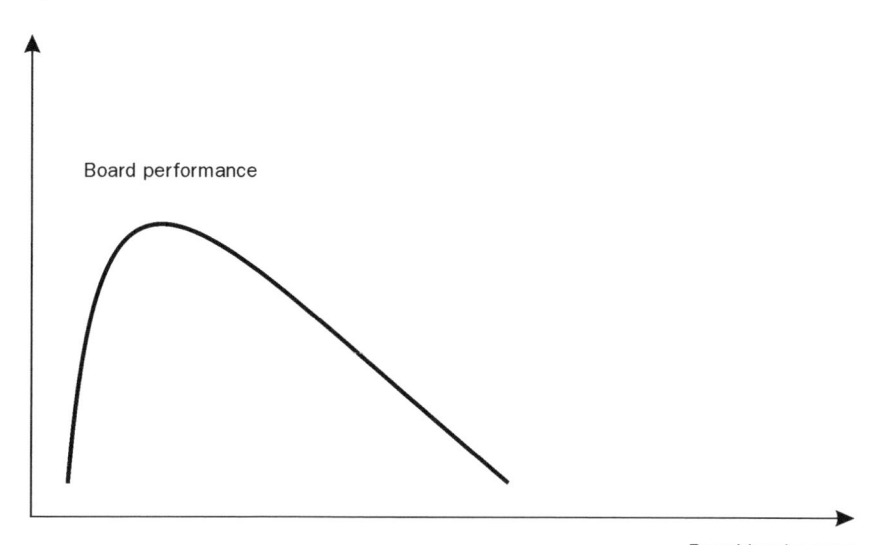

Board performance (y-axis) vs Board involvement (x-axis): curve rises steeply then declines.

authority to overrule executives, non-executive directors have insufficient information to decide whether this is the right thing to do. Even if they retain formal control, Aghion and Tirole show that boards will rationally rubberstamp management decision proposals as long as they have no independent sources of information and if they can assume that the decision proposal is no worse than the benchmark of doing nothing (in other words, assuming that managers and board members have a shared interest in selecting projects that at last cover the opportunity costs of capital). In this case, the agent has the real authority. Boards may recognize this and delegate formal authority to managers who will then want to contribute more information to the board because their interests are safeguarded. In both cases, greater board involvement – understood as overruling of more management decisions or rejection of more project proposals – will harm organisational performance. A formal explanation is provided in the appendix (Appendix 6.2).

Interestingly, it follows from the Aghion and Tirole framework that group decision making may add value when boards retain formal authority if the group decision making structure leads to free riding and thereby creates a credible commitment not to overrule the executives. In this sense, the board may be valuable because it is relatively inefficient. Furthermore, over time the board may build up a reputation for not intervening too much which will allow managers to share more information.

The win-win situation emphasized by management scholars (e.g. Pearce and Zahra, 1991) in which the empowerment of boards does not come at the cost of managerial autonomy corresponds most closely to the situation in which the board delegates significant formal responsibility to the executives who can then feel secure enough against overruling to volunteer more information (Adams and Ferreira, 2007). Aghion and Tirole show that communication (about strategy) will increase in this case, but the board will rationally refrain from overruling the managers and thus, in a formal sense, non-executive board members have absolutely no influence on strategy. It is possible, however, that friendly boards can occasionally come up with ideas which lead to improvements for both managers and non-executives, if the non-executives get better information access. Moreover, the ability to communicate more openly with executives may in itself be valuable for the board (and possibly also for shareholders) which gets a more realistic view of risks and expected returns. Finally, the board retains the right to reject negative NPV projects (which are inferior to the status quo).

As mentioned, certain key decisions – core board activities – cannot be outsourced or shared with the CEO because of conflicts of interest. These include the basic appointment/termination, nomination, control, and remuneration decisions (in contrast executives can and do give advice on the hiring of new executives). For these activities, the marginal productivity of board work will be high. However, for the more managerial tasks, boards face stiff institutional competition. Given limitations on time and information, it will be lucky if the board is able to give much valuable advice to a seasoned executive. This does not mean that coaching, mentoring, strategic sparring, and all the other catchwords are completely devoid of value, but rather that the inspiration from these sources will only add marginally to total value creation in a large company. Moreover, the value of these activities will be highly conditional on the situation. Boards should not always be friendly with managers and sometimes trust can backfire.

Activities such as mentoring or involvement in strategy making which have a positive impact under some circumstances may therefore have dysfunctional effects in other cases. A high level of trust may be conducive to creativity and information sharing, but it can lead to catastrophe when managers are fraudulent. Very elaborate control and incentive systems can be gamed and may suppress teamwork and information sharing, which could reduce risk taking and entrepreneurship and harm performance in that way. Since it is difficult ex ante to determine which contingency will be applicable in a specific company, it may be optimal to simplify board work to the essentials. And certainly, this will hold even more across a range of companies.

The minimum view is therefore that boards will typically delegate 'business as usual' decisions to executives and very rarely intervene in this area. In contrast, they will at least be consulted on major strategic issues, but will typically choose to endorse the recommendations of managers. Moreover, if they disagree with managers they will confer with owners and consultants. Very rarely will they make independent decisions. However, boards will be concerned with strategy in the sense that an articulated strategy enables them some degree of control over the direction of the firm including business risk and expected return. Boards will therefore often insist that the executives have a formal strategy and a budget which they can then use as a benchmark for assessing the development of the firm. The 'unusual' will then come up as deviations from strategy.

The empirical evidence

By and large the empirical evidence is consistent with the proposition that boards do not – on average – matter much to company performance. I consider three types of evidence: studies of board structure and performance, studies of board structure in special situations, and direct studies of behaviour in the boardroom.

Board structure and company performance

Johnson et. al. (1996) summarize an extensive literature review of board structure and company performance as follows:

> *'To our knowledge, there has been no documented evidence of the existence of a unicorn. With tongue slightly in cheek, there can be two general rationales for our failure to 'discover' this legendary species. First, this animal simply does not exist. Second, we have not searched in the right place,*

at the right time, with the right equipment ... In many ways an aggregation and summary of the boards of directors/financial performance/other outcomes literature has this same character. Maybe such relationships simply do not exist in nature. Or, if they do exist, their magnitude is such that they are not of practical importance. Alternatively, given the heterogeneity of typical independent variables. It may be unrealistic to reasonably compare and summarize this body of work.' (Johnson et. 1996 p. 433)

In a subsequent meta-analysis Dalton, Daily, Ellstrand, and Johnson (1998) support this finding for board composition (159 samples, n = 40,160) and leadership structure (coincidence between chair and CEO) (69 samples, n = 12,915):

'The results for the board composition/financial performance meta-analyses suggest no relationship of a meaningful level. Subgroup moderating analyses based on firm size, the nature of the performance indicators, and operationalization of board composition provide no evidence of moderating influences for these variables as well. The evidence derived from the meta-analysis and moderating analyses for board leadership structure and financial performance has the same character, i.e., no evidence of a substantive relationship. These results lead to the very strong conclusion that the true population relationship across the studies included in these meta-analyses is near zero'. (Dalton et al. 1998).

In a survey of the economic literature, Hermalin and Weisbach (2003) conclude that '*..board composition is not related to corporate performance, while board size is negatively related to corporate performance.*' However, the firm size result is based on only two studies, Yermack (1996) for US firms and Eisenberg et al. (1998) for small- and medium-sized Finnish firms, although it has since been supported by other studies (e.g. Andres et al. (2005) and partly by Conyon and Peck (2003)). In contrast Dalton, Daily, Johnson and Ellstrand (1999) in a meta-analysis of 131 samples and 20,620 observations find the opposite: '*...the results for our overall meta-analysis of the board size-financial performance association strongly suggest a nonzero, positive relationship ... these relationships are consistent for market-based and accounting based firm performance measures.*' (Dalton et al. 1999). So there is really no consensus on board size effects.

There are several methodological issues which complicate empirical studies of board structure and performance. The most important is that we have strong reasons to believe that board structure and board behaviour depend upon ownership and capital structure, law, and other governance mechanisms as well as on company performance. Boone, Casares Field, Karpoff & Raheja (2007), Raheja, C. (2005), Baker and Gompers (2003), Denis & Sarin (1999), Hermalin and Weisbach (1998) find that board structure is influenced by ownership structure, board size, company performance, and other economic variables. To estimate the effects of board structure, we need to take this interdependence into consideration, which means estimating simultaneous equation systems with many dependent equations. Very few studies have done this. A recent exception is Bhagat and Bolton (2007), who estimate ownership, governance, performance, and capital structure in four simultaneous equations. They find that board structure (measured by the fraction of independent directors) has no significant effect on firm value and has a negative effect on accounting returns. However, it is difficult to find instrument variables which influence either performance or governance without influencing the others so causality is a problem even in large simultaneous equation models.

All this indicates that boards are part of a complex system of governance mechanisms. In many cases, board structure and board behaviour will be determined by other corporate governance mechanisms in combination with firm-specific variables. For example, large owners often want to be represented on the board. Moreover, even if they are not present at the board, the expectations of large owners can condition board decisions to a very large extent. A board may, for example, feel compelled by anticipated shareholder reactions to fire the CEO after three years of bad performance. Or banks may make demands on board composition as a condition for extending credit to an insolvent firm, and the board may feel compelled to fire the CEO because of manifest or anticipated pressure from creditors. The point is that board structure and behaviour are endogenous, and when this is taken into account, the part of company behaviour and performance which is attributable to the board as such is diminished.

Special situations
There are a number of studies of special situations – e.g. the role of the board in replacing CEOs, shareholder defences, executive compensation, and M&A – and here there is more evidence that boards matter (Johnson et a. 1996, Hermalin & Weisbach 2003). However, the implications for company performance are often unclear. It may be, for example, that independent boards are more likely to replace CEOs when performance is bad, but it is unclear whether this is the right decision. Second, even when performance is measured – as in event studies – it is unclear whether a positive effect on the performance effects of certain types of decisions – like adopting a poison pill – will hold for other types of decisions, as well. In fact, it seems likely that greater independence and more monitoring can have adverse effects on information sharing (Adams and Ferreira, 2007). Finally the observed correlations often run counter to expectations. In a meta study of 38 studies with 69 samples (N = 30,650), Deutsch (2005) concludes that greater board independence is associated with higher executive pay, more unrelated diversification, and more takeover defences – all contrary to expectations in a standard agency model.

What do boards do?
Adams (2005) approaches the study of board behaviour indirectly. She examines the time and compensation of committee work as a proxy for director effort. Using this proxy, she concludes that company boards devote more time to monitoring (audit, compensation, and nomination committees) than to strategy or network roles, but that quite many do have strategy and stakeholder committees which account for respectively 4% and 1% of total director compensation. However, she also finds that most board work (compensation) takes place outside the committees.

Based on a large number of interviews with non-executive directors, Lorsch and MacIver (1989) conclude that non-executive directors are pawns more than potentates vis-à-vis the management, partly because they do not have sufficient time and must rely on the chairman/CEO for most of their information. They also document that most US non-executive directors feel an ambiguous and partly conflicting set of responsibilities to all stakeholders rather than just to shareholders. They conclude that more empowered directors would benefit company performance.

After interviewing 108 non-executive directors, McNulty and Pettigrew (1999) conclude that *'the initiation and generation of strategy are much more likely to be led by executive directors. It is the executive board members, acting outside the boardroom, who tend to generate the content of strategy'*. However, they argue that some boards shape strategic decisions through consultation with the executives (often outside board meetings), while *'only a minority of boards shape the context, content, and conduct of strategy'*. Boards ratify most proposals by the executives (90-95%), but Pettigrew and McNulty maintain that non-executives shape strategy by an ongoing dialogue with the management in and outside board meetings.

All in all, the available evidence is consistent with the proposition that boards do not, on average, matter much to company performance. Board structure seems to influence the direction of decision making, but it is unclear whether this behaviour creates value, and what works in one special situation may be counterproductive in another.

Empowerment and overload

For decades academics have called for empowerment of boards (e.g. Lorsch and MacIver 1989) and many studies have found that boards have, in fact, become more active during the past two decades (e.g. McNulty and Pettigrew, 1999). These changes are often claimed to be influenced by new legislation (e.g. Sarbanes-Oxley – a.k.a. SOX), the diffusion of corporate governance codes, pressure from institutional investors, and the influence of private equity funds (McKinsey, 2007). As noted in section 2, the 'to do list' for boards appears enormously ambitious given the time and information constraints of non-executive board members. Boards should undertake entrepreneurial leadership, strategy proposals setting values and standards for the companies, meetings with major shareholders, and self-evaluation, in addition to a wide range of classical board jobs like hiring/firing managers, checking accounts, and assessing performance.

If the minimum theory proposed here is correct, the call for greater board involvement (e.g. more monitoring) risks lowering company performance. This will happen because boards will make more decisions on the basis of insufficient information and, therefore, make more mistakes.

In addition overruling the executives will make them more reluctant to volunteer information so boards will become less informed than before.

It is difficult to predict exactly how boards will respond to these challenges, but it is possible to identify some plausible outcomes.

Boards may respond by working harder, increasing preparation time, as well as the number and duration of board meetings. This seems to have happened (Price Waterhouse Coopers, 2005; USC and Mercer/Delta, 2005). The risk here is that boards become too much involved in management and thereby lose the mental independence which would allow them to exercise control of management. Aghion and Tirole (1997) predict that more intense monitoring will reduce managerial incentives to take new initiatives and make them more reluctant to share information with the board. Companies may therefore become more risk adverse. Alternatively, boards may feel compelled to make decisions despite inadequate information. This will then lead to inferior decisions.

To deal with many conflicting demands, boards may also adopt a box-checking approach documenting that they comply with corporate governance codes; have adopted standard policies for stakeholders; have policies on business ethics, executive compensation, or other issues; have discussed business strategy and key decisions in the appropriate way; etc. This solution is a bureaucratic, politically-correct way to provide legitimacy for board behaviour. But it has been criticized for bypassing the core objectives of corporate governance: to make good business decisions and ensure value creation (e.g. Lohse, 2006).

Alternatively, board work may be reorganized to become more effective. The organization of boards can change to become more functional and it has already done so to some extent through the increased use of specialized committees which work in parallel – and therefore save time – and which allow a division of labour. To be sure, committee work is partly motivated by a perceived need to separate decisions from the influence of executives, but this does not apply to all committees. Executive committees, strategy committees, and social responsibility committees are to a great extent filled by executives. Moreover, an increasing division of labour between committees, chairs, lead directors, executive directors, and non-executive directors indicates a more sophisticated internal organization of boards. Nevertheless, the basic trade off between management and monitoring remains. Despite additional meetings, boards will never be as well-informed as managers.

Third, boards may outsource more. For example, they can rely more on external advisors like lawyers, auditors, search firms, compensation, and strategy consultants. This also appears to be happening to a significant extent. The risk here is that board work is reduced to endorsing recommendations by these outside consultants whose independence of company management is open to question, since their fees are paid by the company.

Finally, boards may paradoxically come to rely more on managers, for example by asking managers to draft relevant reports and decisions on social responsibility, corporate governance, etc. Obviously, this is contrary to the intention of empowering the board vis-à-vis managers.

Board overload will predictably lead to a substitution by other governance mechanisms.

Owners may become more involved in board decisions at various levels, and in fact board failure in listed companies has provided justification for new business models (e.g. private equity funds), in which owners communicate more directly with managers. For example, institutional investors may seek to take more control of the nomination process for new board members, and they may engage in a dialogue with large owners over who to suggest for the board, and whether this or that candidate is an acceptable CEO. This can then effectively move key decisions outside the boardroom. Large owners may also decide to intervene directly in decisions concerning executive compensation or company policy at shareholder meetings with managers. Nor is it unusual to try to seek investor approval for key decisions like M&A and corporate strategy. Bilateral meetings with major investors imply a communication channel which investors can use to influence the board or, in some cases, to sidestep the board and directly influence managerial decisions.

Moreover, there may be a tendency to increasing interaction between non-executive directors and other stakeholders outside board meetings (McNulty and Pettigrew, 1999). McNulty and Pettigrew argue that non-executive directors can influence the shape and content of corporate strategy in this way, but an equally plausible possibility is that managers can use contacts outside the board meetings to persuade board members of their ideas. Again, major decisions may effectively move out of the boardroom.

It is convenient to distinguish between temporary and permanent overload situations. Temporary overload can occur when boards are faced with isolated decisions which overextend their capacity: for example a major acquisition or the sudden death of a CEO. In this case, minimum theory would imply that board members solicit and implement advice from major shareholders, company managers, and consultants. When the problem is solved, the board will revert to business as usual.

Permanent overload can occur when boards are more or less continuously faced with new decisions. In this case, the prediction would be that boards will devise institutional mechanisms to deal with the new situation. For example, companies which continuously undertake acquisitions will delegate more responsibility for M&A to the management such that only exceptionally large investments will be decision items at board meetings. In the same way large companies which make more large-scale economic decisions will delegate more responsibility to the management team.

Permanent overload can also occur because more responsibility is placed on boards as a consequence of new regulation. Boards will then try to deal with the new situation by increasing use of lawyers, committees, company secretaries, etc. To economize on information scarcity there will predictably be a strong pressure to imitate standard solutions despite a lack of fit with the company's specific situation. For example, family-owned companies routinely adopt the same corporate governance practices as companies with dispersed ownership despite facing very different governance problems.

The overload situation will influence board composition. More experienced board members with alternative sources of income may recognize the control loss and be more selective when accepting new board positions. Less-experienced (or less intelligent) board members will more willingly retain and accept board positions. As a result, board talent may become increasingly scarce.

Discussion

The minimum theory proposed here implies that boards have a comparative advantage in a few classic tasks – evaluating company performance, hiring and firing executives, fixing executive pay, and ratification of major decisions – which managers themselves cannot handle because of conflicts of interest. The expertise which boards accumulate in undertaking these tasks is also useful for business strategy, risk management, social responsibility, and shareholder relations. But given time and information constraints, the marginal value of additional board work declines steeply and becomes negative if boards begin to seriously interfere with the management of the company.

The theory has a number of quantifiable implications which can be tested in further research:
- The board will not make much of difference for performance of the average company
- If anything, board involvement above and beyond the generic board tasks is likely to lower company performance
- Temporary overload will be more likely to occur when boards are faced with critical decisions
- Permanent overload can occur in dynamic business environments with many discrete decisions (e.g. M&A) which are presented at board meetings
- Permanent overload can also occur if regulation and corporate governance codes heap duties and responsibilities on boards without regard for their information and time constraints
- When boards are overloaded, other actors like shareholders, auditors, and managers are more likely to fill in for the board by assuming more prominent governance roles. Examples are shareholder activism, bilateral shareholder meetings, and increased use of auditors or other consultants
- Boards will respond to permanent overload by organizational innovations like committees, lead directors, or company secretaries.

To some extent, testing these hypotheses resembles listening for 'the dog that did not bark' since it is difficult to test the null hypothesis of 'no significance' given the existence of a number of complications related to measurement, controlling for other factors, simultaneity, etc., which could yield the same result. But it would seem to be possible to identify a number of major changes (critical incidents) and then to examine qualitatively to what extent the board was a driving factor behind these changes. The strong form hypothesis would be that the key strategic decisions are effectively made outside the board room – by managers, owners, consultants – so that board members are reduced to go-betweens.

As for management implications, it seems useful to apply minimum theory to define the role of the board in strategic management. Boards clearly must discuss business strategy, for without it they will not be able to evaluate company performance, assess risks, or understand the rationale for major decisions like M&A. Furthermore, without an articulated strategy, they will not be able to evaluate or control the future development of the company. Boards must therefore challenge managers to develop and articulate a coherent strategy which can be used as a benchmark for decision-making. However, boards cannot be expected to make strategy, since they have too little time and information and since an executive role in this respect would conflict with their control role. Boards therefore play a role as enablers rather than as generators of strategy. Their contribution can perhaps best be described as 'vetting' strategy – a term coined by Oracle CEO Charles Philips – to indicate an intermediate position between making and monitoring strategy. It would seem idiotic to ignore ideas and suggestions which come up at board meetings, but to be constructive, they must remain part of the brainstorming rather than decision decrees since only the executives have the capacity to assess their usefulness. Under normal circumstances, the board will therefore not have much of an influence on business strategy or on company performance.

There are exceptions, however, which have been identified in the literature.

In case of prolonged underperformance, boards face the difficult decision of whether to replace the CEO and/or to scrap the current strategy. Both decisions are costly; they leave a decision vacuum in which the board can step in to provide direction and continuity. In this situation boards will predictably turn to large owners or consultants, but if they provide unclear answers, the board will be forced to make independent decisions. The expertise of the board can play a critical role in assessing whether to give the CEO and/or the strategy another chance or to abandon them. A similar situation occurs if the CEO leaves or dies. Typically boards would prefer an orderly succession, but they can act as a safety mechanism in times of crisis.

As a corollary, when the executives are weak (e.g. if the CEO is new or if performance is bad), the board will tend to intervene more (Hermalin & Weisbach, 1998) and ask more questions or be more critical of new decision proposals. In contrast, successful CEOs will become more influential over time (Forbes and Milliken, 1999), and the board will tend to rubber-stamp more decisions.

Another exception occurs when a large owner – perhaps a founder or a member of the founding family – demands a seat on the board and desires to influence the direction of the company. In this case, the board will clearly matter for better or worse. Uniquely talented individuals – the Warren Buffets, Bill Gates, and Phil Knights – may create value in this way: particularly if they have previously held executive positions. Since large owners have their own money at stake, they certainly have the incentive to intervene only when they can create value. However, following the logic of minimum theory, such individuals will de facto typically be executives. For example they often have an office at the company premises and they work full-time rather than part-time. The semi-independent status in the company which we associate with non-executive directors is therefore absent.

References

Adams, Renee B., (2005). 'What do Boards do? Evidence from Board Committee and Director Compensation Data' (March 13, 2003). EFA 2005 Moscow Meetings Paper. Available at SSRN: http://ssrn.com/abstract=397401

Adams, R., & Ferreira, D. (2007, February). A Theory of Friendly Boards. *Journal of Finance,* 62(1), 217-250.

Aghion, P., & Tirole, J. (1995, April). Some implications of growth for organizational form and ownership structure. *European Economic Review,* 39(3/4), 440-455.

Aghion, P., & Tirole, J. (1997, February). Formal and real authority in organizations. *Journal of Political Economy,* 105(1), 1.

Almazan, Andres, and Javier Suarez, 2003, Entrenchment and severance pay in optimal governance structures, *Journal of Finance* 58, 519–547.

Anderson, Ronald C., and David M. Reeb, 2003, 'Founding-Family Ownership and Firm Performance: Evidence from the S&P 500' *Journal of Finance,* Volume 58, Issue 3, 1301-1328.

Andres, de P., Azofra, V., & Lopez, F. (2005, March). Corporate Boards in OECD Countries: size, composition, functioning and effectiveness. *Corporate Governance: An International Review,* 13(2), 197-210.

Baker, M., & Gompers, P. (2003, October). The Determinants of Board Structure at the Initial Public Offering. *Journal of Law & Economics,* 46(2), 569-598.

Bennedsen, M., Francisco Perez-Gonzalez, and Daniel Wolfenzon, 2006, *Do CEOs matter?* Unpublished manuscript, New York University.

Brick, I., Palmon, O., & Wald, J. (2006, June). CEO compensation, director compensation, and firm performance: Evidence of cronyism? *Journal of Corporate Finance,* 12(3), 403-423.

Buffet, Warren. 2003. *Letter to Shareholders.* Berkshire Hathaway Inc.

Corley, K. (2005, March). Examining the Non-Executive Director's Role from a Non-Agency Theory Perspective: Implications Arising from the Higgs Report. *British Journal of Management,* 16, 1-4.

Denis, David J. and Denis, Diane K. 'Performance Changes Following Top Management Dismissals.' *Journal of Finance,* 1995, 50 (4), pp. 1029-57.

Denis, D., & Sarin, A. (1999, May). Ownership and board structures in publicly traded corporations. *Journal of Financial Economics,* 52(2), 187-223.

Deutsch, Y. (2005, June). The Impact of Board Composition on Firms' Critical Decisions: A Meta-Analytic Review. *Journal of Management,* 31(3), 424-444.

Dulewicz, V., & Herbert, P. (2004, July). Does the Composition and Practice of Boards of Directors Bear Any Relationship to the Performance of their Companies? *Corporate Governance: An International Review,* pp. 263,280.

Hermalin, B., & Weisbach, M. (1998, March). Endogenously Chosen Boards of Directors and Their Monitoring of the CEO. *American Economic Review,* 88(1), 96-118.

Benjamin E. Hermalin & Michael S. Weisbach, 2003. 'Boards of directors as an endogenously determined institution: a survey of the economic literature,'

References

Economic Policy Review, Federal Reserve Bank of New York, issue Apr, pages 7-26. [

Hillman, A., & Dalziel, T. (2003, July). Boards Of Directors and Firm Performance: Integrating Agency And Resource Dependence Perspectives. *Academy of Management Review,* 28(3), 383-396.

Huson, Mark R., Malatesta, Paul and Parrino, Robert. 'Managerial Succession and Firm Performance.' *Journal of Financial Economics,* 2004, 74 (2), 237-75.

Lohse, Debora. 2006. Tackling Corporate Governance. Interview with Prof. David Larcker. *Stanford Business magazine.* August

Lorsch, J. and MacIver, E. *Pawns or Potentates.* Harvard Business School Press, Boston, Massachusetts, 1989.

Lynall, M., Golden, B., & Hillman, A. (2003, July). Board Composition From Adolescence To Maturity: A Multitheoretic View. *Academy of Management Review,* 28(3), 416-431.

McNulty, T., & Pettigrew, A. (1999). Strategists on the Board. *Organization Studies* (Walter de Gruyter GmbH & Co. KG.), 20(1), 47-74.

McNulty, T., Roberts, J., & Stiles, P. (2005, March). Undertaking Governance Reform and Research: Further Reflections on the Higgs Review. *British Journal of Management,* 16, 99-107.

Pearce, J. and S. Zahra. 1991. The relative power of CEOs and boards of directors: Associations with corporate performance. *Strategic Management Journal,* 12, pp. 135-153.

Pfeffer, J., & Salancik, G.R. 1978. *The external control of organizations: A resource-dependence perspective.* New York: Harper & Row.

Price Waterhouse Coopers. 2005. What Directors Think. *Corporate Board Member magazine,* published by Board Member Inc.,

Raheja, C. (2005, June). Determinants of Board Size and Composition: A Theory of Corporate Boards. *Journal of Financial & Quantitative Analysis,* 40(2), 283-306.

Roberts, J., McNulty, T., & Stiles, P. (2005, March). Beyond Agency Conceptions of the Work of the Non-Executive Director: Creating Accountability in the Boardroom. *British Journal of Management,* 16, 5-26.

Simon, Herbert, 'The Failures of Armchair Economics,' *Challenge,* Nov.-Dec. 1986, pp. 18-25.

Stearns, L.B., & Mizruchi, M.S. 1993. Board composition and corporate financing: The impact of financial institution representation on borrowing. *Academy of Management Journal* 36: 603-618.

USC/Mercer Delta 2005. Corporate Board Survey Results 2004. March.

Vafeas, N. (1999, July). Board meeting frequency and firm performance. *Journal of Financial Economics,* 53(1), 113-142.

Warther, Vincent A., 1998, Board effectiveness and board dissent: A model of the board's relationship to management and shareholders, *Journal of Corporate Finance 4,* 53-70.

Weber, Max. 1968. *Economy and Society.* New York. Bedminster Press.

Westphal, J. (1998, September). Board Games: How CEOs Adapt to Increases in Structural Board Independence from Management. *Administrative Science Quarterly,* 43(3), 511-538.

Westphal, J., & Bednar, M. (2005, June). Pluralistic Ignorance in Corporate Boards and Firms' Strategic Persistence in Response to Low Firm Performance. *Administrative Science Quarterly*, 50(2), 262-298.

Westphal, J., & Khanna, P. (2003, September). Keeping Directors in Line: Social Distancing as a Control Mechanism in the Corporate Elite. *Administrative Science Quarterly*, 48(3), 361-398.

The tasks of the board according to the combined code

- The board ... is collectively responsible for the success of the company.
- The board's role is to provide entrepreneurial leadership of the company within a framework of prudent and effective controls which enables risk to be assessed and managed.
- The board should set the company's strategic aims, and to ensure that the necessary financial and human resources are in place for the company to meet its objectives and review management performance.
- The board should set the company's values and standards and ensure that its obligations to its shareholders and others are understood and met.
- As part of their role as members of a unitary board, non-executive directors should constructively challenge and help develop proposals on strategy.
- Non-executive directors should scrutinise the performance of management in meeting agreed goals and objectives and monitor the reporting of performance.
- They should satisfy themselves on the integrity of financial information and that financial controls and systems of risk management are robust and defensible.
- They are responsible for determining appropriate levels of remuneration of executive directors (and senior management) and have a prime role in appointing, and where necessary removing executive directors, and in succession planning.
- The board should establish formal and transparent arrangements for considering how they should apply the financial reporting and internal control principles and for maintaining an appropriate relationship with the company's auditors.
- Non-executive directors should be offered the opportunity to attend meetings with major shareholders and should expect to attend them if requested by major shareholders.

The chair and senior non-executive director should
- Hold meetings with the non-executive directors without the executives present.

- Led by the senior independent director, the non-executive directors should meet without the chairman present at least annually to appraise the chairman's performance and. on such other occasions as are deemed appropriate.
- The chairman should ensure that the directors continually update their skills and the knowledge and familiarity with the company required to fulfil their role both on the board and on board committees. The company should provide the necessary resources.
- The chairman should ensure that the views of shareholders are communicated to the board as a whole.
- The chairman should discuss governance and strategy with major shareholders.
- The senior independent director should attend sufficient meetings with a range of major shareholders

The tasks of board committees
- There should be a nomination committee which should lead the process for board appointments and make recommendations to the board.
- For the appointment of a chairman, the nomination committee should prepare a job specification
- The board should undertake a formal and rigorous annual evaluation of its own performance and that of its committees and individual directors.
- The remuneration committee should have delegated responsibility for setting remuneration for all executive directors and the chairman, including pension rights and any compensation payments.
- The (remuneration) committee should also recommend and monitor the level and structure of remuneration for senior management. The definition of 'senior management'. should normally include the first layer of management below board level.
- The board should establish an audit committee to review the company's internal financial controls and to review and monitor the external auditor's independence and objectivity
- and the effectiveness of the audit process, taking into consideration relevant professional and regulatory requirements;
- develop and implement policy on the engagement of the external auditor to supply non-audit services

- review arrangements by which staff of the company may, in confidence, raise concerns about possible improprieties in matters of financial reporting or other matters.
- monitor and review the effectiveness of the internal audit activities.
- have primary responsibility for making a recommendation on the appointment, reappointment and removal of the external auditors.

Source: The Combined Code (2003)

Chapter 6. What Boards do and Should do

Appendix 6.2

When boards retain formal authority, the Aghion/Tirole model implies that both managers and boards maximize their respective payoff functions such that

1) Board utility $\quad u_b = EB + (1-E)e\alpha B - c_b(E)$
2) Management utility $\quad u_m = E\beta b + (1-E)eb - c_m(e)$,

where board effort E ($1 \geq E \geq 0$) is assumed to be synonymous with the probability of correct information about all decision proposals, in which case the board will choose their most preferred project (with payoff B). There remains a probability (1-E) of the board not being informed in which case it must choose the project proposed by management (which is assumed to at least break even). This project will maximize managerial utility and only constitute a fraction α of B ($1 \geq \alpha \geq 0$) and this only if management has made the effort e which with a probability e ($1 \geq e \geq 0$) have informed it sufficiently to make a proposal (alternatively managers will prefer the status quo and make no proposal). Board utility is maximized net of effort costs $c_b(E)$, which are assumed to be an increasing, convex function of E.

In the same way managers maximize the utility function u_m, which give managers a fraction of their maximum utility βb, when the board – with a probability E – is fully informed and chooses its preferred project. In the other case when the board is not informed (with a probability 1-E) and the management is informed (with a probability e), management chooses the project which it prefers (with the maximum pay off b). Likewise managers must deduct effort costs $c_m(e)$ from their utility.

Maximizing these two functions with respect to E and e respectively gives rise to the first order conditions

3) Board utility maximization $\quad (1-\alpha e)B = c'_b(E)$
4) Management utility maximization $\quad (1-E)b = c'_m(e)$,

which show that the board will be more active (monitor more) the higher the possible gains (B), the less effort put in by the agent (e) and the less congruent the objectives of management and the board (α). Moreover, managers will be more active the higher their maximum utility (b) and the less the board interferes (E).

Given the previous arguments for relatively uninformed boards the most interesting and realistic case seems to be when board have little or no information, i.e. when $E \approx 0$ which can for example occur when the marginal costs of information are high $c'_b(E) \rightarrow \infty$. In this case equation 1 and 2 are reduced to

5) $u_b(E) = e\alpha B$
6) $u_m(e) = eb - c_m(e)$

with the first order condition $c'_m(e) = b$, in which case the board has a choice between rubber stamping the decisions proposed by the management (and receive a utility of $e\alpha B$) or remaining passive (and receive zero) and therefore will always choose to rubber stamp since $e\alpha B > 0$.

The more general case is that boards have independent access to a non-zero, but modest amount of information. In this case their involvement (exercise of formal authority) will increase expected returns up to a point beyond which more involvement (more rejections) have a negative impact on board utility. Boards that maximize payoff will recognize this and limit their activity accordingly which implies that they will rubber stamp management proposals.

CHAPTER 7

Ethics as a Governance Mechanism[1]

Contrary to what is often believed, business ethics is not inconsistent with modern economic theory. Both opponents (Friedman 1970) and advocates (Reilly and Kyj 1990) of corporate social responsibility have stressed the inconsistencies. For example Reilly and Kyj (1990) argue that 'Ethics and corporate social responsibility cannot be integrated into business thought if the assumptions of economics are accepted'. This may have been true of certain influential versions of neoclassical economics, but it was not true of Adam Smith (see Sen 1993, Evensky 1993) or classical economists like John Stuart Mill. Furthermore, economics has changed significantly since Friedman (1970). In this chapter I argue that institutional economics contains a rudimentary theory of ethical codes which is limited in scope and far from fully developed, but which may nevertheless be helpful for companies to define what issues an ethical code should address and for policymakers to form realistic expectations of what ethical codes may be expected to accomplish.

I define an ethical code as a set of principles which govern economic behaviour and which may function as a correction to market and policy failures as well as failure of the prevailing social ethic to achieve socially optimal outcomes. Obviously this instrumental view ignores many important issues. It relies very much on standard economic concepts which initially seem controversial when applied to ethical analysis. For example, following a tradition in game theory often applied to prisoners' dilemma games, it will be argued that one ethical code (which induces cooperation) can be said to be more ethical than another (which does not) because it leads to socially optimal outcomes. If one takes into account that there are

---

1. This chapter draws heavily on my paper 'Ethical Codes as Corporate Governance', European Journal of Law and Economics, 2001.

costs of inducing ethical behaviour (cooperation), it follows that optimal ethical codes will depend on those costs. For example, if the costs of the ethical codes are greater then the gains (from cooperation), then an apparently unethical outcome (i.e. no cooperation) may be ethical in a deeper sense. Clearly, this focus bypasses a number of important problems and the range of issues which can be analysed in this way are limited. It is not the intention to give a cost benefit analysis of universal values or basic moral imperatives[2] but to focus on the more marginal issue of whether it makes sense for a company to include a specific issue in its (formal or informal) ethical code. Should an ethical business code support a particular political party? Should it include preferences on which countries or technologies to invest in? Should a company refuse to invest in the arms industry or the tobacco industry? In companies that supply the tobacco industry with important inputs? A line will most likely have to be drawn somewhere.[3] I demonstrate that institutional economic analysis can contribute to defining a normative role for ethical codes as well as to assessing their actual function.

Business ethics as a governance mechanism

Formally, both ethics and economics are concerned with the determination of social values. But while the neoclassical theory of value (Debreu 1959) is concerned with values in the form of relative prices, ethics is normally concerned with *'non-economic'* values (which are not expressed in relative prices – at least not directly). For example, voluntary work is generally considered to be ethical while work for pay is generally considered to be value neutral (neither ethical nor unethical). But since the beginning of the 1970s, a branch of institutional economics also examines non-market institutions. Important modern contributions to the economic

---

2. On the limitations of economic analysis applied to such profound questions see Radin (1996) and Arrow (1997).
3. A European pension fund, PFA, had adopted a set of ethical guidelines which prohibit investment in the arms industry. The fund was criticised in the media when it was discovered that it owners maintain shares in Phillip Morris and other tobacco companies. The company spokesman responded that the fund considered smoking a matter of personal privacy.

theory of ethics include Arrow (1962, 1969, 1973, 1974), Schotter (1981), Sen (1987, 1993), Binmore (1994), Franks (1987), Etzioni (1988) Sugden (1988), Buchanan (1991). A survey is given by Hausman and McPherson (1993).

Much of this literature has been concerned with ethics in general, but here I will attempt to parcel out a specific role for business ethics defined as a code of ethics adopted by a specific company. Ethical business codes adopted by an individual corporation must therefore be distinguished from general ethical codes expressed in the prevailing social ethic. Both actual business codes and the prevailing social ethic must, in turn, be distinguished from ideal ethical codes which (however difficult to define) would lead to (or at least be consistent with) an (unknown) social optimum, i.e. an allocation of resources and set of activities which is considered to be socially optimal with given social objectives. This optimum could include conditions on the distribution of income, attention to the natural environment, etc., but must also – according to standard economic reasoning – be economically feasible and non-wasteful (Pareto optimal). In particular, optimality requires an optimal use of institutions which will be the main concern of this chapter.

Both ethical business codes and social ethics can be regarded as sets of principles which govern (influence) the company's behaviour. In institutional economics an ethical code is therefore a governance mechanism which serves the same purpose as others: to coordinate economic activities. The market or price mechanism is another institution. So is (hierarchical) coordination by way of authority which takes place between bosses and their subordinates in most organizations.

Different mechanisms governing the supply of blood provide an illustrative example of ethics as an economic institution (Titmuss 1971, Arrow 1972, Institute of Economic Affairs 1973). A supply of blood can be obtained from voluntary donors (as often in the UK), it can be bought on the market (often in the US), soldiers can be ordered to give blood, it can even be taken from prisoners (as is known to be the case in some military dictatorships). In principle, a blood firm could even be started in which an entrepreneur employed people with particularly excellent blood vessels (although this would probably be impractical for both medical and economic reasons). A formal or informal ethical code requiring all employees in a company to give blood once a year or encouraging them to do so by (formal or informal) incentives can also be regarded as an institution.

Each of these institutions provide a mechanism which brings about a desired outcome: donors are presumably motivated by ethical codes (good feelings, social status, etc.), sellers are paid according the quantity supplied, employed blood-givers would be paid a fixed salary per month, soldiers and prisoners obey for fear of punishment. A company's motives to adopt an ethical code can be equally diverse: good feeling and social status for managers and employees, a desire to strengthen the company image, or fear of government sanctions. Either way, an ethical code is a set of rules which limits the set of acceptable actions.

Given this simplifying assumption, a choice can be made between alternative governance mechanisms in terms of their relative costs, usually termed *transaction costs*. Obviously, transaction cost must enter into the definition of the social optimum. The lower the transaction cost incurred in attaining a given outcome, the more resources are freed for other purposes. Institutional economics, furthermore, predicts that cost considerations will induce the agents in the economy to choose the least-cost alternative (which minimizes transaction costs).

For example, a national health service responsible for blood supply is faced with a choice of social institutions (i.e. to 'leave it to the market' or to the social ethic, or use various types of government intervention). With a given budget the national health service might consider the cheapest possible way of attracting the necessary supply of blood. Voluntary blood supply may be relatively cheap to administer, but it may be costly to persuade citizens to adopt ethical codes which induce them to give blood. Another possibility is to pass laws obligating citizens to give blood, but this may impose large (hidden) costs.[4] A third way is to leave it to pure market solutions (private businesses or other organizations operating on a commercial or non-profit basis).

In particular, institutional economics predicts that non-market governance mechanisms will arise under conditions of market failure: '... when the market fails to achieve an optimal state, society will, to some extent at least, recognize the gap and non-market institutions will arise attempting to bridge it' (Arrow 1962 p. 21). Market failure arguments can motivate government intervention in the markets, but also other types of non-

---

4. Arrow (1997) mentions that blood giving in Japan is considered such an invasion of the self that all blood is imported.

market institutions: *'Certainly, the government, at least in its economic activities, is usually implicitly or explicitly held to function as the agency which substitutes for the market's failure. I am arguing here that in some circumstances other social institutions will step into the optimality gap.'* (Arrow 1961 p. 22).

As an illustration of this principle, Arrow (1963) argued that a medical ethic among doctors is a way to overcome failures in the market for medical services due to information asymmetries between doctors and patients. Because patients generally lack information about the nature of their illness and effectiveness of alternative treatments, doctors could manipulate them in their own interest. A medical ethic among doctors enforced by powerful collective sanctions helps to overcome this problem (Arrow 1973 p. 139). Arguably, this medical ethic would not have been necessary, had the prevailing social ethic been strong enough to prevent opportunistic behaviour from occurring among all citizens (doctors included). And to the extent that all doctors are motivated by a medical ethic it is not necessary for individual hospitals to introduce their own ethical codes.

These considerations point to a degree of substitutability between different kinds of ethics and tend to support a division of labour between alternative kinds of ethical codes as well as between ethical codes and other institutional arrangements. The implication is that there will be a rationale for ethical codes when alternative governance mechanisms (pure markets, hierarchies, government, the prevailing social ethic...) fail to achieve a social optimum. For example, an ethical business code encouraging all employees to give blood one a year would increase social welfare to the extent that an adequate blood supply is neither generated by market forces or the political systems nor by voluntary action.

The conditions for market failure have been extensively explored in economics. The formal definition of market failure is that prices deviate from total social costs which is predicted by microeconomic theory to occur under conditions of monopoly and externalities combined with significant transaction costs (e.g. the information costs associated with writing and enforcing contracts).

The conditions for government failure are also beginning to be appreciated. If market failures were automatically corrected by government intervention there would be no scope for alternative allocation mechanisms like ethical codes. Although the theory of government failures is less than fully developed, tentative explanations are provided in the public choice literature (for a survey see Mitchel and Simons 1994). For example, powerful interest groups may influence the political process to their advantage at the costs of the general public causing a net reduction of social welfare (Olson 1965). More generally, conditions for successful government interventions are that government is informed about the problem in question and that it has incentives to do something about it.

In contrast, the conditions for social ethics failure have received almost no attention in institutional economics. Arrow (1961) mentions in passing that a medical ethic can also have negative effects if it serves as a barrier to entry that confers monopoly advantages on the medical profession. Elster (1988) gives a series of examples of privately and collectively inefficient social norms: for example informal norms that limit the use of monetary transfers in some circumstances. Theoretically, Douglas North (1990) has emphasized that societies may develop social structures (organizations, ideologies) which lock them into stagnation. A classic sociological study by Banfield (1958) demonstrates that extreme uncertainty (high death rates), low income, and landless peasantry may create an amoral culture oriented only at the nuclear family. It has also been asserted that social values change slowly and that this may put them at odds with optimality in a modern society.

Here I shall propose an alternative view based on Schumpeter (1934, 1938, 1950) which is consistent with these suggestions. In a primitive *circular flow* economy (Schumpeter 1934) economic activity is essentially stable except for stochastic influences (e.g. the weather). Technology is fixed (i.e. there is no technological process), there is no net saving or investment (Schumpeter 1938) as in an economy at level of subsistence, and the standard of living is unchanged from year to year. In this static society, adherence to a finite set of unchanging codes (rituals, customs, social norms) is a viable way of coordinating economic activity. In technical economic terms one can imagine the producers and consumers have already adjusted their plans to a set of equilibrium prices. Once these adjustments have been made, all that remains for producers and consumers to do is to implement their plans which – in a stationary equilibrium – is business as usual.

According to Schumpeter, the role of the entrepreneur and the business firm in this system is to innovate and disturb this circular flow through a process of creative destruction: mainly by setting up new types of production and outcompeting existing producers. This is bound to lead to social upheaval and to challenge existing ethical codes. The entrepreneur will therefore seem unethical when judged by the standards of the existing society. As emphasized by North (1990), powerful interest groups may have a vested interest in the status quo, and they may have produced organizational structures and ethical standards which *lock in* the economy in its present structure.

A social ethic can therefore be unethical if it blocks economic and social progress. Obviously this does not mean that ethics in general is unethical (a viewpoint which was explicitly voiced by Nietzsche). For example, as emphasized by Schumpeter and Weber, capitalism itself is founded on a set of ethical principles (rationalism, hard work, saving). But it can be argued that social ethical standards will tend to be too conservative. For example, this seems to be a natural interpretation of the influential line of research in game theory that models ethics (cooperation) as the outcome of repeated games of the prisoners' dilemma type among selfish individuals (Hausmann & McPherson 1993, Binmore 1994). If so, this will have detrimental direct effects on behaviour as well as spill over effects on policies and markets.

In conclusion, failures in the prevailing social ethic combined with other governance failures creates an important social function for business ethics which appears to be been neglected in the business ethics literature. The next section attempts to develop this viewpoint.

Optimal business ethics

Arrow (1973) explicitly considers the scope for ethical codes of behaviour in modifying the profit maximization objective of business companies. As already indicated, market failures may result from profit maximization with (unpaid for) external effects (e.g. pollution and congestion). In addition, Arrow emphasises the information asymmetries which occur when a firm knows more about its products than the buyer – a parallel to the information asymmetry between doctor and patient. In such cases, for example with regard to product safety, Arrow argues that ethical codes may be desirable because they can increase social welfare, especially if supported by government agencies, trade associations, consumer groups, and individuals within the firm. Assuming that problems of a general and recurrent nature are handled by government intervention or by the general social ethic, ethical codes should mainly be concerned with firm specific issues which the firm is in a unique position to solve.

This conjecture can be applied to environmental management by noting that pollution problems can, in principle, be solved by market mechanisms when markets are complete and when a complete set of property rights exists (which according to the Coase theorem will be the case when transaction costs are insignificant). An implication of this theory is that local pollution problems (e.g. a factory polluting the soil of a neighbouring farm) may be solved by bargaining or court ordering. But if the factory pollutes a lake with external effects on many people, the transaction costs involved in private bargaining may make private ordering unviable. In this case there is scope for alternative solutions among which government regulation by taxation of pollution according to the marginal social costs is often considered to be appropriate to restore optimality. However, in case the government fails to intervene for some reason (information problems, lobbying by pressure groups), the externality problem remains unsolved and the firm can increase overall social welfare by adhering to an ethical code which takes the costs of pollution into account (for example by preventing or cleaning up pollution).

The emphasis on firm-specific issues is consistent with the emerging resource-based view of the firm which sees firm-specific resources and as the fundamental rationale for the existence of firms (Wernerfelt 1984, Collis and Montgomery 1997). A prime example of such assets is firm specific information (core competencies etc.). Firm specific resources can create economic profits and give the firm a certain freedom of action which is absent in perfectly competitive markets that presumably force firms to apply a common set of market-determined standards. For the same reason, firms which have access to proprietary information can take ethical considerations into account.

This is consistent with a Schumpeterian view of the entrepreneurial firm as the bearer of an idea: a piece of new information which is only gradually diffused. As long as this information is unique to the firm, policy markers cannot be expected to use it as a basis for efficient (welfare improving) intervention. Furthermore, the new ideas are likely to meet resistance from an establishment whose value system and ethical standards reflect a vested interest in the status quo (North 1990).

One way to incorporate this into ethical management is for the individual firm to distinguish between general ethical codes to which it must adhere and firm-specific codes in areas on which it has superior information. The general codes should reflect the firm's perception of universal values in business (e.g. the work ethic, honesty, and rationality believed by Weber to be the ethical foundations of capitalism). In contrast, firm-specific codes may sometimes differ from the ethical views held by the rest of society. A biotechnology firm experimenting with technology and products which are uncharted territory for the general public carries a special responsibility both for safety and product standards and an obligation to overcome social resistance (including ethical criticism) from the establishment. In a change resistant environment the social interest may be served by the nurture of ethical codes which differ from the prevailing social ethic.

In conclusion, there is a clear rationale for ethical codes in institutional economics. But this is not to say that the theory is fully developed. Among other things, it suffers from a lack of distinction between ethics and culture or custom, it fails to analyse the importance of conscious choice and learning in ethical decision-making. Furthermore it is open to the criticism of *Nirvana economics* raised by Harold Demsetz in the context of analysing government intervention. The market economy is compared to a theoretical ideal (a state of Nirvana) and if the real world does not live up to the ideal, ethical business codes are somehow (like a Deus ex machina) supposed to restore optimality. Clearly, some refinement is warranted.

Actual business ethics

This section aims to give more content to the functional argument for ethical business codes by examining the mechanisms which induce firms to adopt ethical codes and to what extent they can be expected to adopt optimal (welfare improving) codes.

One way to go about this is to consider to what extent ethical codes are consistent with profit maximization, the standard assumption on firm behaviour in economics. Considering ethical standards as a set of rules which limit the range of acceptable activities, they might be considered to be inconsistent with profit maximization since a profit maximizing firm will offer the same opportunities for profit as an ethically-constrained firm – plus the additional opportunities which may arise from the option to be unethical.

But if ethical codes increase the welfare obtainable in the business, this creates a source of potential profits for the ethically-constrained firm which is not available to the pure profit maximisers and which may outweigh the expected losses due to ethical constraints. In game theory terms, ethical codes are an example of commitment to a certain range of actions and the *value of tying one's hands* has been analysed extensively (for example by Schelling 1960). Tirole (1988) uses the following example:

> *'An oft-quoted example is that of two armies who wish to occupy an island situated between both countries and which is connected to each country by a bridge. Each army prefers to let its opponents have the island by fighting. Army 1, which is somewhat knowledgeable in game theory, occupies the island and burns the bridge behind it. Army 2, then, has no option other than to let Army 1 have the island, because it knows that Army 1 has no choice other than to fight back if Army 2 attacks. This is the paradox of commitment: Army 1 does better by reducing its set of choices.'*

In the same way, firms can benefit by reducing their set of choices. For example, a manufacturer of computers can commit itself to give after sales service free of charge and to hold on to such a commitment even in the event that production of computers will prove unprofitable and will be shut down at a later date. It may be profitable ex ante to make this commitment binding because this will make customers more likely to buy the computer and reduce the probability that production will be unprofitable and thus have to be shut down. An ethical code can have the same function and may thereby increase both profits and social welfare, but to make the scheme work, it is necessary that the firm *burns its bridges* and commits to ethical behaviour even in the event that this should ex post prove to be suboptimal from the company's viewpoint.

Ethical behaviour may also be optimal from a selfish viewpoint in a sequence of repeated games (Schotter 1981, Binmore 1994) in which the stakeholders of a firm get to know each other over time, and where selfish behaviour may be optimal in the short run, but will be punished in subsequent games, and is therefore discouraged. As indicated in the previous discussion, this may be an argument for ethical standards in general more than for business ethics. But if the firm is perceived to be at the beginning of a repeated game, it may have an incentive to commit to a strong code of ethics.

A strong corporate culture or a mission which can motivate employees to make an effort beyond what is immediately selfish are among the important examples of the economic value of commitment (which may arise in prisoners' dilemma games and a number of other games, see Hausman and MacPherson). Studies by Chen, Sawyers, and Williams (1997) and Nwachukwu and Vitell (1977) confirm that corporate cultures can support firm-specific ethical codes. In the theory of clans (Ouchi 1980, Ouchi and Raymond 1983, Alveson and Lindkvist 1993), common values are regarded as an optimal organizational form in unstable environments where there is uncertainty with regard to both means and objectives: for example, in product development where there is uncertainty both about the expected results and the best way to structure the work effort. If socially optimal ethical codes support strong corporate value systems, this may provide an additional argument for their consistency with profit maximization.

In spite of these economic incentives to adopt ethical business codes which are both privately and socially optimal it seems unreasonable to assume that economic forces will always lead to optimality. Access to unique resources may be considered to be a monopoly advantage which the unregulated, uncensored, profit-maximizing firm has an obvious incentive to exploit with as few constraints a possible. In contrast to the finders-keepers ethical defense of profit taking as a reward to alertness (Foss 1997), or creativity (Primeaux and Stieber 1997), it can therefore be argued that the firm privileged by ownership of specific resources also carries a special responsibility to use those resources in an ethical way.

Even though it may be advantageous for the firm to a priori commit to certain values, there are also costs: for example the risk that the world may change so that these values are no longer ethically or commercially viable. The decision to commit to an ethical code can therefore be understood as an irreversible investment decision under uncertainty in which the firm chooses to forsake certain future options, and the cost can therefore in principle be measured by real asset option theory (Dixit and Pindyck 1994). Giving up flexibility by committing to ethical codes is equivalent to giving away put options, the opportunity costs of which is in principle given by the their market value which will increase with uncertainty facing the business. For a profit maximizing company to incur these costs, there must be offsetting benefits (i.e. a value as well as a costs of commitment).

A profit maximizing firm may also find it difficult to commit irreversibly to an ethical code. A standard objection to introducing non-profit objectives in company decision making is that the markets for corporate control will eliminate managers that do not pursue value maximization strategies (e.g. Ehrhardt 1995). Shleifer and Summers (1988) argue that the source of value gains from mergers and acquisitions is a breach of implicit contracts, mainly with employees. Suppose, for example, that a company commits itself to long term employment policies to encourage its employees to invest in human capital dedicated to that particular firm. But what is to prevent takeovers and renegotiation of these implicit contracts in bad times? And if the firm cannot credibly commit itself, will the employees not recognize this and refuse to make the necessary investments in human capital ex ante? Dilemmas like this imply a close connection between businesses ethics and corporate governance. The value of ethical commitments which do not reflect the preferences of company owners is open to doubt. And, if ownership is to function as a basis for long term ethical commitments, a certain degree of stability and accountability is necessary as well. It may not be impossible, for instance, to ensure loyalty to standard ethical codes among institutional investors, but the sustainability of this commitment is open to doubt if the same investors do not commit to a minimum holding period. In contrast to the Anglo-American corporate governance model, more long-term commitment is found in Japanese or German models (e.g. Charkham 1994) which tend to have a much higher degree of ownership concentration and ownership stability.

There is no doubt, however, that it will be in the interest of the profit-maximizing firm to signal a commitment to ethical values if signalling costs are small and if this is perceived to have a positive financial effect (Harrington 1989, Frank 1989). An implication is that business managers will find it in their interest to mimic ethical behaviour to the extent that the public cannot distinguish between honesty and dishonesty. The plethora of ethical business codes with unclear empirical content (small signalling costs) provide circumstantial evidence of this.

Discussion

In this chapter I have analyzed ethical codes as a corporate governance mechanism and the analysis was found to have both normative and descriptive implications for ethical management. It was found that ethical business codes are especially likely to improve social well-being if they concentrate on issues which are specific to the individual firm. It was also argued that optimal firm-specific ethical codes might well differ from the prevailing social ethic. The chapter finally points to some (imperfect) mechanisms which induce firms to adopt optimal ethical codes.

Although I have presented what I believe to be a new approach to the analysis of business ethics, the analysis remains rudimentary in several respects. For example, it has been confined to the standard economic definition of social optimality (efficient use of resources, none-wastefulness). But it is clear that business ethics may also involve a redistribution of resources in favour of the weak. Furthermore, the economic analysis of ethics is still in its infancy. In particular, profit or utility maximization may need to yield to alternative behavioural assumptions.

References

Alchian; Armen A. Uncertainty, Evolution and Economic Theory. *Journal of Political Economy* Vol. 58. June 1950. p. 211-221.

Alveson, M. and Lindkvist, L. Transaction Cost and Corporate Culture. *Journal of Management Studies* vol. 30 no. 3. 1993

Anderson, Elisabeth. The Ethical Limitations of The Market. *Economics and Philosophy*. Vol. 6 no. 2. October 1990.

Arrow, K.J. Uncertainty and the Welfare Economics of Medical Care. *American Economic Review* vol. 53. p. 941-973. 1963. Reprinted in Collected Papers of Kenneth Arrow. Vol. 6. Applied Economics. Belknap press. Cambridge Ma. 1985.

Arrow, Kenneth J. (1969): 'The Organization of Economic Activity' published in Arrow K.J. (1983): *General Equilibrium. Collected Chapters*. Volume 2, Basil Blackwell.

Arrow, K.J. *Gifts and Exchanges. Philosophy and Public Affairs*. Summary. 1972.

Arrow, Kenneth J. *The Limits of Organization*. W.W. Norton & Co. 1974.

Arrow, K.J. Social Responsibility and Economic Efficiency. Public Policy vol. 21. p 303-318. 1973. Reprinted in Collected Chapters of Kenneth Arrow. Vol. 6. *Applied Economics*. Belknap press. Cambridge Ma. 1985.

Arrow, Kenneth J. Invaluable Goods. *Journal of Economic Literature*. Vol. XXXV. June 1997. P. 757-765.

Banfield, Edward C. *The Moral Basis of a Backward Society*. The Free Press. Glencoe. 1958.

Baumol, William J. *Perfect Markets and easy Virtue. Business Ethics and the Invisible Hand*. Blackwell. Oxford 1991.

Binmore, K. *Game theory and the social contract*. Volume 1. Playing fair. Cambridge and London: MIT Press, 1994.

Buchanan, J.M. *The Economics and The Ethics of Constitutional Order*. University of Michigan Press. Ann Arbor 1991.

Buchanan, J.M. *The Demand and Supply of Public Goods*. Chicago. Rand McNally. 1967.

Charkham, Jonathan. P. *Keeping Good Company – A Study of Corporate Governance in Five Countries*. Clarendon Press, Oxford 1994.

Chen, Al Y. S.; Sawyers, Roby B.; Williams, Paul E. Reinforcing Ethical Decision making Through Corporate Culture. *Journal of Business Ethics* 16. 1997. p. 885-865.

Collis, David and Montgomery, Cynthia. *Corporate Strategy. Resources and the Scope of the Firm*. Irwin. 1997.

Danley, John R. Polestar Redefined: Business Ethics and Political Economy. *Journal of Business Ethics* vol. 10. No. 12. p. 915-933. 1991.

Debreu, Gerard. *The Theory of Value. An Axiomatic Analysis of Economic Equilibrium*. John Wiley. New York.1959.

Ehrhardt, M (1995). *The search for Value*. Harvard Business School Press, Boston.

Etzioni, A. *The Moral Dimension*; New York: Free Press, 1988.

References

Elster, John. Social Norms and Economic Theory. *Journal of Economic Perspectives.* Vol. 3 no. 4. Fall 1989.

Evensky, Jerry. Ethics and The Invisible Hand. *Journal of Economic Perspectives* Vol. 7 no. 2. Spring 1993. P. 197-205.

Foss, Nicolai J. Ethics, Discovery and Strategy. *Journal of Business Ethics.* 1997.

Frank, Robert H. If Homo Oeconomicus Could Chose His Own Utility Function, Would He Want One with a Conscience? *The American Economic Review.* Vol. 77. No. 4. September 1987 p. 593-60?

Frank, Robert H. If Homo Oeconomicus Could Chose His Own Utility Function, Would He Want One with a Conscience? Reply. *The American Economic Review.* Volume 79 no. 3. June 1989. p. 594-596.

Friedman, M. (1970): 'The Social Responsibility of Business Is to Increase Its Profits', The New York Times, September 13. 1970, quoted from Hoffman, W. and Frederick, R. E.: 'Business Ethics', McGraw-Hill New York 1995.

Ghemawat, P. (1991): *Commitment. The Dynamics of Strategy,* Free Press.

Grant, C. Friedman Fallacies. *Journal of Business Ethics.* Vol. 10. No. 12. P. 907-914. 1991.

Hamlin, Alan P. *Ethics, Economics and the State.* Wheatsheaf Books. Brighton. 1986.

Harrington, Joseph E. If Homo Oeconomicus Could Chose His Own Utility Function, Would He Want One with a Conscience? Comment. *The American Economic Review.* Volume 79 no. 3. June 1989. P 588-593.

Hausman, D.M. And McPherson, M.S. Taking Ethics Seriously: Economics and Contemporary Moral Philosophy. *Journal of Economic Literature.* Vol. XXXI. p. 671-731. June 1993.

Josephson, Michael: 'Teaching Ethical Decision making and Principled Reasoning', quoted from Hoffman, W. and Frederick, R.E.: *'Business Ethics',* McGraw-Hill New York 1995.

Institute of Economics Affairs. The Economics of Charity. Essays on the Comparative Economics and Ethics of Giving and Selling, with Applications to Blood. London 1973.

Mintzberg, Henry. *'Structuring of Organizations',* Englewood Cliffs. 1979.

Mitchell, W.G. and Simmons, R.T. *Beyond Politics. Markets, Welfare and the Failure of Bureaucracy.* Westview Press. Oxford. 1994.

Noe, T.H. and Rebello, M.J. The Dynamics of Business Ethics and Economic Activity. *American Economic Review.* Vol. 84 no. 3. June 1994.

North, Douglas C. *Institutions, Institutional Change and Economic Performance.* Cambridge University Press, Cambridge 1990.

Olson, M. *The Logic of Collective Action.* Harvard University Press. Cambridge MA. 1965.

Ouchi, W. Markets Bureaucracies and Clans', *Administrative Science Quarterly* vol. 25 no. 1. 1980.

Ouchi, W. and Raymond, L. (1993): 'Hierarchies, Clans and Markets', *Organizational Dynamics* vol. 21 no. 4.

Primaux, Patrick and Stieber, John. Managing Business Ethics and Opportunity Costs. *Journal of Business Ethics* 16. 1997. P. 835-842.

Radin, Margaret Jane. *Conested Commodities*. Cambridge. Cambridge University Press. 1996.

Reilly, B.J. and Kyj, M.J. Economics and Ethics. *Journal of Business Ethics* vol. 9 no. 3. September 1990. P. 691-698.

Schelling, Thomas C. *The Strategy of Conflict*. Harvard University Press. Cambridge Mass. 1960.

Schelling, Thomas C. *Choice and Consequence*. Harvard University Press. Cambridge Mass. 1984.

Schotter, Andrew. *The Economic Theory of Social Institutions*. Cambridge University Press. Cambridge Mass. 1981.

Schumpeter, Joseph A. *The Theory of Economic Development*. Oxford University Press. Oxford. 1978. First English translation 1934.

Schumpeter. J.A. (1950): *'Capitalism, Socialism and Democracy'*, Harper & Row, New York.

Sugden, Robert. Spontaneous Order. *Journal of Economic Perspectives*. Vol. 3 no. 4. Fall 1989.

Sen, A. Does Business Ethics Make Economic Sense. In P.M. Minus (ed). *The Ethics of Business in a Global Economy*. Kluwer. Boston. 1993.

Shleifer, A. and Summers, L. 1988. Breach of Trust in Hostile Takeovers', *In Corporate Takeovers: Causes and Consequences*, edited by Allan J. Auerbach, p. 33-56, University of Chicago Press.

Singer, Alan E. and Singer, M.S. Management-Science and Business-Ethics. *Journal of Business Ethics*. Vol. 16. 1997. p. 385-395.

Titmuss, R. *The Gift Relationship. From Human Blood to Social Policy*. Random House. New York. 1971.

Tirole, J. *The Theory of Industrial Organization*. MIT Press. 1988.

Wernerfeldt, Birger 1984. 'A Resource-Based View of the Firm', *Strategic Management Journal* no. 5. 1984 p. 171-180.

CHAPTER 8

Understanding Corporate Governance Codes[1]

Since the publication of the Cadbury Code (1992), there has been a rapid international diffusion of corporate governance codes containing recommendations on boards, executive pay, disclosure, and investor relations. But there has been little or no scientific evidence to support the recommendations, so it is questionable whether they can be explained by market failures. Instead, based on public choice theory, I propose the alternative hypothesis that the codes reflect rent seeking by institutional investors in a bargaining game with other stakeholders, including investment banks, auditing firms, incumbent owners, managers, and employees. I argue that this hypothesis can explain a number of puzzling features about codes, including their remarkable similarity – the 'one size fits all' approach – and their pattern of diffusion. A study of fifty-two corporate governance codes and a qualitative review of their core contents provide empirical support for the institutional investor hypothesis. The key focus is on empowering boards and making them accountable to minority investors, i.e. capturing the overall control of listed companies. Since it is not clear that these initiatives contribute to overall value creation, an evaluation of the costs of governance is called for.

---

1. This chapter draws heavily on my paper, The Hidden Meaning of Codes: Corporate Governance and Investor Rent Seeking, Published in European Business Organization Law Review, 2006.

Chapter 8. Understanding Corporate Governance Codes

Code puzzles

There has been a virtual explosion in corporate governance codes across the world since the Cadbury Code was first published (Cadbury Commission 1992). Almost every country now has at least one code of corporate governance and some countries like the United Kingdom have updated their codes several times. Recently, the European Commission explicitly endorsed corporate governance codes as a policy instrument: every Member State must have a corporate governance code and the codes should be used along with legislation to implement specific policy goals, such as non-executive directors on boards, board committees, and publicising the pay of individual managers (European Commission 2004, 2005).

And yet, since the beginning the codes have been met with widespread scepticism in the academic community for their lack of a theoretical or empirical rationale (Hart 1995, Daily 2003, Hermalin and Weisbach 2005). The codes are often quite specific in terms of recommendations on the minimum proportion of independent board members, the definition of independence, the ruling that non-executive board members should not be paid by stock options, and the requirement about what information should be disclosed, and so forth. These specific recommendations do not have anything even close to a satisfactory theoretical rationale, and generally they are not backed by any kind of empirical evidence. As a result, researchers tend to conclude that regulation in this area is unlikely to do much good (and if so only by accident) and may, in fact, harm business efficiency by arbitrarily restricting freedom of contract in corporate governance (Hermalin and Weisbach 2005).

The mismatch between research and practice is an interesting puzzle, but it is not the only one in the study of corporate governance codes. For example, it is puzzling why the approach is generally 'one size fits all' towards all companies rather than the tailor-made solutions and exceptions to the rule that theory and common sense would suggest. Moreover, why did the codes appear in the 1990s and not before? Some of the problems that they formally aim to address have been around since the birth of the joint stock company. And why did they acquire the specific content that they have: for example the focus on independence?

In this chapter, I aim to make a contribution to resolving the 'code puzzles' by analysing the nature and function of codes. Previous research has been hopelessly naive in implicitly assuming that corporate governance codes are proposed and adopted because of a need to 'do good'. But this hypothesis is clearly contradicted by the literature, which – as mentioned – has found no systematic theoretical or empirical evidence that codes are likely to improve business efficiency. So we must look for other explanations.

Political economy (public choice theory) has long been sceptical with regard to the efficiency rationale for regulation, and it instead points to rent seeking by interest groups to explain why there is regulation and why regulation takes a certain form (Stigler 1971, Peltzman 1976, Buchanan, and Tullock 1999: ch. 19). If we regard corporate governance codes as a kind of regulation (soft law), the advent of corporate governance codes must be explained by changes in the constellation of interest groups. While there are many stakeholders in corporate governance – including managers, banks, labour unions, auditors, and governments – institutional investors are regarded as particularly important, given the rapidly-increasing share of savings that is channelled through these institutions (e.g., Baums et al. 1993, Becht et al. 2003).

I therefore focus on institutional investors as a driving force in shaping the evolution of corporate governance codes. This hypothesis can explain a number of stylised facts about codes, for example, why they are so similar across the world (they cater to the same investors) and why they appeared during the 1990s (following the massive growth in institutional investment). I develop this perspective theoretically in section 2. A summary statistical analysis in section 3 finds that a sample of fifty-two codes are statistically very similar, focusing in particular on the role of the board, including both member independence and board functions. Section 4 examines how this is implemented in the UK Combined Code in which an empowered, independent board is increasingly regarded as an agent for investors *vis-à-vis* the company and its managers. I conclude that rent-seeking activities by specific interest groups do not necessarily add value for society as a whole and that it is necessary to pay more attention to the costs of codes and other governance policies. Hopefully, an improved dialogue between investors, business, and researchers can contribute to the emergence of a second generation of codes based on solid empirical evidence.

Chapter 8. Understanding Corporate Governance Codes

Corporate governance codes in theory

Corporate governance codes are sets of recommendations on good corporate governance, primarily concerning the structure, organisation, and decision processes of the board, but also to some extent dealing with executive pay, information disclosure, and investor relations. The codes are most often written by committees composed of influential business people at the initiative of a government organisation. Most codes are voluntary on a 'comply or explain' basis in the sense that companies may deviate from the recommendations but need to explain why they do so. They are not law, but they can be regarded as 'soft law', particularly since compliance rates tend to be high (e.g., Laing and Weir 1999, Rayton and Cheng 2004). Rayton and Cheng (2004) find that 98.9 per cent of 402 large listed UK firms have an audit committee and that the same proportion have remuneration committees.

Codes of best practice are found in many other areas: for example, in the form of ethical, professional, and technical guidelines (Héritier 2002). Theoretically, they are a special kind of social institution (Arrow 1969, 1973, Schotter 1981, Thomsen 2001) that can increase overall welfare if they contribute to the solution of market failures that are not adequately addressed by other means (e.g. law or private regulation) and if the costs of writing and enforcing the code do not exceed the benefits (Thomsen 2001).

The question is which market failure are corporate governance codes supposed to address? This is not an easy question to answer since the code writers are often not explicit about the nature of the problem and they certainly do not cloak their discussions in economic vocabulary. Moreover, the relationship between company law and corporate governance codes is often unclear. For instance, codes will occasionally make recommendations that are already included in the law.

Nevertheless, corporate governance codes appear to be concerned with the same themes: for example, transparency, the role of the board, investor protection, fraud avoidance, or how to provide a favourable investment climate to attract international capital. Using the analogy of consumer protection, it appears that the codes are regarded as a solution to asymmetric information problems between investors and companies, i.e., the so-called principal-agent problem (Ross 1973, Jensen and Meckling 1976, MacNeil and Xiao 2005). Firms – or their managers – clearly know much more than investors know about the firm and how it is run. It is well known that information problems of this kind can lead to an undersupply of capital and that these problems can, to some extent, be overcome by regulation and information provision. For example, government regulation may require that the cocoa content in products labelled 'chocolate' is no less than x per cent and that the cocoa content of a chocolate bar must be disclosed on the package. The problem here is that consumers know much less about the true quality of the product and, therefore, cannot make informed decisions. Moreover, producers have an incentive to cut costs and lower quality because this will not affect the price that they can charge to the ignorant consumers.

In the same way, adherence to a corporate governance code appears to be regarded as a guarantee that certain standards of good governance are met and is regarded as a declaration of content. Investors can then invest with greater confidence knowing that these standards are met. Instead of consumer protection, the codes provide investor protection (Cuervo 2002, Aguiliera and Cuervo 2004).

There are several reasons why this kind of quality assurance would appeal to shareholders. Some – the 'widows and orphans' type – clearly do not have the intellectual ability or inclination to undertake it on their own. Others – like institutional investors – want to (and are obliged to) diversify their portfolio over a large number of shares and can save on information costs if they know that all companies meet the specified standards. It is well known that many institutional investors index their portfolio and do not invest much in information collection or bother to vote at shareholder meetings (Zeikel 1978, Cuthbert and Dobbins 1980, Rudd 1986, Woolley and Bird 2003, Clearfield 2005). Some may want to invest in stocks in faraway countries about which they know little and would be assured by minimum standards (Aguiliera and Cuervo 2004).

One concern with this hypothesis is that the principal agent problem is hardly new. It has existed at least as long as the joint stock company itself. The codes, however, are a fairly new occurrence within the past decade or so. The main difference between now and then appears to be that the composition of shareholders has changed from individuals to institutions. Institutions hold larger blocks of shares than individuals and thus may have more of an effect on stock prices. Even more importantly, unlike individuals, they tend to hold a large total number of shares in many companies and so they are able to influence stock exchanges and policymakers. The corporate governance agenda is therefore to a large extent created and shaped by institutional shareholders. The massive build-up of capital in pension funds (Becht et al. 2003) clearly makes them attractive as a source of funding and creates incentives for companies, governments and exchanges to cater to their needs.

Stylised facts and puzzles

The hypothesis that corporate governance codes reflect rent seeking by institutional investors can explain a number of the 'code puzzles', which were raised in the introduction.

1. The mismatch with existing research. Researchers have generally been concerned with the overall performance of firms, but corporate governance codes may have the more limited concern of representing the interests of institutional investors. Thus it is perhaps less surprising that empirical studies have not found any systematic effect of compliance on overall corporate performance (e.g., Laing and Weir 1999).

2. The specificity of the recommendations – for example, in terms of minimum levels of independent board members defined in a particular way – is a puzzle given that the code writers do not know the specific circumstances of the companies they address. But from the viewpoint of institutional investors, who tend to hold shares in hundreds of companies, the specificity makes sense because it makes the codes easy to monitor.

3. The focus on listed companies is understandable given that this is where the bulk of the share investments by institutional investors take place. The same investors are increasingly involved in private equity, but they have not been pushing for transparency or independence in this area, where they tend to take much larger stakes and they tend to have more direct influence.

4. The advent of the corporate governance codes in the 1990s is understandable given the increasing weight and continued massive increase in institutional savings in this period. It is also no surprise that the corporate governance agenda was first launched in the United States and the United

Kingdom, where pension funds began to grow earlier than in most other countries around the world.

5. *'One size fits all'* is no longer a puzzle if one takes into consideration the demand side. While firms are very different, institutional investors around the world are relatively similar. They provide the same standard commodity to their customers using more or less the same financial techniques: in particular portfolio diversification. The one big difference that does emerge from current research is between private and political pension funds (Woidtke 2002). Private pension funds which also cater to corporate customers are generally much more discrete and pragmatic in advocating the corporate governance agenda. In contrast, political pension funds – like TIA CREF or CALPERS – with strong ties to unions or governments are generally much more outspoken.

6. *The strong international similarities* in corporate governance codes are a puzzle considering the large international differences in corporate governance. Why should the codes, relatively speaking, be so similar? Again, one important reason is that while countries are very different, institutional investors are relatively similar across the world. Another reason, of course, is competition for capital in an international market for shares in which UK and US institutions are still very large players.

7. *The contents of the codes* – for example, the focus on independence – is also somewhat of a paradox given that so may other factors like competencies at management and board level may be more important. But such factors are vague and difficult to monitor, and institutional investors have instead been demanding increases in board member independence and corporate transparency. For example, many codes around the world now demand that a majority of board members must be independent of both managers and the majority owners, with whom institutional investors compete for corporate control. The contents of the codes are examined in the following sections of this chapter.

8. *The focus on firms* – rather than, for example, investors – seems to be another example. With few exceptions, existing corporate governance codes focus on what companies and their boards can do to improve corporate governance, while the role of the investors is played down or ignored al-

together. Corporate governance is generally regarded as a set of mechanisms – including ownership structure – which are all-important to a well-functioning corporate governance system. For example, passive investors – who do not bother to vote or monitor firms – may well be a source of inefficiency, because they free ride on other shareholders. Nevertheless, if codes are intended to cater to institutional investors, it is understandable that they mainly concern what companies can do for the investors rather than *vice versa*.

9. *The choice of soft rather than hard law* may be a matter of expediency from the viewpoint of investors as well as companies. Laws take time to change and policymakers may demand an overall social rationale for adopting them. This could mean that the powerful actors may prefer to exercise their influence directly.

While the codes tend to be similar across the world, they are not identical. National codes generally attempt to take into consideration country-specific characteristics like board structure (one or two-tier), employee representation, takeover legislation, and so forth. In public choice terms, they may therefore be regarded as a negotiated compromise between existing stakeholders (e.g., incumbent owners, banks, labour unions, etc.) and the institutional investors. For example, it can be hypothesised that the contents of national corporate governance codes would reflect the relative bargaining power of the institutional investors in different countries.

It is also noticeable that the growth of institutional investment during the 1990s coincided with the deregulation and internationalisation of stock markets (e.g., Thomsen 2003). Internationalisation may have altered the nature of the bargaining game, since it may now be easier for incumbent stakeholders (owners, labour unions, and national governments) to capture domestic institutions and/or to enter into implicit contracts with them. Moreover, given the size and turnover US/UK stock markets, it is understandable that US/UK standards should to some extent be exported to other countries (Thomsen 2003).

Institutional investors have natural allies in their bargaining game with the incumbent stakeholders. For example, auditing firms are not generally opposed to transparency and disclosure, which generates new business for them. Consulting and search firms tend to promote professional non-executive directors, partly perhaps because this is how they earn their living. Stock exchanges, investment banks, and stockbrokers compete internationally for business, and governments also desire large national capital markets. In contrast, incumbent owners (e.g., founding families), employer organisations, employees, and to some extent banks may tend to be opposed to the interests of the institutional investors.

Statistical evidence on codes

There has not been much previous research on the contents of corporate governance codes. This section takes a first step with a summary statistical examination of fifty-two national corporate governance codes gathered from a range of countries around the world.[2]

Subjecting these codes to a statistical analysis (principal components analysis) reveals a remarkable homogeneity (Appendix: Table 1). Ninety-five per cent of the variance is common and can therefore be attributed to a single factor or component. In other words, it is a good first assumption that codes are much alike (and do not display much country-specific variation). A summary description of their contents is found in Table 8.1.

Most of the codes are authorised by governmental organisations, for example, securities and exchange commissions, or by stock exchanges. While stock exchanges are generally organised as private institutions, they do to some extent produce a public good (and they are highly regulated). The rest of the codes are for the most part issued by professional associations. Some institutional investors – like CALPERS – publish their own corporate governance guidelines, but these are not included in the sample.

---

2. Countries: The United Kingdom, the United States, Singapore, Greece, Portugal, Australia, Iceland, Thailand, Hong Kong, the Philippines, Malta, India, New Zealand, Mexico, Malaysia, China, Hungary, Canada, Pakistan, Cyprus, Spain, the Netherlands, Sweden, Belgium, Norway, France, Indonesia, Commonwealth countries, Russia, Romania, Italy, Lithuania, Macedonia, OECD, Kenya, Austria, Bangladesh, South Korea, Denmark, Germany, Poland, Slovenia, Peru, Turkey, Switzerland, Europe, Finland, Brazil, Latin America, Czech Republic, Slovakia, the world (ICGN).

Chapter 8. Understanding Corporate Governance Codes

Table 8.1: Summary statistics of fifty-two international corporate governance codes

Code provision/Code characteristic	Percentage of codes
Authorised by government/stock exchange	65.4
Applies only to listed firms	78.9
Mandatory 'comply or explain' recommendation	61.5
'One share-one vote' recommendation	21.2
Equal treatment of shareholders	73.1
Recommendation on pyramids	19.2
Recommendation on voting caps	21.2
Recommendation on shareholder agreements	13.5
Recommendation on the board of directors	98.1
Recommendation on monitoring role of the board	90.4
Recommendation on advisory role of the board	94.2
Recommendation on board size	15.4
Recommendation on independence of board members	94.2
Recommendation on independence of chairman	7.8
Total n=52 codes	100

Source: The background data for this table was gathered by Morten Bennedsen, Copenhagen Business School (2004).

Generally the codes apply to listed firms only (78.9 per cent), although 20 per cent apply to all firms (listed or not). Admittedly, there are a few codes around the world that apply only to unlisted (e.g., small and medium-sized) companies, but the main focus is clearly on the listed ones.

More than 60 per cent of the codes are adopted on a complete or partial 'comply or explain' basis, whereas the rest are merely recommendations.

As for the contents, almost all codes are concerned with boards (98 per cent), board independence (94 per cent), and the advisory (94 per cent) or monitoring (90 per cent) roles of the board. However, only very few (8 per cent) go so far as to recommend independent board chairs.

In contrast to the many recommendations on board structure and practices, only a minority of the codes contain recommendations on ownership structure (dual class shares, pyramids, voting caps, or shareholder agreements). This is interesting, since some outspoken investors like CALPERS explicitly advocate a 'one share-one vote' policy, which they associate with shareholder democracy. The one ownership issue that does gather general support is 'equal treatment of shareholders', which appears in 73 per cent of the codes.

The contents

In this section, I will discuss what I believe to be the key elements of the UK Combined Code, with occasional references to the Swedish, Danish, and German Codes.

The tasks of the board. The UK Combined Code can be characterised as 'the mother of all codes' which accumulated as a result of regular updates since the publication of the Cadbury Code (1992). It is admirably well-structured, distinguishing between 'Main Principles', 'Supporting Principles', 'Code Provisions', and 'Appendices'. The Code begins with the following memorable sentences:

> **A.1.The Board. Main Principle. Every company should be headed by an effective board, which is collectively responsible for the success of the company.**
>
> ...
>
> The board's role is to provide *entrepreneurial leadership* of the company within a framework of prudent and effective controls which enables risk to be assessed and managed. The board should *set the company's strategic aims*, ensure that the necessary financial and human resources are in place for the company to meet its objectives and review management performance. The board should *set the company's values and standards* and ensure that its obligations to its shareholders and others are understood and met.

Source: The Combined Code (2004), emphasis added.

The key idea here seems to be that entrepreneurship must be balanced with accountability and control. 'Entrepreneurial leadership' and 'value setting' are of course lofty ideals – which few practitioners would associate with normal board work. Certainly, Schumpeter (1934) would have been surprised to see entrepreneurship vested in a committee. The high ideals may be said to constitute the core project of the Combined Code, namely the empowerment of boards. This goes hand in hand with a separation of board and management work, which is evident in the strengthening of independence and committees. In fact, the board is being trans-

Chapter 8. Understanding Corporate Governance Codes

formed from a part of the company to an agency representing shareholders, particularly of course the large institutional investors.

It is interesting to contrast this statement with the much more modest German Code, which of course reflects the context of a two-tier board structure with employee representation:

> 3.2 The Management Board *coordinates* the enterprise's strategic approach with the Supervisory Board and discusses the current state of strategy implementation with the Supervisory Board at regular intervals.
>
> ...
>
> 4.1.2 The *Management Board develops the enterprise's strategy*, coordinates it with the Supervisory Board and ensures its implementation.

Source: The Cromme Code (2003), emphasis added.

There is no mention of entrepreneurship and values here, and it is even clear that the supervisory board does not get involved in strategy making. However, section 3.3 does specify that the supervisory board needs to approve 'transactions of fundamental importance', which 'fundamentally change the asset, financial or earnings situations of the enterprise'. An important difference between the United Kingdom and Germany is of course the magnitude of institutional investment, which is much larger in the United Kingdom.

Independence. As mentioned above, independence is one of the key messages in the Combined Code and its counterparts around the world. The idea is that the majority of the board – and particularly the chair (section A.2.1) – must be independent of the executives in order to control them effectively. The practice of appointing a former CEO as chairman of the board is specifically discouraged (A.2.25). The definition of independent (non-dependence) has become quite strict. A dependent board member is one who:

– has been an employee of the company or group within the last five years;

- has, or has had within the last three years, a material business relationship with the company either directly, or as a partner, shareholder, director, or senior employee of a body that has such a relationship with the company;
- has received or receives additional remuneration from the company apart from a director's fee, participates in the company's share option or a performance-related pay scheme, or is a member of the company's pension scheme;
- has close family ties with any of the company's advisers, directors, or senior employees;
- holds cross-directorships or has significant links with other directors through involvement in other companies or bodies;
- *represents a significant shareholder;* or
- has served on the board for more than nine years from the date of their first election.

Source: The Combined Code (2003), emphasis added.

In particular, the inclusion of relations to significant shareholders is controversial in a continental European setting, where ownership concentration is high and blockholder control is traditionally a key building block of the corporate governance system. This means that the group of shareholders with the strongest incentives to run the company is discouraged from a dominant influence on the board. Note that institutional investors will rarely fit into the category of major shareholders in a single company and are generally not inclined to directly appoint board members for fear of insider trading and compromising their freedom to buy and sell shares in the company.

Another point of criticism is a trade-off between competence and independence. Many of the people who know the company well – present and former employees, founding family, suppliers, lawyers, and so forth – are effectively discouraged from playing a role on the board. The concern here is that the entrepreneurial and strategic direction of British

Chapter 8. Understanding Corporate Governance Codes

companies would be conducted by people with muted incentives and superficial knowledge of the company.[3]

This prospect is in fact underlined by other provisions in the Combined Code. For example, it is stressed that boards should meet regularly without the managers and even without the chairman being present.

The discussions at these meetings cannot possibly reflect any deep knowledge of the company in question. Moreover, the Code expressly recommends that the chairman of the board should have regular contacts with major shareholders (A.2) and even singles out the dialogue with institutional investors as very important (D.1).

> **A.1.3 The chairman should hold meetings with the non-executive directors without the executives present. Led by the senior independent director, the non-executive directors should meet without the chairman present at least annually to appraise the chairman's performance ... and on such other occasions as are deemed appropriate.**
>
> Source: The Combined Code (2003).

The discussion of independence plays almost no role in the German Code (where by law managers cannot sit on the supervisory board, while the employee representative would be regarded as dependent under the UK definition). However, a very similar definition and application has crept into both the Danish and the Swedish Codes, despite the fact that both of these countries have two-tier boards with employee representation.[4]

In fairness, it should be said that the UK Combined Code also recognises the responsibility of the shareholders, in particular the institutional

---

3. Another Combined Code recommendation is that 'Remuneration for non-executive directors should not include share options' (B.1.3).
4. Cf., 3.2.5 of the Swedish Code (2004): 'At least two of the directors who are independent of the company and its management are also to be independent of the company's major shareholders.' Or the Danish Code (2005): 'The independence of the supervisory board ... the Committee recommends that at least half of the supervisory board members elected by the general meeting be independent persons. ... any person related, in terms of business or in any other way, to the company's major shareholder, is not regarded as an independent person.'

investors, for good corporate governance. It even has a section (E) on 'institutional shareholders', who are encouraged to engage in dialogue with companies (E.1), avoid a box-ticking approach in applying the Combined Code (E.2) and 'make considered use of their votes' (E.3). However, these recommendations do not contain much information. Who, for example, would dare to be against 'dialogue' or be in favour of not making considered use of votes?

Discussion

Despite the explosion in codes, researchers of corporate governance have failed to come up with a theory to explain this important phenomenon.

If anything, academic research has tended to examine corporate governance codes from the supply side (i.e., from the viewpoint of the firms that are asked to comply with them). The tacit underlying model seems to have been that corporate governance codes can help repair market failures, although is unclear whether any such market failure can in fact be said to exist. But this line of research has generally failed to provide a satisfactory understanding of codes. For example, there is no systematic evidence that compliance with the codes will in fact tend to improve corporate performance. Moreover, it is questionable whether the agency problem *per se* constitutes a sufficient rationale for codes: for example, whether sophisticated modern pension funds really need legal protection or whether *caveat emptor* should apply.

An alternative is to analyse corporate governance codes from the demand side (i.e., from the viewpoint of the institutional investors which advocate them). In this chapter, I have shown that this approach can explain a host of factors that are difficult to understand from the supply side, for example, the 'one size fits all' approach as well as the timing and diffusion of codes along with massive growth in institutional investment.

If corporate governance codes tend to reflect the preferences of institutional investors, this raises the question of their overall contribution to social welfare. There is nothing illegitimate *per se* about self-interest seeking. Given the increasing proportion of global savings, which is mediated by institutions, it is reasonable to be concerned with how this money can be put to good use. It is not clear, however, that institutional investors are best suited to address corporate governance problems. In fact, it can be argued that institutions are the source of rather than the solution to corporate governance problems because they are bound to prefer diversification of risk to monitoring and, thus, free ride on other market participants.

There are already indications that the costs of governance – including codes as well as other kinds of regulation – have become a serious problem for listed companies. Auditing and compliance costs have increased rapidly, and delistings have increased in both the United States and in Europe. An added concern is that increasing corporate governance bureaucracy at the top management level could have a detrimental effect on overall corporate performance and competitiveness.

A key problem with a narrow demand-side focus is that corporate governance mechanisms constitute a whole that jointly determines the efficiency and performance of firms--including share returns. Interest group politics lead to code provisions which do not improve – or even lower – overall firm performance are therefore unlikely to benefit investors in the long run. One – optimistic – scenario for the future of the codes is that their initial revolutionary spirit will gradually be tempered by pragmatism as the institutions mature professionally. Even today, many of them – for example CALPERS – appear to have become much more flexible in their approach to corporate governance. So, while the first generation of codes has been successful in setting an agenda for corporate governance, an improved dialogue between investors, business, and researchers can hopefully contribute to the emergence of a second generation of codes based on solid empirical evidence.

References

Aguilera, R., and A. Cuervo-Cazurra. 2004. 'Codes of Good Governance Worldwide: What is the Trigger?' *Organization Studies* 25(3): 415-443.

– – – and G. Jackson. 2003. 'The cross-national diversity of corporate governance: Dimensions and determinants'. *The Academy of Management Review* 28(3): 447-465.

Arrow, K.J. 1969. 'The Organization of Economic Activity'. In K.J. Arrow (ed.). *General Equilibrium: Collected Papers*, Vol. 2. Oxford: Basil Blackwell.

– – – 1973. 'Social Responsibility and Economic Efficiency'. *Public Policy* 21: 303-318. Reprinted in *Collected Papers of Kenneth Arrow*, Vol. 6: Applied Economics. 1985. Cambridge, MA: Belknap Press.

Baums, T., R. Buxbaum and K. Hopt. 1993. *Institutional Investors and Corporate Governance*. Berlin: Walter De Gruyter.

Becht, M., P. Bolton and A. Roëll. 2003. 'Corporate Governance and Control'. In G. Constantinides, M. Harris and R. Stulz. *The Handbook of the Economics of Finance*. Amsterdam: North-Holland.

Berle, A.A., and G.C. Means. [1932] 1968. *The Modern Corporation and Private Property*. New York: Harcourt, Brace & World.

Buchanan, J.M., and G. Tullock. 1999. *The Calculus of Consent: Logical Foundations of Constitutional Democracy*. Indianapolis, IN: Liberty Fund, Inc.

Cadbury Commission. 1992. *Code of Best Practice: Report of the Committee on the Financial Aspects of Corporate Governance*. London: Gee and Co.

Charkham, J.P. 1994. *Keeping good company – a study of corporate governance in five countries*. Oxford: Clarendon Press.

Clearfield, A.M. 2005. 'With Friends Like These, Who Needs Enemies? The Structure of the Investment Industry and Its Reluctance to Exercise Governance Oversight'. *Corporate Governance* 13(2): 114-121.

Code Group. 2004. *Swedish Code of Corporate Governance*. Stockholm: Ministry of Finance.

Copenhagen Stock Exchange Committee on Corporate Governance. 2005. *Revised Recommendations for Corporate Governance in Denmark*.

Cuervo, A. 2002. 'Corporate Governance Mechanisms: A Plea for Less Code of Good Governance and More Market Control'. *Corporate Governance* 10(2): 84-93.

Cuthbert, N., and R. Dobbins. 1980. 'Managerial Participation by Pension Funds and Other Financial Institutions'. *Managerial Finance* 6(3): 43.

Daily, C.M., D. Dalton and A. Canelli Jr. 2003. 'Corporate Governance: Decades of Dialogue and Data'. *Academy of Management Review* 28(3): 371-383.

European Commission. 2004. Commission Recommendation 2004/913/EC of 14 December 2004 fostering an appropriate regime for the remuneration of directors of listed companies. OJ 2004 L 385/55.

– – – 2005. Commission Recommendation 2005/162/EC of 15 February 2005 on the role of non-executive or supervisory directors of listed companies and on the committees of the (supervisory) board. OJ 2005 L 52/51.

Fernández-Rodríguez, E., S. Gómez-Ansón and Á. Cuervo-García. 2004. 'The Stock Market Reaction to the Introduction of Best Practices Codes by Spanish Firms'. *Corporate Governance* 12(1): 29-46.

Government Commission. 2003. *German Corporate Governance Code (The Cromme Code)*. As amended on 21 May 2003.

Hart, O. 1995. 'Corporate Governance: Some Theory and Implications'. *The Economic Journal* 105: 678-89. Reprinted in K. Keasey, S. Thompson and M. Wright (eds.). 1999. *Corporate Governance*. Cheltenham; Edward Elgar Publishing Ltd.

Héritier, A. 2002. *New Modes of Governance in Europe: Policy Making without Legislating?* IHS Political Science Series 2002, No. 81.

Hermalin, B.E., and M. Weisbach. 2005. 'Trends in Corporate Governance'. *Journal of Finance* 60(5): 2351-2384.

Jensen, M.C., and W. Meckling. 1976. 'Theory of the firm: Managerial behaviour, agency costs and ownership structure. *Journal of Financial Economics* 3: 5-60.

Keynes, J.M. 1936. *The General Theory of Employment, Interest, and Money*. New York: Harcourt, Brace & World, Inc.

Knight, F. 1921. *Risk, Uncertainty and Profit*. Boston: Houghton Mifflin.

Laing, D., and C.M. Weir. 1999. 'Governance structures, size and corporate performance in UK firms'. *Management Decision* 37(5): 457-464.

MacNeil, I., and X. Li. 2005. *'Comply or Explain': Market Discipline and Non-Compliance with the Combined Code*. Working paper. Glasgow: University of Glasgow.

Shleifer, A., and R.W. Vishny. 1997. 'A survey of corporate governance'. *Journal of Finance* 52(2): 737.

Peltzman, S. 1976. 'Towards a More General Theory of Regulation'. *Journal of Law and Economics* 19:211-40.

Rayton, B., and S. Cheng. 2004. *Corporate Governance in the United Kingdom: Changes to the Regulatory Template and Company Practice from 1998-2002*. University of Bath Working Paper Series No. 13.

Ross, S.A. 1973. 'The Economic Theory of Agency: The Principal's Problem'. *American Economic Review* 63.

Rudd, A. 1986. 'Portfolio Management: Another Look at Passive Management'. *Journal of Accounting, Auditing & Finance* 1(3): 242.

Schotter, A. 1981. *The Economic Theory of Social Institutions*. Cambridge: Cambridge University Press.

Schumpeter, J.A. 1934. *The Theory of Economic Development*. 2nd edition. Cambridge: Harvard University Press.

Smith, A. [1776] 1981. *An Inquiry into the Nature and Causes of the Wealth of Nations*. 1st edition. Indianapolis: Liberty Classics.

Stigler, G.J. 1971. 'The Theory of Economic Regulation'. *Bell Journal of Economics and Management Science* 2: 137-46.

Thomsen, S. 2001. 'Ethical Codes as Corporate Governance'. *The European Journal of Law and Economics* 12(2).

- - - 2003. 'The Convergence of Corporate Governance Systems to European and Anglo-American Standards'. *European Business Organization Law Review* 4(1).

References

– – – 2004. 'Corporate values and corporate governance'. *Journal of Corporate Governance* 4(4).

Woidtke, T. 2002. 'Agents watching agents? Evidence from pension fund ownership and firm value'. *Journal of Financial Economics* 63(2): 99-131.

Woolley, P., and R. Bird. 2003. 'Economic implications of passive investing'. *Journal of Asset Management* 3(4): 303-312.

Zeikel, A. 1978. 'Pension Funds-Indexed Portfolios'. *Journal of Accounting, Auditing & Finance* 1(2): 136.

Chapter 8. Understanding Corporate Governance Codes

Appendix

Table 1: Principal components analysis of fifty-two codes

```
Number of variables = 17
Number of components = 15
Trace = 52
Rotation: (unrotated = principal)
Rho = 1.00
```

Component	Eigenvalue	Difference	Proportion	Cumulative
Component 1	49.5686	47.5732	0.9532	0.9532
Component 2	1.99533	1.80043	0.0384	0.9916
Component 3	0.194896	0.0857861	0.0037	0.9954
Component 4	0.10911	0.0725421	0.0021	0.9975

Note: Components 4-52 are not displayed since they explain a very small fraction of the total variance.

This table shows the result of a principal components analysis that studies to what extent the fifty-two country codes presented in Table 8.1 co-vary and to what extent their contents may therefore may be attributed a single common element (i.e. a 'mother code'). The analysis indicates that this is the case to a large extent.

III. Understanding International Systems

CHAPTER 9

The Anglo-American Market Model and Shareholder Value

While chapters 5-8 examines corporate governance mechanisms chapters 9-13 will examine country models of corporate governance.

In this chapter we take a closer look at the market model of corporate governance and how the model is implemented in the US and the UK.

We include both the company and the country level. At the company level we talk about 'the shareholder value model'. At the country level we talk about 'the market model'. There is, of course, a connection between micro and macro: many more companies in the US and UK tend to conform to the shareholder value model. But the connection is not a 100% complete (1-0-1) correspondence. Even in bank- or control-based governance systems, individual companies may decide to adopt the shareholder value model. Likewise, there are companies in the US which apply a control-based governance model based on e.g. founder ownership.

The ideal model: shareholder value

I list a recipe for shareholder value creation at the company level in table 9.1. Students of corporate finance will recognize much of it as a textbook description of what companies do. The shareholder value model can therefore be said to be 'corporate governance according to the book' (if the book is a textbook in corporate finance).

First and foremost, the company should have only one goal: shareholder value creation. In the shareholder model, the company is a moneymaking machine – an instrument by shareholders to make money: nothing more.

Table 9.1: The shareholder value firm

- One goal for the company: value creation for all shareholders
- Focus on economic value creation: Max (ROIC-WACC)*IC
- Management motivated by stock options
- Ownership diversification (liquidity, risk)
- Shareholder rights (one share-one vote)
- Board control by non-executives
- No barriers to hostile- or friendly-takeover
- Share buy backs and high dividends
- Optimized capital structure
- Focus on core business
- Transparency and good investor relations

So the company will, for example, buy bicycles from China produced by child labour if they are cheaper than bicycles produced at home. It may choose to buy them at home because it fears reactions by customers or by the government, but this decision will be based on a calculation: how much do we profit by producing in China minus how many customers would we lose (and what would that cost) minus expected regulation costs. It will not be based on ethical concerns. Or, alternatively, you could say that the ethical commandment for the manager is to maximize value creation to his employers.

Shareholders can benefit from dividends and share price increases. Since the value of the shares will reflect expected future dividends, the focus will be on how these future dividends can be increased. The guiding principle of the corporation is therefore profit maximization or, in current jargon, shareholder value maximization.[1] The guiding principle is:

SV = (ROIC-WACC)*IC, or

Shareholder Value Creation = (Return on Invested capital – Weighted Average Cost of Capital) * Invested capital.

So for every decision, managers in the shareholder value maximizing company should ask themselves whether the expected returns are greater than the expected costs of capital. The theoretically correct definition of

---

1. According to basic microeconomics profit is maximized net of opportunity costs which obviously include the costs of capital. Shareholder value maximization is therefore exactly equivalent to profit maximization. It just sounds better.

capital costs is the marginal opportunity cost – what would be the return on the best alternative investment. But since it may be difficult to know what that is, it is customary to use the weighted average cost of capital as an approximation. Since shareholders could have alternatively invested in other stocks and bonds, WACC will include interest costs and a risk premium reflecting the risk of investing in that particular company.

So, for every new investment, the management should ask whether it adds value. In the same way, he should go through all the divisions, departments, and activities of the company. If they do not add value, they should be closed down. Obviously it is difficult to do this precisely since there are synergies between different activities, so the value maximizing company may put the burden of proof on the division in question: i.e. 'you have to demonstrate to us that you add value.'

Incentive programs – i.e. carrots and sticks – support the shareholder value philosophy and are part of the package. For top managers, they will often be tied directly to stock prices – e.g. stock options or restricted stock schemes in addition to bonus systems which reward managers as a share of profits or for achieving operational goals. Non-executive directors may be required to buy stock. For ordinary employees, there may be bonus systems and operational performance measures (sales volume, units sold, etc.). The overall idea is alignment of interest between managers and shareholders.

Even ownership structure can be adapted to the shareholder value logic. For large capital intensive companies dispersed and diversified ownership may reduce the company's cost of capital (portfolio diversification removes firm-specific risk for the shareholder portfolio). More generally, the market model assumes an open market for corporate control so that ownership can be allocated to whomever can create most value by exercising ownership (and therefore pay the highest price for it). This implies that the company should have no takeover defences: for example only one share class.

The Board should be controlled by independent non-executive directors motivated by ownership or stock options. Performance incentives and independence imply that the board will be ruthless in firing managers, closing down production, or vetoing mergers if they do not add value.

Share buy backs and high dividends are also part of the shareholder value package. There is no reason for the company to diversify risk. Excess capital over and beyond what is required to fund positive net present value projects should be paid out to shareholders. The company's capital structure should be optimized with sufficient financial gearing to reflect low costs of debt.

The company will sell off unrelated business units and focus on core business because this facilitates transparency and lowers the risk premium which shareholders demand.

Finally, the shareholder value company recognizes that the shareholder is king. It invests liberally in communication with shareholders: for example in transparent and accurate accounting, timely disclosure of relevant information, and good investor relations.[2]

The market based system: ideal model

The macro or system version of shareholder value is 'the market model' which relies on stockmarkets to coordinate economic activity.
Theoretically the market model is a straightforward application of the notion of perfect competition in basic microeconomics. The conditions for the perfect market are:

- Many buyers (shareholders)
- Many sellers (companies/shares)
- Standard commodities (no preferences, one share class)
- Zero transaction costs (low bid-ask spreads, low commissions)
- Market Clearing (centralised exchange)
- Transparency (full information)
- Large markets: liquidity (market size, depth)
- Secure property rights (investor protection)

Applied to the stock market, the presence of many buyers and sellers implies competition so that no individual buyer or seller has a monopoly situation and is able to influence the stock price. Individual market participants are 'atomistic'. The price is determined by aggregate supply and demand. If you want to invest in computers, you do not have to invest in Compaq, but may instead invest in Dell.

The 'standard commodities' assumption implies that a share is a share in the same way that a dollar bill is a dollar bill. There is no difference be-

---

2. Example? http://www.topdanmark.dk/ir/index.php?ID=221)

tween them and investors do not have to care much which share they buy. In particular this implies only one share class.

The assumption of 'zero transaction costs' is an impossible ideal, but trading cost and bid-ask spreads (differences between the price you get when selling and the price you pay when buying) may be so low that they become insignificant.

Centralized exchange implies that the market produces a market clearing price of shares and the large market assumption that it is possible for shareholders to buy and sell significant amounts of stocks and bonds at this price. The market is so liquid that individual investors will not depress prices by selling stock (or raise them by buying).

Transparency (perfect information) implies that new information is disclosed quickly and is instantly reflected in stock prices. Companies, auditors, analysts, and stockbrokers all supply information to the market and thereby contribute to transparency.

Secure property rights imply that investor rights are protected by law (investor protection). For example, they have a right to vote, to receive dividends and to sell their shares. Since we also want standard shares one share – one vote is the logical choice.

In the market system companies are therefore governed by the stock price. If they are not well managed, the stock drops and shareholders can replace management at the next shareholder meeting, or the company can be taken over. If they are well managed, the stock rises, and the company can issue new shares to attract more capital. Capital is allocated to its best (most profitable) use.

The US model

In many ways, the market model is a good first cut description of the American corporate governance system.

The stock market is clearly very large with many listed companies. Ownership is typically more dispersed than anywhere else in the world (so that no individual shareholder can influence the market). There is an enormous industry of information providers (auditors, analysts, rating agencies), which help keep the market informed. Shareholders are empowered by company laws, which punish insider trading, self dealing (tunnelling), and allow shareholders to sue companies for inefficiency.

Apart from making the rules, the government does not interfere with the market. Corporate governance mechanisms like the takeover market, shareholder activists, and performance-based pay provide further impetus for companies to maximize shareholder value.

Much of this is attributable to what might be termed the American corporate governance revolution, which over the past two decades has significantly changed the way US companies are run. The term shareholder value was first coined in the beginning of the 1980s by Alfred Rappaport (1981, 1985). The term 'corporate governance' defined as holding managers accountable to stockholders was first used in the 1960s, but gained momentum in the 1980s when institutional investors began to support the idea. The huge increase in paychecks accompanying the diffusion of performance-related pay during the 1980s and 1990s radically changed the incentive for USA managers and convinced them to support the shareholder value philosophy (Holmström and Kaplan, 2003). During the same periods, new financial instruments have made it easier to finance takeovers and this put further pressure on firms.

US company law appears to be generally consistent with the market model. International comparisons by La Porta et al. (1998) and Djankov et al. (2005) indicate that the US scores high on levels of investor protection and regulation to prevent self dealing among managers. However, US regulation of corporate governance has become highly complex in recent years with the Sarbanes-Oxley Act (a.k.a. SOX), corporate governance codes, self reporting, and other regulation. The US Committee on capital market regulation has recently concluded that regulation has seriously damaged the competitiveness of US capital markets (Committee on Capital Markets regulation, 2006). In the appendix I discuss the costs of Sarbanes-Oxley.

Corporate objectives in the US are *not* legally limited to shareholder value maximization. For example, the company also has a responsibility to creditors (which very often comes up in lawsuits).

However, the prevailing interpretation is that subject to respecting formal obligations to stakeholders '... *a corporation should have as its objective the conduct of business activities with a view to enhancing corporate profit and shareholder gain*' (American Law Institute, 1992). Boards have a fiduciary duty and a duty of loyalty to shareholders – so they can be held responsible if it can be demonstrated that they had other intentions. Boards have a duty of fair dealing to avoid or to resolve conflicts of interest in dealing with third parties. The board also has a duty of care so it must be able to demonstrate that it actually takes steps to see to it that the loyalty to shareholders is implemented in practice. Thus, objectives are consistent with the shareholder value model.

US Ownership tends to be more dispersed than in other countries. The dominant owners are institutional investors who pursue different kinds of portfolio diversification, but who do not take an active interest in individual companies. This is a nice fit with the shareholder model.

However, founders or founding families have a controlling stake in many (1/3) of even the largest listed US companies – including some of the best known US companies like Microsoft, Google, Amazon, and Nike. There is some evidence these companies on average outperform the investor owned companies (Anderson & Reeb, 2004). This indicates that the market model may not be entirely consistent. Perhaps some ownership concentration is more efficient than complete diversified ownership.

US managers also have significant shareholdings in the companies that they manage. This provides incentives but could also make them risk averse. They appear to hedge a significant proportion of it, however.

US Boards are one tier, but a majority of the directors are now non-executive directors free of material ties with the executives. However, in most cases, the CEO remains chairman of the board, which is a significant concentration of power.

Management incentives play an important role in US corporate governance. Managers of large listed companies receive very high pay ($ 15 million per year on average in 2006 according to ISS), most of which is variable. This is 400 times the pay of average workers and much higher than what European managers earn. Pay for performance also fits the market model, although some would claim that the pay levels have now become too high to be defensible from a shareholder point of view (Bebchuk and Fried, 2005).

However, there are also aspects of US corporate governance which are less consistent with the shareholder model. For example, **takeover defences** are widespread. Some of them – 25 – are listed in table 9.2. Gompers et al. (2003) document that most US companies use many defences – some use only a few, others use almost 20. As a result, it is quite difficult to take over a US corporation. It is possible, however, to challenge the legitimacy of takeover defences in court.

Chapter 9. The Market Model: Shareholder Value

Table 9.2: Takeover Defences among the Largest Listed US Firms

Antigreemail	Prohibits buyback from hostile raider lowering incentive to raid
Blank Check	Right to issue preferred stock in case of a takeover attempt – can dilute the stakes of other shareholders
Business Combination	Delay of transactions with large shareholders – delays the process and makes it more expensive for the acquirer
By-law and Charter	Amendment to by-laws and charter can rule out hostile takeover or make it more costly
Classified boards	Only a certain proportion of board members can be replaced each year – delays a takeover and makes it more expensive
Compensation plans	Cash out after control change – managers and employees can cash in on their performance pay in case of takeover – makes takeover more expensive
Contracts	Indemnification of board members – relieves them of responsibility
Control-share cash out	Acquirer has to offer the same high price to all shareholders – makes it more expensive to achieve control
Proportional voting	The entire board is elected by a shareholder coalition with majority
Directors Duties	Stakeholder rights must be considered in certain companies and jurisdictions
Dual Class Shares	There are two share classes with different voting rights
Fair Price	Acquirer has to pay the same price to all shareholders (two-tier bids)
Golden parachutes	Managers get compensation if they are fired
Indemnification	In charter/by-laws
Reduced Liability	Reduced Liability of directors
Pension parachute	Company pension funds cannot be captured by raider
Poison pill	Board option to issue shares at a discount in case of a takeover attempt – dilutes the ownership share of raider and makes takeover more expensive
Public Voting	Makes some investors – banks, private pension funds – fear reprisals
Severance pay	Acquirer must pay severance pay regardless of whether managers are fired
Silver parachutes	Golden Parachutes for ordinary employees
Special meeting	Call requirements
Supermajority	A qualified majority (e.g. 2/3) is required for merger approvals
Unequal Voting rights	Voting caps (no shareholder can vote more than x%) or less voting power for new shareholders
Written consent	Certain decisions require unanimity among shareholders

Source: Adopted from Gompers et al. (2003)

By and large, we can conclude that corporate governance in the US is quite consistent with the market model with two major exceptions:

1) The balance of power between managers and shareholders is tilted in favour of managers. In part, the weakness of shareholders is unavoidable given dispersed ownership, but is strengthened by takeover defences and 'duality' (that most CEOs are also chair the boards). This is why Mark Roe famously characterized US governance by 'weak owners and strong managers' (Roe, 1994). This may also be the reason that US managers are paid so well. From a European perspective, it would be relatively easy to split chairs and CEOs, and this is recommended by Jay Lorsch, a leading US governance researcher. But many American business practitioners resist the idea.
2) Regulation appears to have become too bureaucratic in recent years up a point which lowers company and stock market performance.

The UK corporate governance model

UK corporate governance is in many ways similar to that of its old colony: the US. The stock market is large compared to the size of the economy. Ownership is dispersed. The dominant owners are institutional investors. The board system is one-tier. There are both executive and non-executives on the board, but the majority of the board members are non-executives. Managers of listed companies are paid by performance using stock options and bonus schemes.

Following closer scrutiny, however, there are some subtle differences which appear to have considerable influence on corporate governance practices.

Firstly, company law is less bureaucratic and cumbersome. The UK has not adopted Sarbanes-Oxley and therefore its enforcement is much less rigid. As a result, foreign companies currently find it more attractive to have shares listed in London than in New York. This is not to say that the UK has not had its share of bureaucracy. But the regulation has been less stringent and has been of a different kind. Beginning with Cadbury (1992), the UK has relied more on self regulation (i.e. corporate governance codes) which were written by business people. This has probably led to lower costs of governance.

181

Secondly, ownership is slightly less dispersed than in the US – at least partly because the percentage of private shareholders is smaller. Moreover, the distribution of shares among large investors is more even (Barca and Becht, 2003). On average, the largest owner of a British company holds 5% and the share of the second largest owner is not much lower. Moreover, because of informal networks within the business elite (i.e. the 'old boys' clubs'), investors find it easier to act in concert. This means that the 5-10 largest owners (which are normally institutional investors) have a direct influence on company managers. The UK system may therefore be described as 'Pension fund governance'. In consequence, owners are somewhat stronger, and managers are somewhat less powerful than in the US.

With regard to board structure in the UK, boards are somewhat smaller, which should theoretically add slightly to their effectiveness (Conyon and Peck, 2003). Moreover, as one result of the corporate governance debate, it has now become best practice to separate the positions of CEO and chairman of the board. This means that non-executive directions have more influence on company behaviour.

Finally, again partly as a result of less powerful managers, executive pay is much lower for similar sized companies and the use of takeover defences is more limited. Since Cadbury (1992), there have not been any major financial scandals in the UK of the Enron, Tyco, WorldCom type.

In summary, the market model of corporate governance seems to have been applied more faithfully in the UK than in the USA. The UK model has attracted widespread admiration and, unlike Sarbanes-Oxley, British style corporate governance codes have been imitated around the world.

The only exception seems to be that the objectives of corporate governance in the UK seem to be somewhat broader than shareholder value maximization. For example, contrary to views commonly expressed in textbooks on corporate finance, UK directors now face a complex set of responsibilities to ALL stakeholders. Consider the UK 2006 companies act: § 172. Duty to promote the success of the company, part (1):

> *'A director of a company must act in the way he considers, in good faith, would be most likely to promote the success of the company for the benefit of its members as a whole, and in doing so have regard (amongst other matters) to*

(a) the likely consequences of any decision in the long term,
(b) the interests of the company's employees,
(c) the need to foster the company's business relationships with suppliers, customers and others,
(d) the impact of the company's operations on the community and the environment,
(e) the desirability of the company maintaining a reputation for high standards of business conduct, and
(f) the need to act fairly as between members of the company.'

Some would regard this as a more civilized and less brutal approach to corporate governance, but it is a deviation from the pure shareholder model. Whatever benefits there may be in adopting a stakeholder view, a multi-valued –and possibly partly conflicting – objective function beyond profit or value maximization does not make it easier for company directors to make decisions or for shareholders to hold them accountable (Jensen, 2001).

Evaluating the market model

Students of corporate finance may be tempted to believe that the market model is optimal because it has been demonstrated empirically that stock markets tend to be efficient. But this is a mistake. There are at least 3 definitions of market efficiency.

1. Arbitrage efficiency: No Easy Money

The most basic form of market efficiency is that it is not possible to make money on investing by following a set of rules, however complex they may be. If it were, we would theoretically expect that this opportunity would be ceased and exploited by arbitrage until the point at which this was no longer possible. This is the type of efficiency which is examined in the finance literature. However, it is a weak form of efficiency since stock prices generated randomly by a computer in the basement of the New York Stock Exchange would also be impossible to predict based on any kind of information (i.e. they would be strong form efficient in finance jargon). Nevertheless few people would call this market efficient in a real sense. What appears to be missing is that truly efficient markets must provide accurate information about fundamental values.

2. Value efficiency: Stock markets reflect fundamental values (+/-)

A stronger efficiency is therefore that stock prices reflect the fundamental value of firms. This is what is required if stock prices are to lure capital to its most efficient use. Leaving some room for noise in stock prices, Fisher Black has defined an efficient market as a market in which stock prices 90% of the time are within a factor two of their fundamental value. Value investors like Warren Buffet explicitly seek to invest in companies in which there is a discrepancy between stock prices and fundamental value (i.e. where the company is undervalued or at least not overvalued). However, even value efficient markets need not be governance efficient. Consider, for example, a company which has issued shares without voting rights and where the managers 'live it up' at the expense of the shareholders and they refuse to pay dividends. The stock price might be very low reflecting the dim prospects for shareholders. But it might not matter if the managers do not care.

3. Governance efficiency: efficient monitoring and capital allocation

The strongest form of efficiency is that the governance system monitors and allocates efficiently such that capital is put to its most productive use. This necessitates a mechanism which translates market and other signals into action at the company level – for example a shareholder meeting, a vigilant board, or a stock option scheme for managers. This mechanism is what we call corporate governance.

While it is generally assumed the stock markets are arbitrage efficient, it is less clear that they are value efficient. If they were, it would probably be more difficult for investors like Warren Buffet to make money. To form an impression, you may want to look at the evolution of the NASDAQ index which first rose by a factor of 17 during the 1990s and then fell by 2/3 from 2000 to 2003 (the scales are logarithmic), but has since more than doubled. If there is a story about fundamental values which can explain this, I would like to hear it. In contrast, it is relatively plausible that the markets first overvalued and then perhaps undervalued the average NASDAQ stock. Since the index reflects large numbers, the volatility of individual stocks was clearly far greater.

If the market is not value efficient it is of course debatable what role society would give it in the allocation of capital. Intuitively, based on the above evidence, this should be a very limited role. For example, stock option programs must have systematically miscalculated managerial compensation over the past decades and we have no reason to believe that it will be more accurate in the future. Moreover, can we maintain that hostile takeovers will increase efficiency if stock prices do not reflect fundamental values? Or is it safe for institutional investors to index their portfolios?

But failures in US governance do not mean that other systems did better. While it seems likely based on this argument that US governance could be improved, it is dangerous to compare a real corporate governance model to a theoretical ideal (The Demsetz fallacy of comparing real world institutions to a theoretical Nirvana), particularly since hindsight is, after all, the 'most exact science'. Other national stock markets also experienced stock market fluctuations over the same period of time, and even if their companies were (and are) less sensitive to stock market signals, this does not necessarily mean that their long term corporate governance is better. If they are less sensitive to the stock market, what is the guarantee that they allocate capital more efficiently?

In international comparison, the US/UK governance system appears to be very competitive in terms of economic growth, profit rates, and market valuations. The loss of competitiveness which was observed in the beginning of the 1990s has since been replaced with successes in IT, biotechnology, and almost all sectors of the economy. Japan which seemed to be an economic threat at the time has since experienced a decade of problems which appear to be partly attributable to its corporate governance. New listings go to London or New York and not to Frankfurt or Berlin.

To most observers, the market model, therefore, seems superior to other corporate governance models around the world – at least in the current economic climate. The verdict is still out, however. It is clear that the stock markets of the UK and the US have significant advantages in terms of market size and historical position. Would they have performed equally well without these advantages? Can the market model be successfully imitated by other countries or will that have undesirable side effects or their economies? Has the market model been damaged by overregulation? These are some of the difficult questions which must be answered to evaluate whether the market model will continue to be competitive in the next decade. When we know the answer 10 years from now, it will be too late; the more interesting question will be what is competitive in the next decade after that. The point is that the world is changing and so is the optimal governance system.

A more sophisticated, but perhaps less useable, answer can be derived from fundamental reasoning. The market model is a system of corporate governance which emphasizes markets: particularly stock markets. The system will work well in circumstances when markets tend to flourish and it will do badly under conditions which lead to market failure. If the challenges ahead involve greater information asymmetries, externalities, and asset specificity, non-market types of governance could be more competitive. If we will see lower transaction costs, the market based governance systems will thrive.

References

Bebchuk, Lucian Arye and Fried, Jesse M., 'Executive Compensation as an Agency Problem'. *Journal of Economic Perspectives,* Vol. 17, Summer 2003.

Holmström, Bengt R. and Kaplan, Steven N., 'The State of U.S. Corporate Governance: What's Right and What's Wrong?' (September 2003). ECGI – *Finance Working Paper* No. 23/2003. Available at SSRN: http://ssrn.com/abstract=441100.

Rappaport, A. 1981. Selecting strategies that create shareholder value. *Harvard Business Review.*

Rappaport, A. 1986. *Creating shareholder value the new standard for business performance.* Free Press, New York.

Appendix 1

Sarbanes-Oxley

On July 30, 2002 the Sarbanes-Oxley Act (Public Company Accounting Reform and Investor Protection Act of 2002 abbreviated as SOX) was approved by the US Congress by a vote of 423-3 and by the Senate 99-0. In signing it into law, President George W. Bush stated that it included *'the most far-reaching reforms of American business practices since the time of Franklin D. Roosevelt.'* (The New York Times, July 31, 2002). The act contains 11 sections including provision on the following issues:

- Disclosure of mandatory 'control of controls systems' related to financial reporting, which must be attested by independent auditors (section 404)
- Financial reports to be signed by chief executive officers and chief financial officers (section 302)
- Rules on auditor independence (term limits for leading auditor, prohibition against combining consulting and auditing, etc.).
- Creation of a Public Company Accounting Oversight Board (PCAOB), a semi-private institution, which is to supervise the auditing profession.
- Mandatory independent audit committees to oversee the relationship between the company and its auditor
- Ban on personal loans to any executive officer or director
- Accelerated reporting of insider trading
- Prohibition on insider trades during pension fund blackout periods
- Significantly increased criminal and civil penalties for violations of securities law
- Protection of whistleblowers who leak information to the public

The direct costs are considerable. A survey of 224 largest public firms in the USA by Financial Executives International with regard to the direct costs of complying with Section 404 of the Sarbanes-Oxley Act finds that the average first-year estimate is almost $3 million for 26,000 hours of internal work and 5,000 hours of external work, plus additional audit fees of $823,200, or an increase of 53% (Zhang, 2005).. Although the direct cost tends to decrease over time, compliance costs still average 3 million dollars per company and amounts to 2-3 % of revenues for small companies (The Economist 21. May 2005).

These direct cost estimates do not include opportunity costs of time or behavioural effects: for example the uncertain effects of having managers sign off on their responsibilities down the organization or the opportunity costs of top management time spent on auditing and control issues. At the same time other regulatory changes – like corporate governance codes from both NYSE and NASDQ – have contributed with more regulation. Some commentators argue that the administrative costs of these initiatives have spurred delistings from American exchanges (Block, 2004; Engel et al., 2005; Marosi and Massoud, 2005; Kamar et al., 2006; Leuz et al., 2006) and have led international companies to list elsewhere, e.g. in London. The report issued 30. November 2006 by the Committee on Global Capital Markets regulation concluded that US capital markets are losing their competitiveness and that regulation costs play a leading role in this shift ((Hubbard, 2006, 2007; Hubbard and Thornton 2007, Committee on Global Capital markets Regulation, 2006).

The complexity of regulation is no doubt increased by the new US enforcement regime, which delegates extensive power to the SEC and to the PCAOB to engage in a specific dialogue with companies which – in the eyes of the regulator – do not comply with the law.

In sum, Sarbanes-Oxley is a complex contribution to a field of practice which is already extensively regulated by company law and best practice codes.

Although Europe has not been subject to the rigors of Sarbanes-Oxley, she has also had her fill of regulation. There are new EU directives on transparency (2004), prospectuses (2003), transparency, market abuse (2003), takeovers (2004), and financial instruments (2004). Moreover, all European countries have now adopted corporate governance codes on a 'comply or explain' basis.

Much of the new corporate governance regulation can be regarded as 'second generation' in the sense that it deals not just with control of executives (i.e. 1st generation regulation) but with control of control (which I will here define as 2nd generation): Auditors are to control internal control procedures which are designed to control the executives. The PCAOB – and audit committees – are to control the auditors who exercise control over the executive through the annual report. Boards which control the executives are to be more accountable to shareholders. One obvious outstanding question remains. Why are the same institutions which are believed to have failed in a number of instances – auditors, boards, shareholders – now assuming an even greater role in corporate governance. When the original control did not work – or rather were *claimed* not to work – the response was to implement more control on the controls. Perhaps third generation controls are not far off.

Sarbanes-Oxley has been heavily criticized by US business practitioners.

First of all, SOX is – by any standards – a complex piece of legislation. The text is long (66 pages), and it covers many different aspects of company behaviour and the creation a new quasi-governmental institution. It was enacted under perceived time pressure (stock prices were falling), and even some of its proponents argue that it was sloppily written and internally inconsistent. It is unquestionable that bundling so many initiatives in one law made it a very complex piece of legislation.

Second, it was enacted 'top down' contrary to the US common law tradition and despite protests from business leaders. A series of laws with time for discussion would no doubt have given business more time to adjust and would be met with less resistance.

Third, the rationale was unclear and disputed from day one. More than anything else, falling stock prices were the aftermath of the internet bubble. Symbolically, the law was very much directed at Enron and Arthur Andersen, which had already been severely punished by bankruptcy. Despite a relatively simple – easily communicable – storyline in the Enron/Anderson story, the law went well beyond prohibiting Enron-type practices: introducing sections 302 and 404 to address problems related to the internal consistency of accounting which has very little to do with the top-level fraud in Enron.

Fourth, SOX involved many different people so that implementation could not be left to complexity-loving experts (for example, section 302 had branch managers all the way down testify that their accounting was correct accordingly to certain vaguely-defined and imperfectly-understood standards).

Fifth, the penalties for non-compliance were severe: up to ten years in prison – more severe than sentences for manslaughter. Moreover, the law was religiously enforced. Understandably, this combination of ambiguity and severity created widespread anxiety.

Sixth, the easiest solution to avoiding collusion between companies and their auditors – requiring companies to change their auditing firm at regular intervals – was avoided.

In conclusion, most of the complexity of Sarbanes-Oxley appears to derive from two provisions – 302 and 404 – which were relatively peripheral to the central theme of the law. Although bad cases make bad law, prohibiting certain types of Enron-like behaviour (i.e. personal loans to board members and managers) would have been relatively easy to explain to the public.

CHAPTER 10

Bank Governance in Germany

Corporate governance in Germany differs from the market model by using banks as intermediaries between savers and companies. In this chapter we examine German corporate governance focusing on characteristics which deviate from the market model such as bank leadership, two tier boards, and employee representation.

Bank governance in theory[1]

The relationship between a company and its bank is perhaps the single most important of all business relationships after ownership relations. The relationship creates obvious links between the two parties via the credit relationship which may more or less completely determine the activities of individual firms and which has, in some cases, led to the bankruptcy of even large banks. In addition to capital transfer, bank relationships involve information transfers to assess the financial risks involved in the company's activities. Generally, they are multi-functional involving many kinds of financial services such as short term credit, long term loans, new equity issues, payment systems, portfolio management, as well as various kinds of advice (Holland 1994). Banks have enthusiastically endorsed the messages of relationship building, and relationship banking has become a catchword among bankers since the beginning of the 1980s.

---

1. This section draws heavily on my unpublished working paper, The Duration of Business Relationships. Banking Relationships of Danish Manufacturers 1900-1995.

A higher level of information, trust and resource commitment may enable banks to better assess the risks involved in a company's business and thus to extend more credit, give better advice, etc. Hodgman (1963) found in a series of interviews that *'bankers preferred to lend to applicants who were most likely to maintain long term deposit relationship with them'* (Holland 1994). Likewise, companies may be willing to take on more debt if they have developed close banking relationships over time. In addition, Holland (1994) emphasizes that close relations are regarded as implicit insurance for both banks and companies. Companies expect the bank to help them in hard times, and in turn, banks expect companies to give them a relatively certain share of their regular bank business. Social bonds (Håkanson and Snehota 1995, chapter 5) also appear in relationship banking. Thus, Donaldson (1969) found that finance officers *'placed considerable emphasis on the importance of cultivating a close relationship with the lending officer – a relationship usually regarded as a highly personal one involving mutual trust and continuous communication'* (Holland 1994 p. 369).

In accordance with practice, the economics literature views bank relationships as a way to overcome credit rationing and adverse selection under asymmetric information (Stiglitz and Weiss 1981, Diamond 1984). Information asymmetries between lenders and borrowers may cause lenders to limit the supply of capital which may have unfortunate effects if

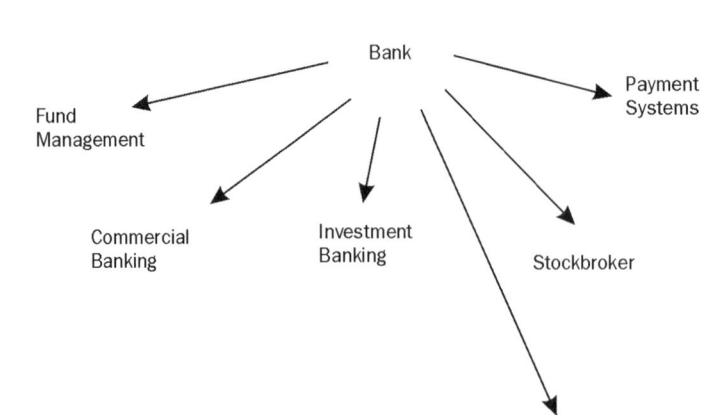

Figure 10.1: Universal Banking

profitable investments cannot be funded and especially so in times of financial distress (Stiglitz and Weiss 1981). Long-term relationships may provide banks with better information on the nature of the company and its business which may reduce these problems. In comparison with anonymous bond markets, banks are in a better position to monitor the borrowers (Fama 1985). Furthermore, the prospect of future business is an added incentive for banks to provide 'bridging finance' for a client in trouble. This implies significant survival value of a close bank relationship from the viewpoint of the company.

From the viewpoint of the bank, reduced information asymmetries may in some cases overcome credit rationing and may generate extra business or, in other cases, may help to avoid bad loans. Furthermore, bank loans may also spill over into other kinds of bank business including cash management, short term credits, transactions, and investment banking. A loyal customer base implies a secure source of revenue. And a better understanding of the clients is in itself an important asset which may support new product development, marketing, etc.

This would seem to imply that bank relationships are particularly valuable (and durable) when companies are credit rationed: e.g. when they have insufficient equity or internal funds to finance their investments.

Bank monitoring and financial control may reduce managerial discretion and agency costs. For example, banks have an obvious interest in persuading companies to avoid managerial inefficiency and unprofitable projects which endanger their ability to repay loans. Close relations with other companies may also provide a valuable source of advice on recruitment, acquisition targets, restructuring, etc.

In contrast to this rosy picture, more recent research has stressed a dark side of banking relationships. Greenbaum et al. (1989) argue theoretically that the interest rate charged by banks on loans to a company will increase in the duration of the relationship which predicts that companies will eventually switch banks as competitors give them a better offer. Sharpe (1990) argues that relationship banks gain access to an information monopoly which they can exploit to the firm's disadvantage unless checked by reputation.

Bank leadership in Germany

Traditionally, banks have played a central role in German economic development. Companies have turned to their 'house banks' for credit, investment bank services, asset management, transactions, and all other financial services. Germany's tradition for universal banks – which combine all of these services in one bank – allowed banks to grow large and thereby better able to manage large accounts with undue financial risk. The tradition was – and is – therefore to finance companies by long term bank debt more than by issuing equity to the stock market.

Moreover, many company pension funds are not separately funded, but remain part of corporate liabilities and do not, therefore, add to the size and liquidity of the financial markets.

German banks are allowed to posses controlling stakes in non-financial firms and historically they have done so to a considerable extent. Thus, bank capitalism has led to more ownership control of large German firms than we find in large US firms. Since the major banks concentrate their shares in large companies, the combined share of the three largest banks may easily add up to a majority of the votes.

In addition to direct ownership, German banks act as custodians for ordinary shareholders and may represent them at shareholder meetings. This further increases their power at shareholder meetings. German banks also control the votes of mutual funds, whose shares they can vote if necessary.

Moreover, bankers are allowed to sit on the supervisory boards of non-financial companies, which again adds to their power.

Altogether, German banks dominate corporate governance in Germany through ownership, ownership representation, board membership, and lending relationships. Moreover, there seems to be an implicit understanding that a lead bank will step in and provide bridging finance in case of a financial crisis in one of its debtors.

However, the German model appears to be changing. In global competition with other banks and stimulated by new tax laws (which no longer tax appreciation on long term shareholdings when the banks sell them), German banks have sold off shares and reduced loans to large German companies in recent years. Moreover securitisation – selling loans to investors – may have weakened the loan monitoring role of banks. Whether this change will completely renew German corporate governance remains to be seen.

Two-tier boards with employee representation

Germany has a mandatory two-tier board system. All companies must have a supervisory board (Ausichtsrat) and a management board (Vorstand), whose roles very much resemble those of non-executive and executive directors in the UK. Overlap between the two boards is prohibited.

The supervisory board is charged with many of the same functions as boards in the US and UK:

- to review the performance of the company and take steps to avoid bankruptcy,
- to monitor the performance of managers and to replace them if necessary,
- to ratify major decisions (e.g. M&A).

Employees have a right to elect up to half of the board members in larger corporations, but the shareholders maintain a voting majority since the vote of the chairman is decisive in case of a deadlock. As mentioned, bankers may also sit on company boards which could theoretically tip the balance in favour of stakeholder viewpoints (see below).

In addition to employee representation at the board level, many decisions concerning labour issues must be discussed in work councils before they can be put into practice.

The management board (Vorstand) is a collective decision-making body appointed by the supervisory board. It is headed by a CEO (Sprecher), but in principle differences of opinion are settled by majority voting.

Other characteristics of German corporate governance

The German **legal system** is civil law which according La Porta et al. (1998) is associated with less protection of minority investors. However,

La Porta et al. (1998) note that the quality of enforcement in Germany is very high so that property rights are well protected.

Incentive pay is gaining ground in Germany, but is clearly less widely and extravagantly used than in the UK and US. Pay levels are lower, and so is the performance sensitive share of total pay.

Why is Germany different?

Charkham (1994) suggests a cultural explanation: German corporate governance reflects deeply-held views of how companies should be run and of the relationship between business and society. Private ownership is not a goal in itself, but is subordinate to the public interest. Ownership involves obligations as well as rights. The purpose of a company is to provide goods and services for the population: not to make money. These views – though difficult to verify – seem consistent with a strong industrial tradition in German business. Unlike in the UK, considerable social prestige is traditionally attached to engineering and physics, but not to economics and finance. 'Wer nichts wird wird Wirt' (Wirt is inn-keeper or short for Wirtschaftler/economist: he who does not become anything becomes an economist – bright people become engineers, philosophers, or lawyers).

According to the cultural view, the industrial tradition – valuing the company as such (das Unternehmen an sich) – promotes long-term thinking, stakeholder interest, and survival of the corporation is the overall goal. It is translated into long terms of office for executives who continue after retirement as supervisory board chairs. Conservative accounting seems to fit the picture.

Another related view turns to politics. There is a strong social democratic tradition in Germany, and the German Christian conservatism has traditionally been more social and less liberal than the conservatives and Republicans in the UK and the US. Social democracy emphasized co-determination which led to employee representation. It may also be that Social Democrats found it easier to regulate banks and therefore preferred the bank-based model.

Evaluation of the German model

Germany is clearly a very rich society despite recent unification between East and West. GDP per capita is the same as in the UK, but 1/3 lower than the US.

It is questionable whether the bank-based German governance model has contributed adequately to the profitability and competitiveness of German corporations during the past decades. The banks themselves seem on the way to replacing it with a more market-oriented style of governance.

The board system – particularly employee representation – has been met with significant criticism in the business community. It seems to have led to larger supervisory boards; the average size is now 15 members (Andres et al. 2006), compared to 7 in the 1970s. Schroeder and Shrader (1988) find that supervisory boards go through the motions (i.e. limit decisions) to what is legally required. Gorton and Smid (1998) argue that firms with employee representation have lower performance and lower risk which is what you would theoretically expect: all else equal, employees have an interest in protecting their jobs and so they would want to influence their companies to risk less. If there is a trade off between risk and return, the greater risk aversion should lead to lower returns (figure 10.2).

Figure 10.2

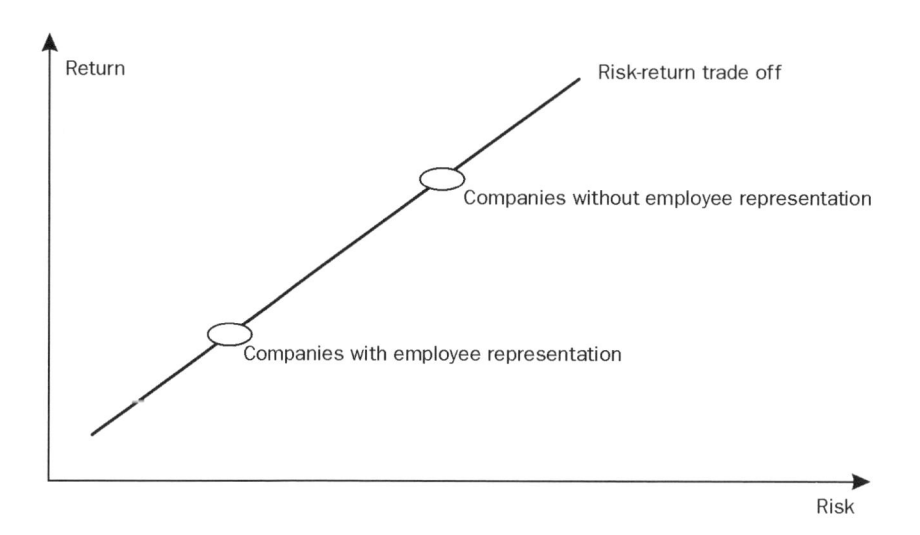

The same logic can be applied to other parts of the German corporate governance system. Banks are naturally risk averse because they lose by downside risk, but they do not gain by upside risk. Banks would, therefore, naturally induce companies to take less risk, which would then lead to less risk taking and lower returns. As powerful actors in the German corporate governance, banks and employees share a common interest in not inducing risk-taking pay by performance pay for executives.

At the macro level, all this might be expected to show up in less entrepreneurship and lower economic growth than would otherwise have been the case. If so, the lower risk taking will only be in the short-term interest of employees and banks, because both stand to benefit more than anything else from higher economic growth. This may be one reason why both bankers and unions now seem more susceptible to economic reform.

References

Diamond, D. W. 1984. Financial intermediation and delegated monitoring. *Review of Economic Studies* 51. 393-414.
Donaldson. G. 1969. *Strategy for Financial Mobility*. Harvard Graduate School of Business Administration. Division of Research.
Fama, E. 1985. What's different about banks. *Journal of Monetary Economics* 15.29-39.
Greenbaum, S.I., G. Kanatas and I. Venezia. 1989. Loan pricing under the bank-client relationship. *Journal of Banking and Finance* 13. 221-235.
Holland, John. Bank lending relationships and the complex nature of bank-corporate relations. *Journal of Business Finance and Accounting*. 21(3).367-393.
Houston, Joel and James, Christopher. 1996. Bank Information Monopolies and the mix of private and public debt claims. *The Journal of Finance* 60(5). 1863-1889.
Moriarty, R., R. Kimball and J. Gay. 1983. The Management of Corporate Banking Relationships. *Sloan Management Review*. Spring. 3-15.
Sharpe, S.A. 1990. Asymmetric information, bank lending and implicit contracts: A stylised model of customer relationships. *Journal of Finance* 65(4). 1069-1087.
Stiglitz, Joseph E. and Andrew. Weiss. 1981. Credit rationing in markets with imperfect information. *The American Economic Review* 71(3).

CHAPTER 11

Relational Governance in Japan

Theoretical considerations

Relational governance involves ongoing relationships between market participants and other members of society. Instead of coordinating economic activity purely via the price mechanism, relationship governance involves additional formal or informal contractual obligations. For example, instead of just buying and selling the parties, an ongoing relationship may make mutually-binding long-term contracts, or they may partially internalise the transaction by buying stock in each other. Social mechanisms like reputation and culture may reinforce or replace formal contracts.

Oliver Williamson (1975, 1985, 2005) has persuasively argued that such contractual governance can be (transaction) cost effective when the relationship is:

- ongoing and long-term (i. e., characterized by a high frequency of transactions) and
- characterized by dependency (asset specificity).

For example, long-term contracts and ownership integration can insure the parties to the transaction against opportunistic behaviour and thereby can increase their incentive to make transaction-specific investments.

Complete integration will involve a merger between the firms involved in a transaction, but a complete merger will involve a loss of local autonomy and incentives in the individual firms which may reduce economic efficiency. An alternative – hybrid – mode of organization is relational governance where firms form associations by partial ownership, interlocking boards, long term contracts, and social relationships. Such partial integration may promote trust and cooperation between the firms involved.

Relational governance may also be extended to a wider group of stakeholders like employees or consumers whose loyalty is a valuable asset for the firm. For example, a company which treats its employees well and does not fire them unless it is absolutely necessary will build up loyalty in the workforce which makes employees less likely to change jobs. Among consumers, a track record of providing superior value at low prices will build brand loyalty.

By stabilizing economic relationships, relational governance can reduce risk – for example employment risk –and if market participants are risk averse this will be a competitive advantage.

The Japanese model

Japanese corporate governance has a number of special characteristics which separate Japan both from continental Europe and from the US/UK.

Keiretsus (company groups) are the dominant ownership mode for large listed firms. At first glance, ownership is very dispersed and comparable to the US or the UK, but closer scrutiny reveals that companies in a company group tend to hold shares in each other so it is usually impossible for an outsider to take over a Japanese company against the wishes of its management. Some keiretsus are formed among former subsidiaries in Japanese Zaibatus – family-owned business groups – which were broken up during the US occupation after the Second World War. Others are formed around 'main banks'. And yet others – vertical keiretsus – a formed along the supply chain so that a firm and its suppliers are united by ownership.

Even in the absence of ownership ties, **industrial networks** between a firm and its suppliers tend to be highly stable and to be regarded as part of an ongoing relationship rather than as a set of spot market transactions.

Bank finance rather than equity finance is the predominant mode of capital provision. There are many similarities to the German bank-based model, but in Japan, US-style ownership ceilings were imposed during the occupation, and this prevented Japanese banks from taking a dominant role in corporate ownership. It appears that relational governance is practiced over a wider range of business relationships in Japan. However, 'main banks' are reported to play a leading role in many company groups.

The board system is one tier. Boards tend to be very large – often 30-40 members – and composed primarily of company managers. Of the few outsiders, most come from other companies in the business group. Consequently, board control of managers is virtually absent.

Employee relations are characterized by lifetime or, at least, long-term employment. Japanese managers – salary men – tend to work in the same company throughout their careers. A system of enterprise unions – rather than trade unions – means that employees in the same company tend to be members of the same enterprise union.

Government intervention has traditionally played some role in Japanese society. For example, bank credit was politically directed at certain sectors of the economy, and large parts of Japanese businesses are protected from international competition by tariffs and by other trade barriers.

Incentive pay is used to a much smaller extent and average pay levels are much lower than in the US. Moreover career progress seems to be determined by seniority more than performance. However, company-wide bonus systems for all employees provide a collective incentive.

Company law is in the civil law tradition imported from Germany. Although Japan scores highly on formal measures of investor protection, the level of shareholder influence is very limited. Japanese companies are famous for holding their annual meetings on the same day which effectively prevents small shareholders from attending most of them. Moreover, the meetings are deliberately kept very short: for example thirty minutes.

Aoki (1988) has called the Japanese model **'contingent governance'**. Under normal circumstances, management is left to its own devices. But in times of crisis, the main bank steps in and leads a rescue operation which takes charge of the subsequent restructuring. Bank relationships thus reduce credit constraints in bankruptcy and financial distress. They provide an important source of insurance in an economy with a very small government sector and without a social safety net – e.g. without employment insurance. In addition, inflexible labour markets make it difficult to find a new job. The closed markets for corporate control function appear particularly important under these circumstances.

Chapter 11. Relational Governance in Japan

Japanese culture is a popular explanation for differences in corporate governance. In her 1945 classic 'The Chrysanthemum and the Sword,' Ruth Benedict argues that the Japanese 'shame' culture is more social than the individualistic 'guilt' cultures of the West and that social motives like 'honour', 'obligation', or 'duty' play a much stronger role. Correspondingly, Charkham (1994) argued that Japanese corporate governance is shaped by mutual obligations between the company and its employee, a strong corporate family feeling, and decisions based on consensus and social responsibility. However, cultural stereotypes seem inconsistent with the dramatic changes in corporate governance during the past century (see below), while Japanese culture has presumably remained unchanged. Apparently corporate governance is not determined by culture, although culture may clearly be one of the important background variables.

The Keiretsu system

An example of a keiretsu is the Mitsubishi group, which consists of the following companies:

Asahi Glass Co., Ltd. Mitsubishi Gas Chemical Company, Inc. Mitsubishi Shindoh Co., Ltd.
The Bank of Tokyo-Mitsubishi UFJ, Ltd. Mitsubishi Heavy Industries, Ltd. Mitsubishi Steel Mfg. Co., Ltd.
Kirin Holdings Company, Limited Mitsubishi Kakoki Kaisha, Ltd. Mitsubishi UFJ Securities Co., Ltd.
Meiji Yasuda Life Insurance Co. Mitsubishi Logistics Corp. Mitsubishi UFJ Trust and Banking Corp.
Mitsubishi Aluminium Co., Ltd. Mitsubishi Materials Corp. Nikon Corp.
Mitsubishi Cable Industries, Ltd. Mitsubishi Motors Corp. Nippon Oil Corp.
Mitsubishi Chemical Corp. Mitsubishi Paper Mills Limited Nippon Yusen Kabushiki Kaisha
Mitsubishi Corporation Mitsubishi Plastics, Inc. P.S. Mitsubishi Construction Co., Ltd.
Mitsubishi Electric Corp. Mitsubishi Rayon Co., Ltd. Tokio Marine & Nichido Fire Insurance Co., Ltd.

Mitsubishi Estate Co., Ltd. Mitsubishi Research Institute, Inc. Related Organizations/Others
Mitsubishi Fuso Truck & Bus Corp.

Today the members are regarded as independent companies after the break up in 1945.

Mitsubishi Corporation, the core of the Mitsubishi Group, is Japan's largest general trading house (sogo shosha), whose functions encompass business relationships across the entire value chain of business for its corporate clients:

- **Sales Agency:** Sales and exports for manufacturers
- **Marketing**
- **Purchasing**
- **Logistics (transport and storage)**
- **Finance**
- **Processing and producing goods**
- **Investment,** e. g building plants and establishment of subsidiary and affiliated companies
- **Business Intelligence:** gathering, analyzing, and supplying information on international affairs, legal matters, and market trends
- **Business Consulting**
- **Technology search:** R&D and technology transfers
- **Joint projects** Cooperating with business partners, M&A, Joint Ventures, network formation.

Keiretsus are groups of companies loosely connected by cross ownership: sometimes also by a joint name (logo) and a common management philosophy. The shareholdings by group members – and sometimes also by business partners outside the group – are extremely stable and constitute an effective defence against hostile takeover. There are fewer ties between company groups

It is unclear to what extent group members actually exercise their ownership. In some cases, executives from other group companies sit on the board, and some loose coordination apparently takes place at monthly 'Presidents' meetings'.

There are said to be two types of keiretsus: horizontal and vertical.

Chapter 11. Relational Governance in Japan

Horizontal keiretsus – like Mitsubishi – consist of companies in different industries. Traditionally there was only one company per industry and thus, meant there were no competitors. But more recently, there are examples of competition between group members. The result is a spiders' web of small ownership shares (figure 11.1).

There is often a 'main bank' at the centre of such keiretsus which handles all their banking business.

Figure 11.1: A Horizontal Keiretsu

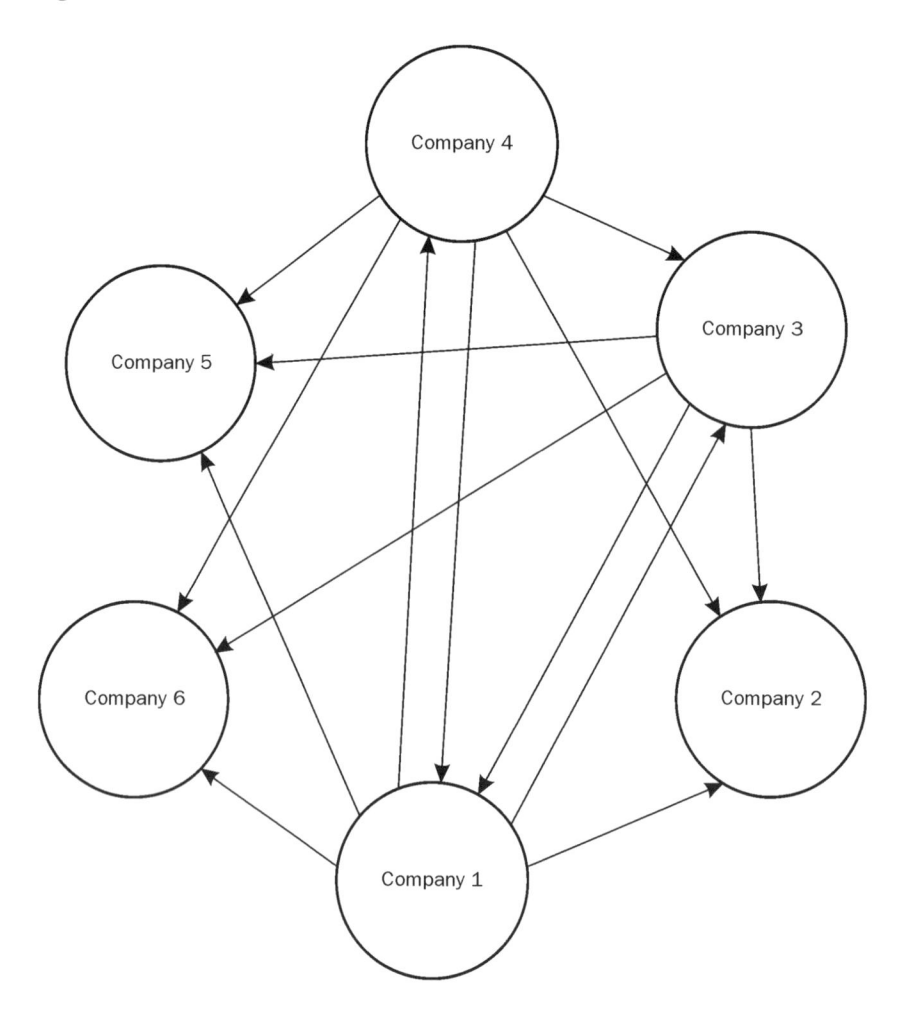

Vertical keiretsus – like the Toyota group – consist of firms in the same value chain from raw material to production to distribution. There is typically one leading firm which controls the chain which contributes to coordination of activities along the supply chain (figure 11.2).

Figure 11.2: A vertical Keiretsu

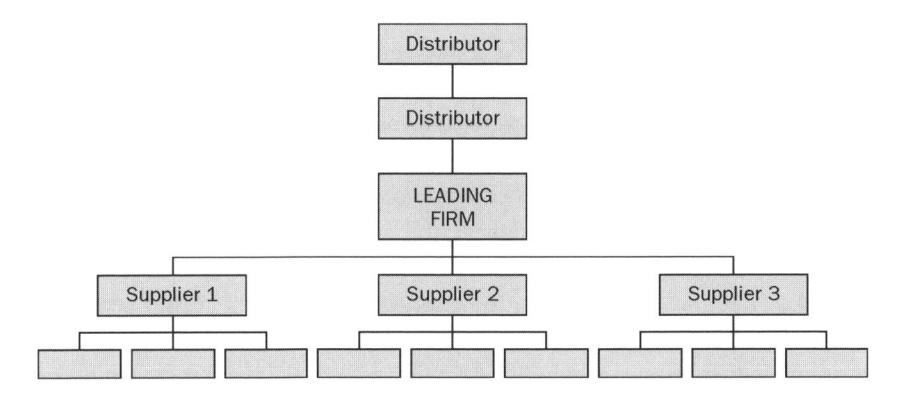

Many Japanese management innovations – like the Just in Time System – seem to spring from this type of coordination. This is consistent with 'Williamsonian' advantages of relational contracting.

History of Japanese corporate governance

As told by Morck and Nakamura (2003), Japanese corporate governance has undergone dramatic changes during the past century.

Up to the 1930s, the dominant ownership structure was Zaibatsus – family-owned business groups – which combined a wide range of business companies in a conglomerate structure with a pyramid structure of ownership relations.

During Japanese militarism from 1930-45, Japan was effectively run as a planned economy. Government-appointed board members dictated what companies had to do to assist mobilization and industrialisation by plan. Bank credit was particularly tightly controlled.

After the war, the US occupation authority dictated a number of reforms in corporate governance. The Zaibatsus were held to be part of the Japanese war machine and broken up. Ownership was dispersed to employees, and from 1945-50, Japanese corporate governance was run according to the shareholder model--for example with many hostile takeovers.

From 1950-1990, companies reacted with cross shareholdings as a takeover defence, and the cross shareholdings increased when foreigners were allowed to buy shares. This led to the formation of the modern day keiretsus.

In the after war period the Japanese economic was highly successful. Over these 4 decades Japan caught up with and overtook most western economies in terms of GDP per capita and world market shares. Japanese corporate governance was widely admired and regarded as a source of competitiveness.

But at the end of the 1980s, the country experience a huge bubble in property and equity prices, the collapse of which has lead to a period of economic stagnation up to present time. Corporate governance problems are widely blamed. For example, banks have been unable or slow to liquidate bad loans because of keiretsu ties.

However, some Japanese companies like Toyota and Sony with a strong international orientation have been able to excel despite the stagnation of the domestic economy. Many of these companies are newcomers outside the keiretsus or zaibatsus and found it difficult to sell to the domestic market which was controlled by the old establishment.

Changes in the Japanese model

As a result of the prolonged crisis, corporate governance has been much debated. But nothing much has happened. A few companies like Sony have reduced board size and internationalized their boards, but this is clearly an exception.

However, Japanese firms appear to have reduced their stockholdings and international ownership has increased. In some cases, this has lead to significant restructuring and improved competitiveness. For example, the partial Renault/Nissan merger in 1999, where Renault took over 44.3% of the ailing Nissan, (Nissan holds 15% of Renault) and installed Caslos

Ghosn as new CEO, is a well-published success story. Ghosn sold off shares in other companies so that 1394 Stockholdings were reduced to 4 and he managed to trim 20% of supply costs over a few years. Ghosn also sold off some business; for example, seat production was sold to Johnson controls. This turnaround to profitability and growth was widely acclaimed as a role model.

Evaluation of the Japanese model

Japan is now one of the 20 wealthiest countries in the world on a par with the UK and Germany. There was a time when the Japanese model worked.

However, the country has been in relative stagnation for almost 20 years and some of this appears to be related to corporate governance. In particular, friendly shareholders, creditors, and boards combined with low-key incentives and domestic monopoly power provide little motivation for change, particularly not for dramatic restructuring which is probably what is needed if Japan is to resume its high growth rates.

There do not seem to be any quick-fix solutions, however. It may be necessary for companies to internalise social functions – like employee relations or social responsibility – in a country where the government sector is so small and markets are so inflexible that becoming unemployed is equivalent to dropping permanently out of society.

Nevertheless, given increasing competition from China, Japan cannot rest on its laurels for long.

References

Charkham, J., 1995, *Keeping Good Company: A Study of Corporate Governance in Five Countries*, Oxford: Oxford University Press.

Ronald J. Gilson; Mark J. Roe. 1993. Understanding the Japanese Keiretsu: Overlaps between Corporate Governance and Industrial Organization. *The Yale Law Journal*, Vol. 102, No. 4. (Jan., 1993), pp. 871-906.

Kester, W.. 'Industrial Groups as Contractual Governance Systems.' *Oxford Review of Economic Policy* 8, no. 3 (autumn 1992): 24-44..

Morck, Randall K. and Masao Nakamura Frog in a Well Knows Nothing of the Ocean: A History of Corporate Ownership in Japan, p. 367-459. In Randall K. Morck, editor. 2005. *A History of Corporate Governance around the World: Family Business Groups to Professional Managers*. The University of Chicago Press, 2005.

CHAPTER 12

Family Business with East Asia as an example

In this chapter, we analyze family ownership. Family ownership is the most common corporate governance model around the world. I take look at what family ownership is, outline its strengths and weaknesses, summarize its economic performance, and describe the means of keeping control. As an example, I use family business in East Asia.

Family business defined

A privately-held firm is simply a firm whose shares are not publicly-listed. A **closely held firm** is a firm owned by a few shareholders. Most privately-held firms are closely held.

Founder ownership means that the firm is currently owned by its founder. Founder ownership may be called first generation of family ownership, but most first-generation firms never make it to the the second generation. In some cases – like Bill Gates in Microsoft – the founders themselves regard it as a bad idea. Second-generation ownership means that a firm is owned by one or more of the founder's children. Third-generation ownership firms are owned by the grandchildren. In fourth-generation firms, we sometimes talk of 'cousin ownership'. To add to the confusion, we sometimes talk about family ownership as including founder ownership and sometimes excluding first generation ownership.

Personal ownership means that a company is owned by a single person. This person need not be the founder – for example a restaurant may be personally owned, without having been inherited. Most small shops are believed to be acquired – not inherited. Even in large companies you sometimes see management buy outs.

209

Families can play a continuum of roles in their companies. In Table 12.1, I classify some of them in a matrix.

Table 12.1: Family roles in business firms

		Management	
		Professional	Family
Ownership	Dispersed (outsiders)	Investor governance	Family management
	Family (insiders)	Family governance	Owner-management

Source: Burkart, Panunzi, Shleifer (2002).

In an **owner-managed** company, the owner (acquirer, founder or family) manages the company.

The family may choose a professional manager, in which case we can talk about **family-governed** companies. In many cases, family members will retain seats on the board and thereby specialize in corporate governance.

If the founder/family sell its shares, but continues to mange the company, we talk about a '**family managed company'**.

In the founder/family sells its shares to outside investors and steps down from management and board positions, we get an **investor-owned** (i.e. professionally managed) company.

The different roles are important because – as we shall see – they may have very different implications for company performance.

Above and beyond the business relations, families have other characteristics which add to the complexity of family firms. It is customary to illustrate this by drawing a three sphere diagram (figure 12.1).

There are the family, the firm, and the funds. Some members of the family may work in the firms, while others do not. Some of the family's funds may be invested in the firm, while others are not. For business families, the three spheres are connected, so what happens in one sphere influences the others.

Figure 12.1: Complexity of family firms

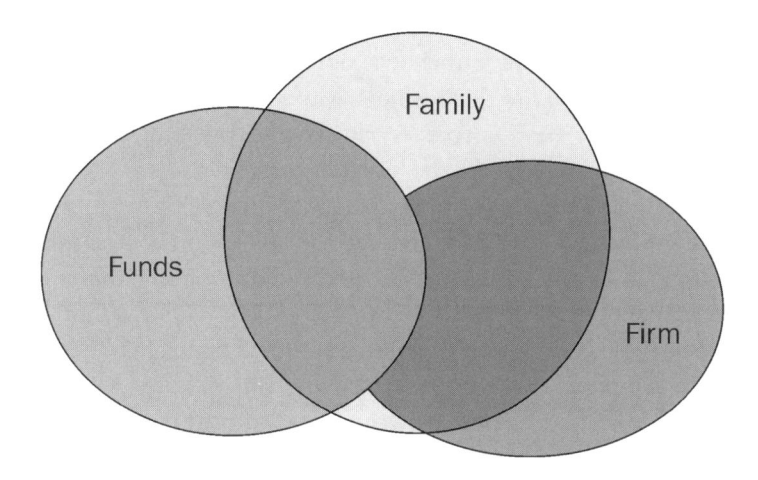

For example, illness or death of family members may lead the family to sell the firm even though family managers are not directly affected. The presence or absence of offspring will influence whether the family wishes to continue the business.

The family's non-firm funds will also influence the firm. Succession – continuation of family ownership – is more likely if siblings outside the firm can remain independently wealthy. Large families may put pressure on the firm to pay high dividends even though the firm has profitable investment opportunities.

The costs and benefits of family ownership

Personal ownership (1st generation, founder ownership) has many attractive characteristics. From an agency theory viewpoint, it solves the moral hazard problem because the owner has both the power and the incentives to make efficient decisions. It also solves the adverse selection problem because the owner has an incentive to sell if she is in not the 'best owner'. If others can run the business more profitably – or 'better' all things included from the viewpoint of the owner – she has an incentive to sell.

Founder-managers in particular are self-selected to be good owners. They could choose to sell out, but choose not to, which implies that they are particularly committed to the business. Moreover, among many start-ups which failed, they have succeeded. It is no surprise, therefore, that founder-owned companies tend to be high performers.

From a management point of view, personal ownership may be particularly competitive because it involves a clear allocation of responsibility with a single individual. Ideologically and philosophically, many people value personal ownership because they associate it with freedom.

But there are also costs which may to be weighed against the benefits. **Risk aversion** is a result of having a large ownership stake (e.g. 100%) in a single firm. Given the trade off between risk and return, risk aversion will in many cases reduce company performance because there are profitable projects which are not implemented. **Capital constraints** are closely connected to risk aversion. Unlike joint stock companies, personally-owned companies cannot issue an unlimited amount of shares to the public (if they want to remain personally owned). **Entrenchment** means that it may be difficult to replace owner managers who do not realise that they are not the best managers. Entrenchment effects will often be combined with age effects.

Family ownership (2nd generation and on) has many of the advantages of personal ownership, i.e. continuing personal ownership. Family-owned business may benefit from loyalty among family members and employees, and large families may act as a source of insurance (if a family member is in trouble or needs start-up capital, they may help financially).

Family ties are no doubt conducive to trust, and in the absence of formal institutions – justice, law, and enforcement – family business may be the only effective way of doing business. For example, the Medicis of Florence or the Jewish merchant families used family members in different countries and locations as an infrastructure for financial transactions and transportation of goods during the middle ages.

However, there are also costs of family ownership. The selection mechanism is different from that of personally-owned companies since inheritance is no guarantee of ability. In general, in the average firm, we must expect to see regression towards the mean in the next generation.

Figure 12.2

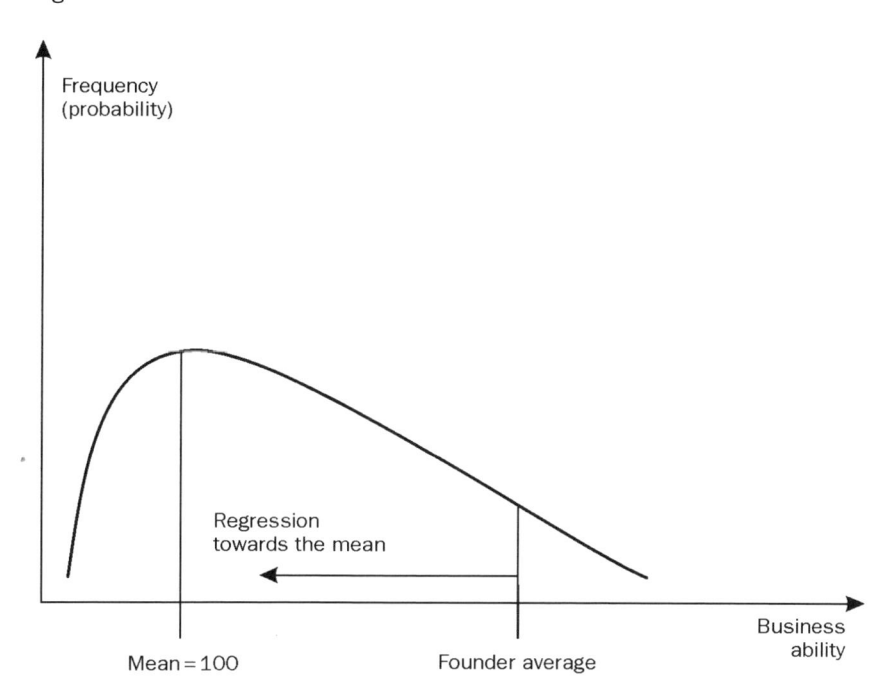

```
Frequency
(probability)
```

Regression towards the mean ←

Mean = 100   Founder average   Business ability

The founder-owners are self selected to be better than average in terms of business ability (IQ, initiative, and other characteristics necessary to succeed in business). But their sons and daughters will probably be no different from the mean, and even if they are genetically slightly 'better equipped' they will statistically be worse than their founder parents (whose genes are mixed with the other parent's). We will therefore see 'regression towards the mean' (as observed by Sir Francis Galton among the British nobility). Theoretically, therefore, we cannot expect second generation owners to do as well as their parents, but there seems to be no reason that they cannot do just as well as other businesses.

Consider the daredevil Danish entrepreneur Simon Spies who founded and successfully managed a large charter travel agency. Spies was known for his eccentric lifestyle and his penchant for young girls lead him to marry one of them – Janni Spies – just before he died. Taking over the company and managing it with the help of her brother and other bad advisors, it took her two years to take the company down. Several thousand jobs were lost.

Moreover, there are special problems in family firms which are very much part of this mode of governance. While family ties can be a source of competitive advantage, the mirror image – **nepotism** – implies that family members are sometimes given jobs which they are not capable of and therefore mismanage the firm more or less. An added consideration is **family conflict**, which can be more emotional and therefore more difficult to resolve than conflicts among rational, professional managers. There are many examples of family feuds taking even large firms down.

Family ownership and economic performance

Family business has bad press. There are many politicians, journalists, and researchers who are ideologically opposed it.

Nevertheless, several studies have found that family firms perform very well compared to professionally-managed, investor-owned firms. Some results by Anderson and Reeb (2003) from the largest US firms (S&P 500 index) are reproduced in table 12.2.

Table 12.2: Family ownership in large US Firms Standard and Poor's 500 Industrials (Anderson & Reeb 2003)

	Family firms	Others
Number of Firms	141	262
Family ownership %	18	0
Board independence %	43.6	61.1
Founder- managed %	14.5	0
Heir-managed %	30.4	0
Outside CEO (%)	55.0	100.0
Firm value	1.6	1.3
ROA %	6.1	4.7

The first surprise in this table is that family business is fairly common even among large listed US firms. 1/3 of the S&P can be characterized as family firms, either because they are managed by members of the founding family (family management), because the family owns a controlling share (family ownership), or both. Of the family firms, 55% are managed by an outside CEO, 15% are managed by the founder, and 30% are managed by a descendant.

The second surprise is that the family firms perform better than the investor-owned firms. Firm value (q) – a measure of market valuation – is 25% higher and so are profit rates. Apparently, they must be doing something right despite their 'communist' critics.

Table 12.3 by Amit and Villalonga – on a similar but larger sample of large listed US firms – examines differences between founders and heirs.

Table 12.3: Firm value (no. of firms) in Large Listed US Firms (Amit and Villalonga 2004)

	Founder Ceo	Heir Ceo	Outside Ceo	Total
Founder chair	3.12 (215)	1.61 (10)	2.81 (73)	3.0 (298)
Heir chair	- (0)	1.74 (306)	1.81 (78)	1.76 (384)
Outside chair	- (0)	- (0)	1.94 (359)	1.94 (359)
Total	3.12 (215)	1.74 (316)	2.04 (510)	2.17 (1041)

According to this table, the best of all worlds would be to have a founder-CEO with a mean firm value of 3.12 compared to an average of 2.17 for the entire sample. In contrast, heir CEOs do substantially worse than average (average q=1.74) depending whether or not their father continues as chairman of the board. Companies with a professional CEO do much better than heir-managed firms, particularly if the founder stays as CEO. However, the difference between an heir chair/CEO (1.74) and a professional chair/CEO (1.94) is insignificant.

Altogether, this evidence indicates that founder-ownership is a blessing associated with superior performance whereas there is not much of a difference between family-managed and professionally-managed firms. Certainly the second generation family firms do not do better than those which are professionally-managed. This is consistent with agency theory, as argued above, and with regression towards the mean.

Chapter 12. Family Business with East Asia as an example

Family control mechanisms

Families can retain control of their firms by several direct and indirect means. First, they may choose not to share ownership by issuing shares to the public. Alternatively, they may sell shares but retain control by various control mechanisms, which all involve deviations from the proportionality principle (One share – one vote): dual class shares, pyramids, shareholder agreements, etc.

Dual class shares – or more precisely, differential voting rights – usually signify the existence of more than one class of shares of which one class has more voting rights than the others, while they have the same dividends – or cash flow – rights.

In table 12.4 I provide an example.

Table 12.4: Dual Class Shares: An Example

	A-shares	B-Shares
Voting rights	1	0.1
Number issued	1000	10000
Held by	Family	Outsiders
Share of vote (control)	50%	50%
Share of Dividend (cash flow)	10%	90%
Ratio	5:1	5:9
Difference control-cash flow	40%	-40%

A founding family decides to split its shares into two classes (before listing, as long as the family holds 100% of the shares, there is no problem with this): 1000 A shares with 1 vote per share and 10000 B shares with one vote per share. The B shares are then listed on a stock exchange and sold to the public. The new investors now have 50% of the shares – minus perhaps one B share which the family keeps to itself. The public now holds 90% of the shares (more precisely 90.9%) and has a right to a similar portion of the dividends, but only 50% of the votes. With 1 B share in addition to the A shares the family has a majority of the votes and the ability to win most votes at a shareholder meeting. This gives rise to some agency problems: for example, the family can refuse to pay dividends and instead elect family members to sit on the board and pay them sky high fees.

We can calculate the disproportional between vote and cash flow rights as a difference:

Control rights – cash flow rights of the family = 50% – 10% = 40%
Control rights – cash flow rights of outside investors= 50% -90% = -40%.

Or we can calculate it as a ratio:

The family has vote to cash flow rights of 50%/10% = 5:1.
Outside investors have vote to cash flow rights of 50 %/90%= 5:9.

Dual class shares are widely used in most countries around the world. They were banned from US exchanges for a while, but are currently allowed again. Note there may be more than two classes of shares, so we might have A, B, and C shares.

Pyramids are another control mechanism in which the family maintains the majority of the shares in a company, which owns the majority of the shares in another company, which owns the majority of the shares in a third company, etc. An example is given in figure 12.3.

If the family holds 51%, we can then calculate its share of the total capital invested as a function of the number of levels in the pyramid:

Table 12.5: Control and Capital investment in a pyramid structure (example)

Companies in Pyramid	Family's share of capital	Board members appointed by family	Outsiders share of total capital invested
1	51%	100%	49%
2	26%	100%	74%
3	13%	100%	87%
4	7%	100%	93%

Thus, with 4 companies in the pyramid, the family can control the entire structure – e.g. appoint all board members in all 4 companies – with only 7% of the capital. Again, this may give rise to type II agency problems between majority and minority owners: for example if the family refuses to pay dividends.

217

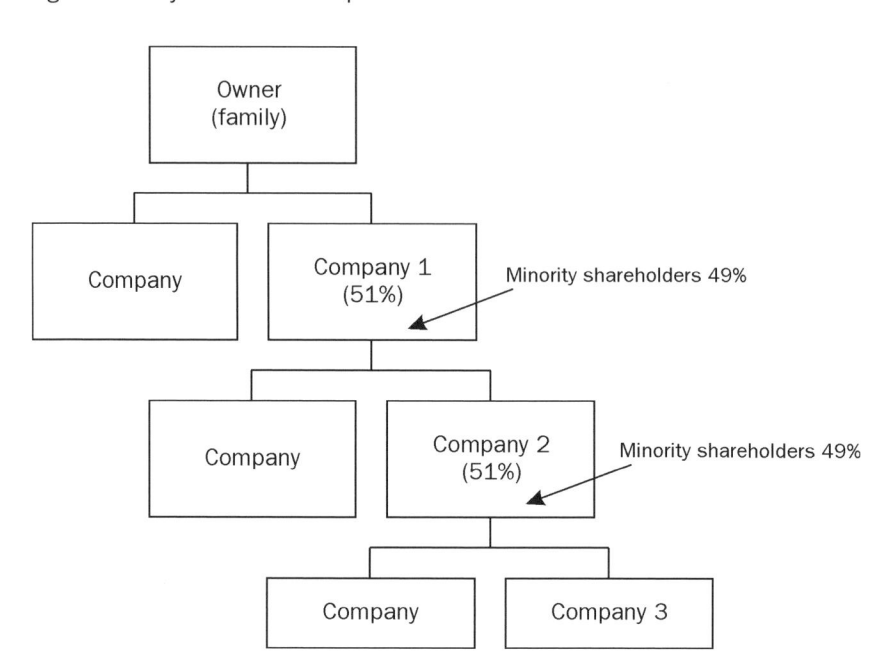

Chapter 12. Family Business with East Asia as an example

Figure 12.3: Pyramids: An example

```
                    Owner
                   (family)
                   /      \
            Company    Company 1 ──── Minority shareholders 49%
                        (51%)
                        /    \
                  Company   Company 2 ──── Minority shareholders 49%
                             (51%)
                             /    \
                       Company   Company 3
```

As an example, if the bottom company (4) sells a piece of property worth 200 million for 100 to its closest parent company (no 3), which resells it to company 2 for 50 which resells the privately held family company for 25, the family makes 200-25=175 million at the expense of the minority investors who have no power to prevent it. The minority investors, therefore, depend completely on the legal system for the protection of their interests.

Other kinds of control mechanisms include shareholder agreements, cross holdings, and voting caps. **Shareholder agreements** can, in principle, specify anything legal – so that dual class shares for example are a special kind of shareholder agreement.

Cross holdings can also help maintain control. A family can control two companies with 20% of shares in each company if they both hold 30% in the other company.

Voting caps limit the voting rights of any single owner to a certain maximum (e.g. 10%). This makes it more difficult for an outsider to challenge family control even though the family has sold its shares.

Should dual class shares be prohibited?

The critics of family enterprise often argue that dual class shares should be prohibited. So do eager European bureaucrats and politicians who would rather that the smaller companies of small countries would be taken over by the large companies in the large countries (called 'restructuring' and 'efficiency' in the jargon). Another argument – more politically correct and therefore more widely-used – is that common standards are necessary to create a common European capital market which can be competitive with the USA. A third, very understandable, argument is from the British: if they can take over our firms, why can we not take over theirs? A fourth argument is that managers of pension funds believe that the value of their shares will increase (which would benefit just about everyone these days).

However, there are a few important counterarguments.

First, where is the externality? Nobody forces people to buy dual class shares. Government intervention requires an argument.

Secondly, some companies with dual class shares are well-managed and value their ability to make long-term decisions (e.g. A P. Møller Mærsk, the Wallenberg companies) or to be socially responsible (e.g. Google, Novo Nordisk, Nike). Should they be punished just because some people do not like dual class shares?

Third, prohibiting dual class shares may lead to delistings and fewer new listings because families value control. This would lead to fewer listed companies.

A large recent study for the EU Commission concluded that there is no case against dual class shares (Burkhart and Lee 2007). Subsequently, the EU Commission dropped plans to take action in this area.

Ownership and control in East Asia

In two seminal papers, Classens et al. (2000, 2002) study ownership and control in listed East Asian firms. They find that family ownership is the most common ownership model in eight East Asian countries with Japan as a clear exception. Half of the listed companies – often more – are family-owned (only 10% of companies in Japan where family ownership of the largest companies was abolished after the Second World War). Government ownership is fairly important in Singapore (24% of companies) but this is also an exception.

The – typically Chinese – business families in East Asia use various mechanisms to maintain control: direct minority ownership, pyramids, cross holdings, etc. In this way they have been able to establish big business groups. On average, the value of the assets controlled by the 15 most important families account for 40-50 % percent of the gross domestic product: much more in Hong Kong (84 %) and Malaysia (74 %).

The average cash flow to voting rights ratio of the largest owner is 80 % – i.e. the owners vote 20% more shares than they have dividend rights to.

Table 12.6: Votes and cash flow rights of the largest Owner

Country	Cash Flow	Voting	Ratio
Hong Kong	24.3	28.1	86.5 %
Indonesia	25.6	33.7	76.0 %
Japan	6.9	10.3	66.8 %
Korea	14.0	17.8	78.5 %
Malaysia	23.9	28.3	84.4 %
Philippines	21.3	24.4	87.6 %
Singapore	20.2	27.5	73.4 %
Taiwan	16.0	19.0	84.3 %
Thailand	32.8	32.3	101.7 %
East Asia 9	15.7	19.8	79.4 %

Source: Classens (2000)

In an estimate of the effect of ownership structure, Classens et al. (2000) find an overall positive relationship between cash flow rights and firm value (figure 12.4).

This is consistent with a classic agency logic: a larger share of cash flow rights will give the largest owner a larger incentive to maximize value in the absence risk aversion and capital constraints. After all: it is their own money.

However, the authors also find that disproportionality has a negative effect on firm value (see figure 12.5).

Figure 12.4: Largest owner's share and firm value (Classens et al, 2002)

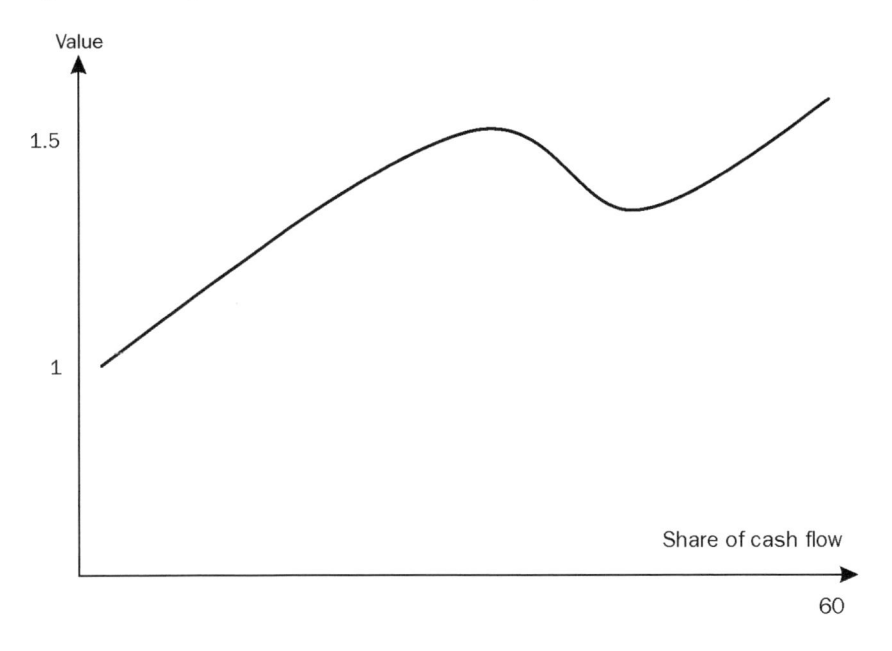

Figure 12.5: Disproprotionality and firm value (Classens et al, 2002)

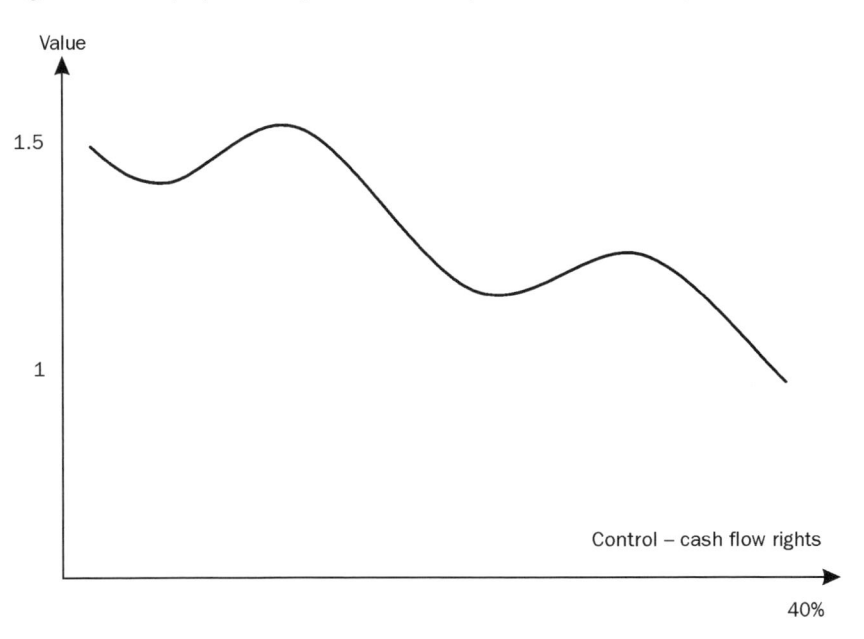

Chapter 12. Family Business with East Asia as an example

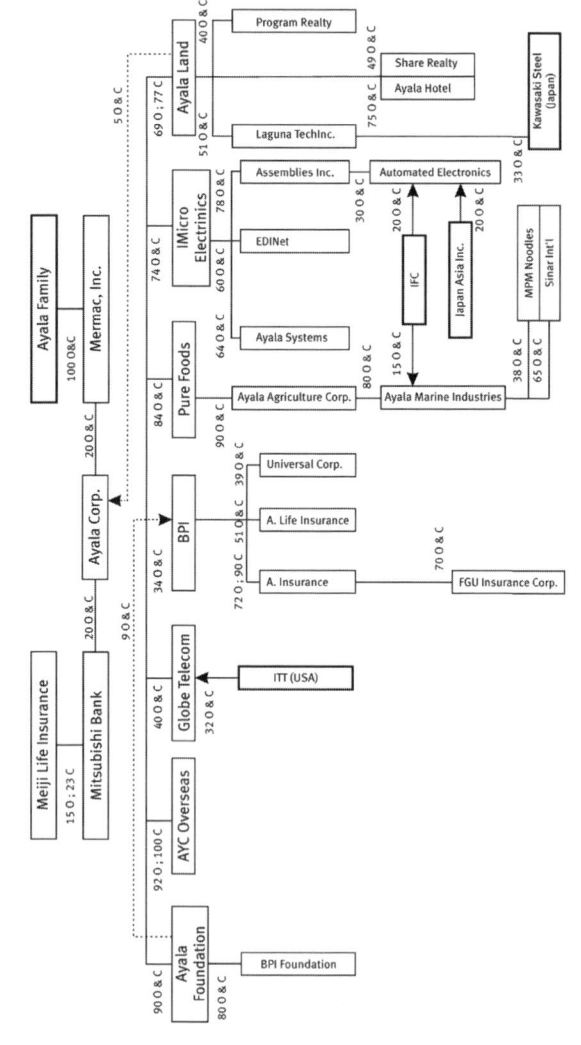

Figure 12.6: A Glimpse into the Li Ka-Shing group

The Li Ka-Shing group (Hong Kong). The principal shareholders are shown in thick-bordered boxes. Ownership stakes are denotes with 'O' and control stakes are denoted with 'C'. Pyramidal holdings are denoted with thick lines and cross-holdings are denoted with dotted lines. The difference between ownership and control at any given node implies that shares with superior voting rights have been used. Star TV, Husky Oil, CIBC, Cheung Kong, Hutchinson Whampoa, Cavendish International, Hong Kong Electric, China Strategic Invest, Dao Heng Bank, Consoli-dated Electric Power, Pacific Concord, Peregrine, Hopewell Holding, Guoco Holding, Woo Kee Hong, Kumagai Gumi, Evergo, Kwong Sang Hong, and Lippo are publicly traded. Suntec City, Cluff Resources, Peregrine Invest, Asia Commercial, HK China Ltd, and Chee Shing are closely-held companies

Source: Claesssens et al. (2000)

222

So while family ownership appears to have a positive effect on family business, this is attributable to the beneficial effects of economic incentives rather than to family control. A high degree of disproportionality between ownership and control invites type II agency problems and investors react by discounting the value of the company's shares.

An example of a family business in east Asia is the Li Ka-Shing group which was named after the Hong Kong Billionaire Li Ka-Shing. Li Ka-Shing controls one of the oldest British trading houses from the 19th century – or 'hongs' of Hong Kong – known as Hutchison-Whampoa. The group is involved in trading, cargo, and container operations, logistics, warehousing, engineering, and retail sales. With an estimated net worth of $13 billion Mr. Ka-Shing is one of the richest men in the world.

In figure 12.6 (from Classens, 2000) I provide a picture of the Li Ka-Shing conglomerate, which consists of 25 companies, including Hutchison Whampoa. Cheung Kong is the sixth largest, Hong Kong Electric Dai Heng Bank is the 22nd largest: all are very large listed companies in Hong Kong.

For example, the Li Ka-Shing family controls 34% of the vote in Hong Kong Electric with 2.5% of the cash-flow rights to the pyramid chain: Cheung Kong – Hutchison Whampoa – Cavendish International – Hong Kong Electric.

References

Anderson, R. and D. Reeb (2003). Founding-Family Ownership and Firm Performance: Evidence from the S&P 500' *Journal of Finance*, 58 (3): 1301-1328.

Bertrand, M. and A. Schoar (2006). The Role of Family in Family Firms. *Journal of Economic Perspectives*, 20, 73-96. Spring.

Burkart, M. and S. Lee (2007). The One Share – One Vote Debate: A Theoretical Perspective. ECGI Working Paper Series in Finance. *Finance Working Paper* N°. 176/2007.

Claessens, Stijn., Djankov, Simeon., and Lang, Larry. H.P., 2000. The separation of ownership and control in East Asian corporations. *Journal of Financial Economics* 58, 81-112.

Claessens, S., S. Djankov, J.P.H. Fan and L.H.P. Lang, 2002. Disentangling the Incentive and Entrenchment Effects of Large Shareholdings, *The Journal of Finance*, 57, 2741-71.

Villalonga, B., and R. Amit (2006). How Do Family Ownership, Control, and Management Affect Firm Value? *Journal of Financial Economics* 80(2): 385–417.

CHAPTER 13

Corporate Governance in Scandinavia[1]

Scandinavia consists of 3 small countries in Northern Europe: Denmark, Norway, and Sweden.

These countries share many characteristics which have implications for their corporate governance.

They are small (5-8 million inhabitants) and homogenous. This means that informal social networks are easily formed, and that informal governance mechanism like reputation and culture are more effective than in large countries.

They are rich countries even in comparison to other high-income OECD and European countries with Norway being the richest of the three.

They have a history of social democratic governments. All three countries have high government expenditure, which are reflected in the world's highest marginal tax rates (Gwartney and Lawson, 2006). Social democracy shows up in employee representation on boards, for example. It also shows up in Norway's many government-owned companies, although the social democrats have historically been reluctant to intervene directly into the business sector and remain so in Denmark and Sweden.

They are very internationally-oriented (e.g. exports or imports to GDP). International product market competition is a strong disciplining mechanism for large Scandinavian companies.

1. This chapter draws heavily on my paper with Christopher Edling, Trond Randøy, Evis Sinani, and Anna Staffsudd 2007. Corporate Governance in Scandinavia: Comparing Networks and Formal Institutions. European Management Review. Forthcoming.

According to La Porta et al. (1998), they belong to the special legal family of Scandinavian civil law, which is characterized by somewhat higher investor protection than other civil law countries, but lower than in common law countries such as the UK and the US.

They receive top marks on almost all variables when it comes to enforcement such as efficiency of judicial system as well as accounting standards. Note also the high risk and credit-worthiness ratings that all Scandinavian countries have received. The World Bank rates the Scandinavian countries consistently highly on both society and government quality as well as on regulations and rule of law. Indeed, both when considering the measures separately as well as together, the Scandinavian countries are rated among the best governed countries in the world. See table 13.1 for a comparison of the World Bank index, the investor protection index and the anti-selfdealing index.

Table 13.1: Rating of countries by different indices

	World Bank Index	Anti-director index	Anti Self-dealing index
Finland	5,35	3,5	0,46
Netherlands	5,23	2,0	0,21
Denmark	5,16	4,0	0,47
Luxembourg	5,08	2,0	0,25
United Kingdom	4,98	5,0	0,93
Sweden	4,96	3,5	0,34
Norway	4,94	3,5	0,44
Ireland	4,75	4,0	0,79
Austria	4,72	2,5	0,21
Germany	4,64	2,5	0,28
Belgium	4,03	2,5	0,54
Portugal	3,84	3,5	0,49
France	3,69	4,5	0,85
Spain	3,67	5,0	0,37
Hungary	2,99	2,0	0,20
Italy	2,90	2,0	0,39
Greece	2,62	2,0	0,23
Czech Republic	2,61	4,0	0,34
Poland	2,26	3,0	0,30
Slovakia	1,59	3,0	0,29

Source: Djankov et al. (2005), The World Bank

Comparative governance

In table 13.2 I have summarized the governance systems of the 3 countries. For reference I place them between the bank-based Germany System and the market-based British system.

Table 13.2: Corporate Governance in Scandinavia

	Germany	Denmark	Norway	Sweden	UK
Owner concentration	Medium	High	Medium	Medium	Low
Owner Identities	Banks Families	Families Foundations Coops	Government Foreign	Business groups	Institution. Investors
Board System	Two Tiers	Two tiers	Two tiers	Two Tiers	One Tier
Insider share	-	-	-	(+)	+
Employee Representation	+	+	+	+	-
Bank Influence	++	(+)	(+)	+	-
Performance pay	(+)	(+)	(+)	(+)	+
Legal System	Civil	Civil	Civil	Civil	Commmon
Listed firms '99	1043	242	191	292	2292
Listed firms '04	872	175	175	300	2073
Market Cap % GDP	55	68	39	137	158

Ownership. All three countries have a significant degree of family ownership among listed companies (as most other countries across the world including the US) and, in all of them, foreign ownership has increased significantly since the 1990s. Moreover, institutional investors have increased their share of the stock market in all three countries. However, each country combines these elements with unique, country-specific structures. Denmark has some of the world's largest farm cooperatives and is also characterized by a large number of industrial foundations which own and operate business companies. Indeed, Denmark is special in a Nordic perspective, as about two thirds of listed firms are controlled by a majority shareholder (Eriksson et al., 2001; Krüger Andersen, 2004; Lausten, 2002; Rose and Mejer, 2003). In Norway, the government owns many business companies. Traditional industries like shipping are still controlled mainly by families, but resource intensive business like oil and power as well as banks are now, to a large extent, owned by the state (La Porta et al., 1998; 2002b; Oxelheim, 1998; Randøy and Nielsen, 2002). As for Sweden, it has a tradition of large business groups and large industrial firms, which is reflected in its large stock market, as socialist governments, labour unions and industrialists together favoured large firms in the economy. Half of the stock market has long been controlled by the two business spheres of Handelsbanken and Wallenberg. Although foreign and institutional ownership has increased recently, they have to a large extent kept their dominance of the stock market. (Agnblad et al., 2001; Collin, 1998; Högfeldt, 2004).

Thus, Scandinavian countries have a long tradition of strong owners. They achieve this control by dual class shares, pyramids, and cross-shareholdings, where Denmark emphasizes dual class shares, Norway pyramids (a few) and dual shares (a few cases), and Sweden uses all three to a much larger extent than the other two and indeed the rest of the world (La Porta et al., 1998). Majority ownership is also more common in Denmark and Norway. Despite this, there is little evidence of owners expropriating personal gains from minority shareholders (Dyck and Zingales, 2004; Nenova, 2003).

Boards. Board structure in the three countries is formally very similar. While company law in all three countries prescribes that there must both be one or more responsible managers and a supervisory board to appoint managers and approve significant decisions, Scandinavian boards have been described as both one-tier and two-tier and even semi-two-tier boards. I classify them as two-tier boards, because by law there must be both a management function and a board function in all joint stock companies, and these functions must be independent.

The boards are quite strong (independent) vis-à-vis managers and have long been composed of mainly non-executives. CEO duality is not allowed by law. Moreover, by law boards are in charge of the overall management of the corporation and must decide on all major issues. Formally, they only delegate decision power to managers. In practice, the management is in charge of the day-to-day business of the company, while the supervisory board monitors, hire/fires, and ratifies (often rubberstamps) all major decisions.

The most specific characteristic of Scandinavian boards is, however, the mandatory employee representation. Employees are allowed a 1/3 representation and they participate in the board work on equal terms with members appointed by the general meeting with the same duties, rights, and responsibilities. As such, they must represent the interest of the company and not (at least not legally) the interests of the employees. This system seems to work in the sense that it does not do much damage in most cases, although (or perhaps because) employee representatives are known to be quiet in board meetings. Some would argue that employee board representation has helped to foster a sense of solidarity in Scandinavian societies. The Scandinavian experience is different from that of Germany which has up to 50% employee representation.

However, even in board structure there are some differences. Norway has adopted a system of boards of representatives in-between shareholder meetings and supervisory boards. Sweden endorses a seat for the CEO on the supervisory board, but the Danish corporate governance code advises against it. In both Norway and Sweden, nomination committees composed of major shareholders have come to play an important role in determining board composition.

Banks. The Scandinavian countries have traditionally been categorized as bank- or relationship-based corporate governance systems. However, there have been considerable changes since the 1990s. Whereas Denmark has greatly increased both total domestic credit provided by the banking sector as well as its domestic credit to the private sector, Sweden has done the opposite. In contrast, Sweden's market capitalization now resembles the traditional market-based economies (USA, UK) in terms of market capitalization to GDP. Stock market turnover to GDP is also much higher in Sweden in 2000. Furthermore, IPOs approach Anglo-American levels and, in the case of Norway greatly exceeds them, whereas M&A activity is on a par with the US, with the exception of Denmark (La Porta et al., 1997; Pagano and Volpin, 2005). At face value in 2000, we would therefore characterize Sweden as market-based, Denmark as bank-based, and Norway as somewhere in-between, but with relatively less-developed financial markets. Nevertheless, banks in Scandinavia are not as influential as in Germany. In Denmark, banks do not represent shareholders at annual meetings, bankers cannot sit on supervisory boards, and banks may not own large blocks in non-financial companies. Historically, banks have been more powerful in Sweden; both the main spheres have a bank at the centre (The Wallenbergs were bankers operating though Skandinaviske Enskilda Bank).

Incentives. Stock options are now commonly used in all three countries, and CEO pay has increased, although it is still at a low level when compared to the UK. Sweden has by far the highest pay levels and uses more variable pay; thus, it comes closer to a market-based governance model.

The **legal system** is, as previously mentioned, Scandinavian Civil Law. Generally, Scandinavian countries do not score too high on the La Porta et al. measures of investor protection, but shareholder rights are quite advanced, and shareholders have more power to nominate directors and to suggest items at shareholder meetings than they have in the USA.

The stock market is small – close to the German level – in both Denmark and Norway. But the Swedish stock market is now much bigger and closer to the UK than to Germany in terms of size. Much of this is attributable to a few large companies.

Altogether, there are many powerful similarities between the Scandinavian countries, but there are also quite a few differences between them. In particular, Sweden seems to have become much more of a market model over the past decade. Norway has become a filthy rich, but half-nationalized oil economy. Denmark appears to be stuck with its miniature, but relatively efficient firms.

Evaluating the Scandinavian model

While it is difficult to classify Scandinavia unambiguously on a scale between market and bank, it is clear that standard US corporate governance model of 'strong managers and weak owners' and its related problems do not fit. On the contrary, Scandinavia has weak managers who are pressured by strong owners, independent boards, and strong labour unions. Thus, classical agency (type I) problems are much less serious than in the

UK. One indicator of management weakness is that CEO pay has not increased to same extent as in the US.

Moreover, the strong owners in Scandinavia appear to be relatively decent – perhaps because of socialization and perhaps because social democratic politicians have historically been 'breathing down their necks'. For example, the value spread between voting and non-voting shares – an indicator of expropriation risk – is quite low.

Finally, stakeholder issues do not seem to be more serious in Scandinavia than in other countries. In fact – because of employee representation and strong labour unions – employees seem stronger in Scandinavia than anywhere else in the world – with the possible exception of Germany.

So, it is be possible to argue that Scandinavia is a 'sweet spot' with no serious corporate governance issues on the horizon.

But it is also possible to argue that Scandinavia has too few governance problems and pays a price for its strong owners and strong unions. The price is opportunity cost. A small US state like Delaware now has GDP per capita of $ 67.000 compared to $ 34.000 in Sweden, $ 36.000 in Denmark, and $ 43.000 in Norway. Average US per capita GDP is now $ 44.000 – much higher than in Scandinavia. But small homogenous countries should not be compared to the US average. Small, homogeneous, well-educated and well-developed countries should be able to do much better than that.

One of the reasons for American dynamism is a strong capital market which will inevitably involve ownership dispersion and agency problems. It also involves dramatic restructuring, takeovers, and other issues which seem unpalatable to the cosy Scandinavian consensus. The point is that the gains of dynamic capital market – or more generally of a dynamic market economy – may well be worth it.

References

Agnblad, J., E. Berglöf, P. Högfeldt, and H. Svancar. 2001. Ownership and control in Sweden – strong owners, weak minorities and social control. In Barca, F., and Becht, M. (Eds.), *The control of corporate Europe*. Oxford: Oxford University Press.

Barca, F. and M. Becht. 2001. *The Control of Corporate Europe*. Oxford University Press, Oxford, UK.

Baums, T. 1994. The German Banking System and its Impact on Corporate Finance and Governance. Aoki, M. and Patrick, H., eds. *The Japanese Main Bank System*. Oxford University Press, Oxford, UK.

Booth, J.R. and D.N. Deli. 1996. Factors affecting the Number of Outside Directorships held by CEOs. *Journal of Financial Economics*. 40(1), 81-104.

Coffee, J.C. 1999. The Future as History: The Prospects for Global Convergence in Corporate Governance and its Implications. *Northwestern University Law Review*. 93, 641-708.

Coffee, J.C. 2001. Do Norms Matter? A Cross-Country Examination of the Private Benefits of Control. *Columbia Law and Economics Working Paper* No. 183.

Collin, S-O. 1998. Why are these islands of conscious power found in the ocean of ownership? Institutional and governance hypotheses explaining the existence of business groups in Sweden. *Journal of Management Studies*, 35(6): 719-746.

Demirguc-Kunt, A., and R. Levine. 1999. Bank-based and market-based financial systems: Cross-country comparisons. *World Bank Policy Working Paper* No. 2143.

Denis, D.K., and J.J. McConnell. 2003. International Corporate Governance. *Journal of Financial and Quantitative Analysis*. 38 (1), 1-36.

Durnev, A. and E. Han Kim. 2002. To Steal or Not to Steal: Firm Attributes, Legal Environment, and Valuation. *Working Paper*, University of Michigan Business School.

Dyck, A. and L. Zingales. 2002. 'The Corporate Governance Role of the Media,' R. Islam, *The Right To Tell: The Role Of Mass Media In Economic Development*. Washington, D.C.: World Bank, 2002, pp. 107-40.

Dyck, A., and Zingales, L. 2004. Private benefits of control: An international comparison. *The Journal of Finance*, LIX: 537-600.

Eriksson, T., E. Strøjer Madsen, M. Dilling-Hansen, and V. Smith. 2001. Determinants of CEO and board turnover. *Empirica*, 28(3): 243-257.

Fama, E.F. 1980. Agency Problems and the Theory of the Firm. *Journal of Political Economy*. 88(2).

Franks, J., C. Mayer and S. Rossi. 2004. Ownership: Evolution and Regulation. European Corporate Governance Institute *Working Paper* 09/2003 (revised 12/2004).

Franks, J., C. Mayer and S. Rossi. 2005. Spending Less Time with the Family: The Decline of Family Ownership in the United Kingdom. Randall K. Morck, eds. *A History of Corporate Governance around the World: Family Business Groups to Professional Managers*. The University of Chicago Press, 581-607.

Granovetter, M. 2005. The Impact of Social Structure on Economic Outcomes. *Journal of Economic Perspectives*. 19(1), 33-50.

Gugler, K. 2001. *Corporate Governance and Economic Performance*. Oxford University Press, Oxford.

Gwartney, J.D., and Lawson, R.A. 2006. The impact of tax policy on economic growth, income distribution, and allocation of taxes. *Social Philosophy and Policy*, 23(2): 28-52.

Hallock, K.F. 1997. Reciprocally Interlocking Board of Directors and Executive Compensation. *Journal of Financial and Quantitative Analysis*. 32(3), 331-344.

Högfeldt, P. 2004. The history and politics of corporate ownership in Sweden. Cambridge, MA: National Bureau of Research, National Bureau of Economics Working Paper 10641.

Johnson, W.B., S.M. Young, and M. Welker. (1993). Managerial reputation and the informativeness of accounting. *Contemporary Accounting Research*, 10(1), 305.

Kogut, B. and G. Walker. 2001. The small world of Germany and the durability of national networks. *American Sociological Review*. 66(June), 317–335.

Krüger Andersen, P. 2004. The takeover directive and corporate governance: The Danish experience. *European business law review*, 15(6): 1461-1475.

La Porta, R., F. Lopez-de-Silanes, A. Shleifer and R. Vishny. 1997. Legal Determinants of External Finance. *Journal of Finance*. 52 (3), 1131-50.

La Porta, R., F. Lopez-de-Silanes, A. Shleifer and R. Vishny. 1998. Law and Finance. *Journal of Political Economy*, 106 (6), 1113-55.

La-Porta, R., F. Lopez-de-Silanes, and A. Shleifer. 1999. Corporate Ownership around the World. *Journal of Finance*. 54 (2), 471-517.

La-Porta, R., F. Lopez-de-Silanes, and A. Shleifer. 2002a. Investor protection and corporate governance. *Journal of Financial Economics*, 58(1-2): 3-27.

La-Porta, R., F. Lopez-de-Silanes, and A. Shleifer. 2002b. Government ownership of banks. *The Journal of Finance*, 57(1): 265-301.

Lausten, M. 2002. CEO turnover, firm performance and corporate governance: empirical evidence on Danish firms. *International Journal of Industrial Organization*, 20(3): 391-414.

Lazear, E. P. 1995. 'Corporate Culture and the Diffusion of Values,' in T*rends in Business Organization*. H. Siebert, ed. Tübingen, Germany: J.C.B. Mohr, pp. 134–40.

Milbourn, T. T (2003). CEO reputation and stock-based compensation. *Journal of Financial Economics*, 68(2), 233-262.

Morck, R. and M. Nakamura. 2005. A Frog in a Well Knows Nothing of the Ocean: A History of Corporate Ownership in Japan. Randall K. Morck , eds. *A History of Corporate Governance around the World: Family Business Groups to Professional Managers*. The University of Chicago Press, 367-459.

Morck, R., D. Stangeland and B. Yeung. 2000. Inherited Wealth, Corporate Control, and Economic Growth? In Randall Morck, eds. *Concentrated Corporate Ownership. National Bureau of Economic Research Conference Volume*, University of Chicago Press, Chicago

Nenova, T. 2003. The value of corporate voting rights and control: A cross-country analysis. *Journal of Financial Economics*, 68: 325-351.

North, D.C, 1991. Institutions. *Journal of Economic Perspectives*. 5(1), 97-112.

Oxelheim, L. 1998. 'Regulations, institutions and corporate efforts – The Nordic Environment' in Oxelheim, L. et al. Eds. *Corporate Strategies to Internationalise the Cost of Capital*. Copenhagen: Copenhagen Business School Press.

Pagano, M., and Volpin, P.F. 2005. The political economy of corporate governance. *The American Economic Review*, 95(4): 1005-1030.

Pedersen, T. and S. Thomsen. 1997. European Patterns of Corporate Ownership. *Journal of International Business Studies*. 28(4), 759-779.

Prowse, S. 1995. Corporate Governance in an International Perspective: A Survey of Corporate Control Mechanism among Large Firms in the U.S., U.K., Japan and Germany. *Financial Markets, Institutions & Instruments*. 4(1), 1-63.

Randøy, T., and J. Nielsen. (2002). 'Company Performance, Corporate Governance, and CEO Compensation in Norway and Sweden', *Journal of Management and Governance* 6: 57-81

Roe, M.J. 1991. A Political Theory of American Corporate Finance. *Columbia Law Review*. 91: 10-67.

Roe, M.J. 1994. *Strong Managers, Weak Owners: The Political Roots of American Corporate Finance*. Princeton University Press, Princeton, New York.

Rose, C. and C. Mejer. 2003. The Danish Corporate Governance System: From Stakeholder Orientation Towards Shareholder Value. *Corporate Governance: An International Review*. 11(4), 335-344.

Shleifer, A. and R.W. Vishny. 1997. A Survey of Corporate Governance. *Journal of Finance*. 52(2). 737-783.

Tadelis, S. 1999. What's in a Name? Reputation as a Tradable Asset. *American Economic Review*. 89(3), 548–563.

Vives, X. 2000. Corporate governance: Does it matter? X. Vives, eds. *Corporate Governance*. Cambridge University Press, Cambridge, UK, 1-15.

Weiss, Y. and C. Fershtman. (1998). Social status and economic preference: A survey. *European Economic Review*, 42(3-5), 801-820.

World Bank Development Indicators. 2007-04-01. wwww.worldbank.org

IV. Conclusion

CHAPTER 14

Corporate Governance beyond the Hype

Corporate Governance has become a fashion wave during the past two decades. Apparently, the term was first used in the beginning of the 1960s to signify shareholder democracy, but it did not really gain ground until it was endorsed by institutional investors during the 1980s and 1990s (Becht et al. 2003). Since then, the concept has spread to include investor protection, corporate social responsibility, and board work. The best practice recommendations of Cadbury (1992) were a milestone, and similar recommendations and practices have spread throughout the world. Now we have Sarbanes-Oxley, several EU directives, national code committees, corporate governance policies in all major corporations, recommendations for NGOs, cooperatives, and family firms, as well as vibrant debates on executive compensation, takeover defences, diversity, and social responsibility. As a crude indicator of growing interest, I track Google references to corporate governance in figure 14.1.

The accuracy of this measure is open to discussion, but no matter how you measure it, there is little doubt that the public interest in corporate governance has increased enormously in recent years and it will not disappear in the near future. One reason is the phenomenal ability of the subject to mutate. The term corporate governance used to mean shareholder democracy. Then it was identified with hostile takeovers, shareholder value, and stock options. Later it became synonymous with board control to avoid accounting irregularities. It might mutate once again into corporate social responsibility. All the while, the concept has been expanded while it miraculously maintains its identity. Corporate governance has become a common denominator for many subjects in corporate finance and company law.

Chapter 14. Corporate Governance beyond the Hype

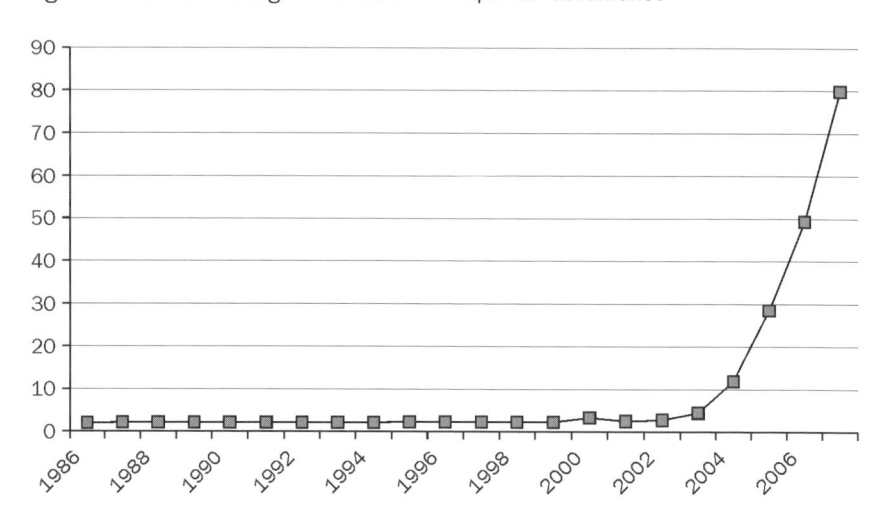

Figure 14.1: Million Google references to Corporate Governance

A fashion trend of this size will inevitably involve a lot of hype as populists, consultants, politicians, and special interest groups try to capture it for their own purposes:

- Institutional investors want power and recognition
- Consultants would like to sell more services
- Academics love an excuse to write more papers
- Rating agencies profit directly from an increasing interest in governance
- Auditors use professional standard setting to create a lucrative niche for themselves
- Investment bankers desire more business (M&A, IPOs, Privatization)
- Politicians like to champion popular causes like the 'overpayment' of CEOs
- Bureaucrats demand more regulation to get more resources and to be more important
- The media demands scandals to sell newspapers and commercials.

In contrast, managers and controlling shareholders have confined themselves to passive resistance. Many have only grudgingly accepted the new ideas and silently hope that they will go away. One reason is, no doubt, that corporate governance has very much been phrased as a question of what companies (managers) can do for minority shareholders so that discretionary power is challenged. Another reason is, perhaps, that they have found it difficult to see gains in company performance, which is their main concern.

It would be easy, therefore, to dismiss corporate governance as a fad, but this is almost certainly a mistake. The corporate governance debate – misguided though it often may be – can be seen as a logical consequence of the massive build-up of pension funds and other savings which we currently witness, and which will continue in the in next decades. These trillions of savings need to be channelled into profitable investments for society to be able to progress, and for the present generations to be able to live as comfortably as possible on their pensions. It is up to the fund managers to invest as profitably as possible and to use their influence to make their companies as profitable as possible. Since the pension funds are agents for almost all ordinary citizens, the funds have an obvious interest in an enlightened shareholder value maximization which includes social responsibility. Luckily, there are an unprecedented number of opportunities for profitable investment in information technology, biotechnology, alternative energy sources – not to mention globalization and emerging economies. So there is every chance of success; we need merely to construct the system to make it happen. This system is what I call corporate governance.

Good corporate governance

So what is good corporate governance? How can we get it right?

The first rule of the game is that there are no general recipes. There a number of different corporate governance mechanisms which can be applied more or less intelligently to the individual company given its situation. So the first conclusion is that the gurus who claim to know what is 'right' – and there are many of those – should be handled with caution. If they are right, they are right by accident. So be sure to strike them from the list of invited guests. One kind of guru is the preacher/moralist. Another kind is the investor-activist who is really only interested in short term share price appreciation. A third kind of guru is the lobbyist or client company, whose wealth depends on a special interest group. A fourth guru is the businessman who has experience from two to three companies and who wants to apply his enormous wisdom to all the rest of the world. A fifth guru could be the academic with a purely theoretical solution.

A common example is that investors and advisors will often want a founding family to sell out and to leave, partly because the professionally-managed investor-owned firm is their benchmark, and partly because this will make it much easier for them to make money. To be sure, exit is sometimes the best strategy, but there are also many instances in which both the company and the family are better served by having the family stay.

A second recommendation is that corporate governance is no end in itself. The reason why we have corporate governance is to ensure value creation. So if there appears to be a conflict between corporate governance and value creation, it is artificial; corporate governance should yield.

A third recommendation is that corporate governance is not a management tool. It is a tool – or rather a toolbox – for owners to control and direct managers. So when managers start to talk about mobilizing owners or getting the board to create value, it is time to be aware.

While it is not possible to tell you what to do with your company or country without knowing what company or country we are discussing, it is relatively easy to give examples of good and bad corporate governance. Good corporate governance enhances and creates value. Bad corporate governance destroys value. I have listed some examples in figure 14.2.

At the country level, good corporate governance is about ensuring freedom of enterprise and property rights including freedom of contract. Cost-effective and timely enforcement is critical. Red tape (including overregulation), unreliable and corrupt courts, and slow enforcement can make the system break down. The rules should be as simple as possible, but no simpler than that (i.e. no rules can also be a problem). For example, many international investors demand a discount before investing in China, because they are unsure if they will get their money back.

At the ownership level, value-creating governance comes about by ensuring the optimal match between the company and its owners. The

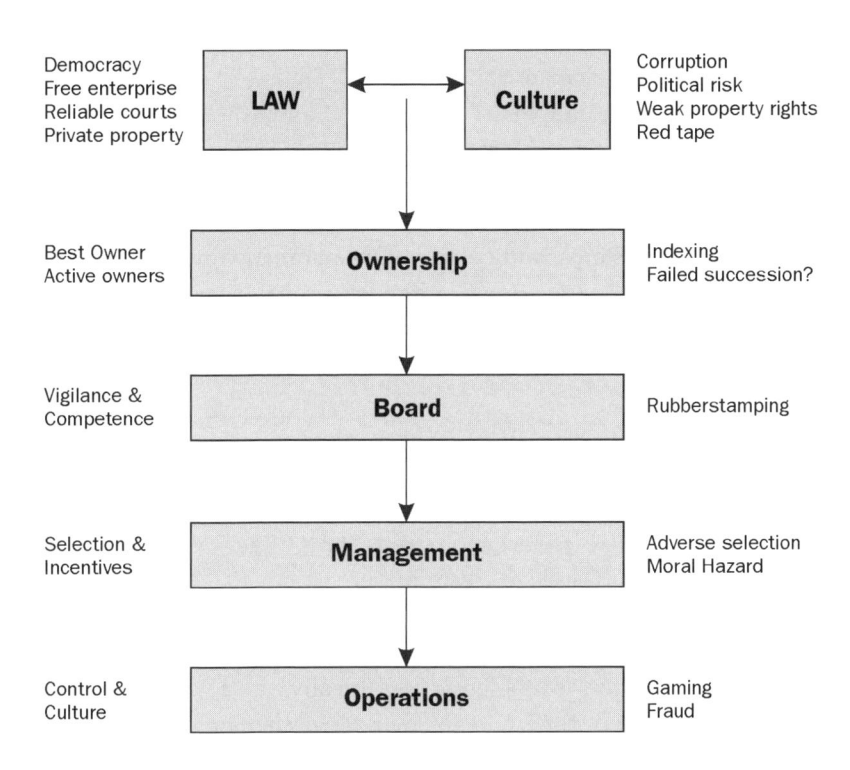

Figure 14.2 Corporate Governance and Value Creation

Democracy / Free enterprise / Reliable courts / Private property	**LAW** ↔ **Culture**	Corruption / Political risk / Weak property rights / Red tape
Best Owner / Active owners	**Ownership**	Indexing / Failed succession?
Vigilance & Competence	**Board**	Rubberstamping
Selection & Incentives	**Management**	Adverse selection / Moral Hazard
Control & Culture	**Operations**	Gaming / Fraud

competence, capital, incentive, and agility of the owners needs to be matched against the needs of the company. When this goes well, the owners will take an active interest in the company and will step in (e.g. replace managers) if things go wrong. In contrast, bad corporate governance comes about when shareholders do not bother to exercise their ownership rights; for example, many investors do not even bother to show up at shareholder meetings. Another classical instance of bad ownership is failed succession: the 'stupid son' inherits the firm from his clever father and takes it downhill faster than lightning strikes.

At the board level, good corporate governance requires that independent, vigilant board members exercise effective control, block value-destroying acquisitions, coach if necessary, and occasionally come up with a good idea or a useful contact. But there are also many examples of bad boards which rubberstamp management proposals, approve stupid proposals, and do not contribute anything to firm value.

Management makes the real difference, so they must be selected carefully and motivated to create value by well-designed incentive systems. If not, there are many examples of incompetent and self-serving managers who destroy value for the shareholders.

Finally, even the finest laws, owners, boards, and managers will make no difference if the decisions they make are not implemented. The management, control systems, and culture of the company must be optimized so that decisions are implemented and management (as well as the board) gets correct information about what is happening in the company.

Corporate governance reviews

So what should we do about it in practice? I recommend that companies review their corporate governance every three years and take steps to change it if this would seem to create value.

A corporate governance review is an evaluation of a company's governance. It may be produced by insiders (e.g. the board) or by outsiders who consider investing in the company. Ideally, the review results in a small (i.e. 5-10 page) paper where the major issues are noted.

Since corporate governance is usually relatively stable, annual reviews do not make much sense. Every third year – or in connection with major changes – may be a better interval.

1. A good place to start is to consider whether there is a governance problem in the company. The best way to find out is to consider the company's economic performance, particularly the return on capital, shareholder returns, and market value. To assess performance, the company should be benchmarked to some standard: for example competitors or an index of companies in the same industry. Even for a well-performing company there is a question whether it could have performed even better with a different governance structure. However, for companies that produce excellent result, there is a natural inclination to assume that they must be doing something right, and, 'if it ain't broke, don't fix it!'.

2. A second step is to attempt to verify to which extent the company's performance appears to be influenced by governance issues. Tough competition, unforeseen changes in business conditions, stock market fluctuations, or bad luck may all influence company performance. The question to ask is whether this would have been much different with another type of corporate governance. Surprisingly, the answer is often 'no'!

3. The review will then go through different corporate governance mechanisms, often concentrating on a few of them, asking whether a different type of ownership, board, incentive system, capital structure, or information system would be likely to improve company performance. The review will ask questions like: is the company capital-constrained? Would it benefit from going private? Do the board members have adequate expertise to evaluate company performance?

Internal reviews will have the opportunity to interview board members and managers about the efficiency of board meetings and other inside information. There will typically be a considerable satisfaction with the status quo in internal reviews, but nevertheless some important topics for further discussion will arise. External reviews will often be more critical because of a tendency to discount uncertain information.

Index

Adverse selection 34-38, 49
Agency problem 17-21, 25-39
Analysts 54
Asymmetric information 26-27, 32-39
Auditors 53-54
Bank Governance 68-69, 191-98
Bank ownership 93
Bank-Based model (see also Bank Governance) 52
Banks 229-230
Board 18, 50-51, 62, 66-68, 101-125, 129-133, 228-229
Board Committees 108
Board systems 66-67
Cadbury Code 151,153, 161
CEO 111
Competition 55
Comply-or-explain 56
Control-based system 64-66
Convergence 73-76
Corporate governance codes 27, 55-56, 151-166
Corporate governance mechanisms 60-63, 85-96
Corporate ownership 94
Country models 71-72
Creditors 51-52
Cross holdings 218
Dual class shares 216-217, 219
Empire building 30
Employee representation 68, 195
Entrenchment 30
Ethics 135-147
Excess expenditure 29
Family ownership 93, 211-220
German Code 162
German model 93, 146, 194, 197-198
Government ownership 94-95

Incentive system 52-53
Insiders (i.e. executives) 68
International systems 64-71
Investor ownership 93
Investor protection index 47
Japanese Model 200-202, 206-207
Keiretsu system 202-205
Keiretsus 200
Large Owners 49-50, 62
Law 45-48,62
Legal systems 70-71, 230
Management board 67, 162, 195
Managerial labour market 55
Market model 176-177, 183-186
Market-based system 64-66, 68,
Mechanisms of Governance 41-57
Media pressure 56
Moral hazard 33-34
Moral Standards 42-44
Non-executive directors 67
One tier system 66-67
Owner identity 90-94
Ownership 85-96
Ownership and performance 89-90
Ownership structure 87-89
Performance pay (see also Incentive system) 70
Personal ownership 211-212
Pyramids 217-218
Reputation (see also trust and reputation) 62
Sarbanes-Oxley 187-190
Scandinavia 225-231
Scandinavian model 230-231
Self dealing 29
Separation of ownership and management 28
Shareholder agreements 218

245

Shareholder pressure 50
Shareholder Value model 173-176
Stakeholder 19-20
Supervisory board 66
System effects 57
Takeovers 54
Transaction cost 90-92

Trust and reputation (see also reputation) 44-45
Two tier system 66-67, 195
UK Combined Code 161, 162-164
UK corporate governance model 183
US model 177-180
Voting caps 218